SO THIS IS

SHOW

BIZ!

CLEO ANSTETH

SO THIS IS SHOW BIZ!

MTFoster Books

P O Box 7155

Warner Robins, GA 31093

Copyright © 2012 Michelina T Foster

ISBN: 1481009826
ISBN-13: 978-1481009829

DEDICATION

To all serious musicians, composers, arrangers,
Performers, representatives, and lovers of music
Who know and have seen the changes
In the music industry … and lived through them.

Most importantly to my Dear Wife, Alice,
Who stood by me during all the ups and downs of
Our musical rollercoaster -- our married life.
I thank her for keeping "her promise"
To me and our Family.

Cheers, Dad

CONTENTS

Acknowledgments   1

1   A Typical Day   3

2   The Erwin Booth Revue - 1946   18

3   The Nick Gray Orchestra - 1950   28

4   The Transition - 1955   55

5   The Survivor - 1970   57

6   Steve Post – Musician - 1980   126

7   The Trip   232

8   Biography of Cleo F Ansteth   322

So This Is Show Biz!

ACKNOWLEDGMENTS

It has been many years since this manuscript has seen the light
Of day again. Thanks to +Michelina T Foster for copyrighting,
Re-typing, editing, and arranging for its publication.

Chapter 1

So This Is Showbiz!

Stan Bernstein arrived at his office at the usual time. It was 10:00 AM and he paused before opening the door which stated **Stan Bernstein Artist Management.** He wondered if *artist management* adequately described what he had been doing for the past 20 years. Then he decided it wasn't important, because he was thinking of packing it in and retiring in the near future. Stan opened the door, said "Hi" to his secretary and asked, "Are there any messages?"

Helen Hall replied, "You had a call from Mr. Sonny Cross. The details are in a note on your desk. You'll find it on top of the morning mail."

He went into his office, removed his coat, sat at his desk and examined Helen's note. It stated: Mr. Sonny Cross - telecom- 9:30 AM. 'Tell Stan to call me back as soon as he gets in. He can reach me at 702-555-8555. That so-called artist he booked into my room has gone too far this time. I've had it with all his crap.'

Stan looked at the 555 prefix number and noted that it wasn't the prefix of the Las Vegas Strip Hotel where Sonny worked as entertainment buyer. He assumed it to be Sonny's home phone and realized that it wasn't a good omen. Stan wondered what his client, Jerry Ross, did this time. Rather than have Helen be the go-between, Stan decided to place the call. It might give him an edge with Sonny, and he probably would need one.

"Hello Sonny. This is Stan returning your call. What can I do for you this morning?"

"You can straighten out that son-of-a-bitch, Jerry Ross. Do you know what he pulled last night?"

"No Sonny I haven't heard a thing."

"That egomaniac disrupted my show room with another one of his little boy tantrums. Ten minutes after the first show was supposed to go on, I received a call from the showroom. No one was on stage, and the audience was getting restless. They were applauding and raising hell - in hopes of getting something started. I tried to call Jerry's dressing room but the line was busy. The first thing that raced through my mind was fear. I wondered if someone had slipped through our security system and nailed Ross. Then I thought he might be sick, so I hurried to his dressing room."

"What did you find when you got there?" Stan asked.

"I found out that Ross was just being difficult. His secretary stopped me in the outer lounge area and said 'Mr. Ross was in conference'. I started to walk past her, but she stepped in front of me and blocked my entrance. She had a telephone in her hand and was talking with Jim. I heard her say, 'Mr. Ross is ready to go on, but he wants to be sure that the showroom is ready for his performance. Last night, he heard dinner dishes being cleared from a table during his second song. It disturbed him, so he's merely giving the staff adequate time to make sure that it doesn't happen again tonight'. My God, Stan, our customers aren't a bunch of cattle. If some of them take a little longer with their dinner, we can't steal their food before they are finished. That's no way to treat paying customers or guests."

"I agree Sonny, but your contract with Mr. Ross clearly states that dinner dishes will not be removed during his performance. This hasn't been a problem during previous engagements. Perhaps your showroom staff is getting lax. Why don't you check into it and tighten up procedures if you think it's necessary. I don't doubt what you're saying, but I'd like to hear the other side of the story before we get too involved with this incident. I will contact Mr. Ross this afternoon and then get back with you."

"All right, Stan, that sounds fair, but let me tell you how the rest the evening went with your *superstar*. I want you to have the complete story before you call him. When I was finally permitted to see Ross, the only other person in the room was Mark Hudson. Good grief, Hudson is his conductor and these guys see each other all the time. Ross was telling Hudson how he wanted the sequence of the show revised. After he finished with the line-up, he changed his mind again and said, 'as long as we're getting started late, let's shorten the show. Pull the Shitty-Hitty Medley.' Wow, what a medley to pull! One of the high points in his show is that medley. You know the one I mean, Stan, he introduces it as, 'a medley of my hit records from the 60s.'"

"Yes Sonny, I'm familiar with that medley."

"A lot of people expect him to sing those songs. They would be disappointed if they didn't hear them during a Jerry Ross performance. Well, I blew my stack and asked if they could hear all the noise coming from the showroom. I insisted that they start the show immediately, and told them the audience would probably tear the place down if they didn't."

Stan asked, "Did those comments get any action?"

"No. Ross just glanced at me and said 'don't interrupt me, Sonny. This is important! I'll be with you in a moment'. Stan, I just stood there like a hired hand... waiting. I was dumbfounded. Ross gave a few more instructions to Hudson and then told him that, 'that was all'. As Hudson left the room, Ross said, 'alright Sonny it's your turn. What can I do for you?' I wanted to punch him out, but I kept my anger under control and asked if he was ready to go on stage. He told me, 'of course. As soon as Hudson starts the overture, I'll be on my way.' When the show finally started -- 30 minutes late, I was a basket case."

"I can well imagine", Stan said. "Tell me Sonny, how did Ross handle this situation after he got on stage?"

"With his usual charm and a bunch of lies, when the audience died down after his first number, he really conned the audience. Ross told them that he got caught in traffic on the way to the hotel. Then he went into a song and dance about running through the back entrance and being stopped by our security people. He said they wouldn't let him continue on his way until he gave proper identification. After three or four minutes of making jokes about our security procedures, he had the audience loving him and hating the hotel."

While Sonny rambled on, Stan was thinking: This was Jerry's last engagement at the Strip Hotel under his current contract. Year after year, the hotel had provided him with 8 to 10 weeks work. This gave Jerry a solid financial base and minimized the amount of touring necessary to maintain his lifestyle. Stan wondered if Jerry was losing his mind.

When Sonny wound down, Stan asked, "By the way how is showroom attendance holding up during Jerry's engagement?"

"It's very good. We're averaging about 85% filled, but that doesn't give Ross the right to carry on like a spoiled brat."

"You're right, Sonny, and I appreciate your giving me all of the details on last night's incident. After I've talked with Jerry, I'll return your call."

"Okay Stan, so long for now."

Helen came in and announced, "Vic Bailey just called to let you know the preliminary promotional proposal is ready."

"Is that the one for Carl Kay's new record?" Stan asked.

"Yes. He would like to set up a meeting and have his people review it with you. Are you still planning to leave on your vacation tomorrow?"

"Yes, Helen. Ask ole Vic to forward the proposal. I don't think we want to meet with his people until we have had a chance to look at his cost figures. I'll be calling you off and on throughout my trip. You can review the proposal and give me the high points over the phone. It will take another two months for the recording company to complete its sweetening and mixing, so we still have plenty of time to wrap up the promotional end of it. I'll be back in two weeks, so let's delay the meeting with Vic and his people until I return. If their cost figures appear to be in line, we'll get together with them sometime after the first of the month."

When Helen left, Stan reached for the bottle of nitroglycerin tablets. He slipped one under his tongue, and a minute later he felt better. He sat by the window looking out over Wilshire Boulevard and wondered about the series of events that brought him to Beverly Hills, California. He certainly didn't plan any of it.

Stan started to daydream and remembered the first significant event. It occurred during 1944, the year he was drafted into the Army. After basic training was completed, he was assigned to a Special Service Band. The band played dance music at various officers' clubs and occasionally went on USO tours. It was a 16 piece band: five reeds, three trumpets, three trombones, drums, guitar, piano, bass, and the leader doubled on vocals and trumpet. Stan played the third alto chair. He felt fortunate to be in the band, because he did not consider himself to be an outstanding musician. The lead alto man felt the same way about Stan and criticized him continuously. If it wasn't phrasing, it was intonation, dynamics, attack, etc....

The lead alto man was Steve Post, and he was a dedicated musician. Steve was a conservatory graduate, and had played with some of the name bands prior to being drafted. Without question, Steve was the best musician in the unit. In addition to playing a lead alto, he wrote special arrangements for the band. Steve was not a compulsive arranger. If the leader asked him to write a chart he would comply.

Therefore, most of his arrangements were background music for vocals performed by the leader. However, when the band was performing extended USO tours, Steve would re-orchestrate music for various acts to fit into the instrumentation of the service band. It annoyed him if only eight or ten men were playing, and the rest just sat and held their horns because they didn't have specific parts to play. By the same token, if an act came on tour with arrangements that included full string sections and/or French horns, Steve would pick up their important lines and incorporate them into the existing service band's instrumentation. Most of the USO acts were surprised and pleased with Steve's orchestrations.

During this period, Stan Bernstein became an adequate performing musician. This was a result of two things: the opportunity to play every day, and Steve Post's constant constructive criticism.

Stan was jolted from his thoughts by the ringing of the telephone. Helen said, "It's Jerry Ross calling for you. Are you in?"

"Yes, Helen, I'll take it. Hello Jerry, what are you doing up so early? I was going to call you in another hour or two."

"I'm up early because I'm angry, really angry. Last night, Sonny Cross tried to lean on me."

"Jerry, I heard Sonny's side of the story earlier this morning. He said your first show went on 30 minutes late last night."

"That's right, and it will happen again tomorrow night if I hear dishes being picked up while I'm on stage tonight. Hotel employees throughout the showroom are getting slipshod. Last night, during one of my monologues, I heard two musicians carrying on a conversation. Besides being unprofessional in their behavior, they don't seem to realize that the audience comes to hear me, not them. Their conversation was distracting. Hudson called a special rehearsal for today in hopes of cleaning up some of their rotten sounds. Yesterday, I informed the hotel's music contractor of specific musicians I don't want to see on that stage if, and when, I return for future engagements. Stan, even the lighting is getting unpredictable. During my opening number last night, I reached down to shake hands with the young woman sitting at the center stage table, and the spotlight didn't follow me down. While I'm trying to sell myself to the audience and get them in a receptive mood, the spotlight was on my conductor's backside and I was in the dark. Everybody is goofing off and getting away with it. If Sonny won't straighten them out, I'll do the job for him. I'm not going to tolerate unprofessional behavior from supporting personnel during my shows."

"Of course, I understand," Stan replied. "I'll relay these complaints to Sonny, and I feel certain that he will initiate appropriate corrective actions."

"I'm glad someone is certain of something, and I wish I could depend on it. Look, Stan, I know Sonny is new on the job and still trying to establish cordial relations with the staff, but it's time for him to start acting like an entertainment director. There are too many deadheads in that showroom. If Sonny tightens up procedures, you won't have any more problems with me."

"Good. I know he will appreciate hearing that! I'll call Sonny back and pass on your comments." Stan looked at his watch. It was another hour before his appointment with Norma Anderson, so that would give him more than enough time to call Sonny Cross. He placed the call and tried to smooth things over. When Sonny's mood became more cordial, Stan asked him if he was interested in starting negotiations on a new contract with Jerry Ross.

"No. I'm not interested in offering Ross another contract. I haven't even considered it, and this fact has nothing to do with last night's fiasco. Our management people believe entertainment costs are getting out of hand. Although we're known for our superstar policy, I have been asked to obtain price quotes on Revues and Broadway Shows. Our Star Policy will continue for a few more months to honor existing contracts, and then I believe we will be trying something different. Now this is confidential information, Stan, so don't spread it around."

"You have my word. I'll keep my mouth shut, but I'm surprised."

"So am I, but that's the way the ball bounces. As yet, we don't have a firm management commitment for a change in our entertainment policy, but the price differentials certainly make it look attractive. I may get into a bind during this transitional period, and if I do, I'll have to scratch for temporary entertainment. Would you mind giving me the dates Ross has open through the next five months?"

"Not at all. Here they are, Sonny..."

The talk with Sony wasn't as disagreeable as he had anticipated. Stan hoped his next task would turn out the same way, but he had his doubts.

Norma Anderson had called a few days earlier and asked Helen to set up an appointment. When Stan found out about it, he had mixed feelings about the meeting. He considered Norma an old friend, but sometimes friends and business don't mix very well. The first time they met was in 1946. He was still a performing musician, and she was one of the chorus girls in the Erwin Booth Revue. The Revue was booked throughout the summer at state and county fairs. Norma's career started to blossom a few years later; first with Broadway shows and then the Hollywood musicals. Stan even had her for a client for a short time before her third marriage: but when his initial contract ran out, Norma's husband (Jack Enders) decided that he would be her personal manager. Stan heard that the divorce turned out to be a very bitter experience for Norma.

When she arrived at the office, Stan greeted her with genuine warm affection. They reminisced for a while, and then Norma asked him, "Would you consider taking me back as a client?"

"Norma, every agent in this business would like to have you as a client. I would say yes this very second, but I'm planning on retiring in the near future."

"It must be very nice to be in that position," she replied.

"It sure is, and I feel very fortunate. The man upstairs must like me, but you know the feeling. I happened to drive past your house the other day and said to myself, 'that place must be worth at least $400,000'."

"It's up for sale."

"Well, with the children raised and you being single again, it probably is too big for your needs."

"It's not that Stan, the place is simply eating me alive. The overhead is unbelievable, and I can't afford to live there anymore."

"You must be kidding," said Stan.

"I wish I were but I'm not. Jack did a poor job of investing my money, but the worst part was his gambling. I had no idea how much money he lost until we started divorce proceedings. I won't bore you with all the details, but the truth of the matter is, I'm broke and must go back to work."

"I'm sorry to hear that, Norma. I don't want to offend you, but if you need money, I could loan you a few dollars."

She laughed and asked, "Do you really think that you can trust me?"

"Why not? If I can't trust another Jew, I've got big troubles."

That comment helped break the tension and Norma asked, "You remember when we were with the Erwin Booth Revue, and I asked if you'd loan me thirty dollars until payday?"

"Yes, I remember. We were having a late-night birthday party for you, and one of your boyfriends from Chicago showed up. He had enough money to get himself to wherever it was we were performing, but he didn't have anything left for the return trip. I think he was going to hitchhike home. You asked me for thirty dollars so he could take the bus. Norma, why did you ask me? At the time, we had only known each other for a few weeks."

"You were the only one at the party who looked like he might have an extra thirty dollars," she said laughingly.

"As always, you overestimated my financial resources. I found it flattering, but not factual. At the time you asked for the loan, I recall being a little drunk. When I woke up the following morning, I had second thoughts about how free I was with my money. I also remember that you paid me back at the end of the week. Norma, if you're serious about going back to work... how would you feel about performing in a production show at Lake Tahoe?"

Norma replied, "I'm serious about it, and I'll consider almost anything."

"Let me tell you about this possibility, and we'll see if it grabs you. Last week, Benny Fisher called and told me his new production show was in trouble. They maintained a star policy for years, and their regular customers aren't interested in seeing a show without a headliner. Attendance is down, but the hotel doesn't want to abandon the show. I guess they put a lot of their own money into it. So now they're thinking about featuring one name performer in the show to see if it will boost showroom counts. They won't consider paying anyone the kind of money you made a few years ago - when you were on the Silver Circuit. However, working conditions would be excellent, and you would only be on stage for about 30 minutes during each show. The hotel will take care of any music and costume expenses, and you'll be guaranteed a minimum of three months continuous work. If this sounds interesting, I'll have Helen attempt to get Benny on the phone."

A few minutes later, Stan was asking Benny Fisher if he had found a suitable headliner. Benny replied, "We're negotiating with a few people, but nothing has been firmed up. Do you have someone in mind?"

"Yes," Stan replied. "How would you feel about having Norma Anderson in your show?"

"I would like it, but you know that we're not willing to spend the kind of money she demands. No, it would be out of the question. I couldn't even make a tentative offer that would fall into her salary ballpark, but I wish I could. You think she might be interested in working with our show?"

"I don't know, Benny, it was just a thought. Earlier today, I happened to run into her, and she expressed a strong desire to get back to work. I think she's looking for something that will take her mind off the recent divorce."

"How did she look?" Benny asked.

Stan smiled at Norma and said, "She looked just fine, lovely as always."

After a short pause, then he told him, "Well, I must admit, this is a possibility I hadn't considered. Are you handling her account again?"

"No. This is just something between friends. As a matter of fact, Doris and I are going on a long overdue vacation tomorrow. However, if you would care to discuss your show with Norma, I could contact her and relay your thoughts."

"Okay, why don't you do that," Benny said. "If she shows any interest, tell her we will be happy to send down our plane and pick her up. She will be a guest in the hotel while we discuss business."

"Benny, if I can't wrap this thing up today, will it be alright to have Helen make the phone calls and necessary arrangements?"

"Sure, I always enjoy talking with Helen. Where are you going on your vacation?"

"We plan on driving up Route 1 and stopping whenever we see anything of interest," Stan replied.

"That certainly sounds restful, but if you get bored when you're passing our way, take a detour over to our place and say hello."

"Thanks, Benny, we may do that."

Stan hung up the phone, turned to Norma and told her, "The first thing we must do is find someone to represent you. Bennie is a seasoned, astute negotiator, so you're going to need first-class help. Do you have someone in mind, or would you prefer to have me recommend a few people?"

"No, don't bother. I can take care of that myself."

"Norma, why put yourself in that position? It's not your forte."

"It may not be my strongest ability," she said, "but I learned a lot about that end of the business from Jack. He had many faults, including being a lousy husband, but he knew how to negotiate a contract. I truly believe I can do it."

"All right Norma, but I think you've lost your marbles. If you insist on trying it on your own, let's get Helen in here and fill her in on your plans."

They reviewed the telephone conversation with Benny Fisher and agreed that Helen would call him the following afternoon. The arrangements for Norma's trip would be scheduled at Benny's convenience, and if at all possible, a time when he would be under a minimum amount of stress. When Helen returned to his office, Stan asked Norma if there was anything else he could do for her.

"Yes Stan, I'll take that loan."

He wrote a check for five thousand dollars and handed it to Norma. She put the check in her purse without looking at it.

She started toward the door, then turned and said, "Thanks. I'll return the money as soon as I can. If I get the job at Lake Tahoe, you'll receive your usual 10% commission."

Stan started to protest, but Norma hurried from the room without looking back. After a few minutes, Helen walked in and asked, "Have you looked at the mail yet?"

"Not all of it," he replied, "but I did see something we should take care of. That new rock group, Swift and Company, wondered what my reaction was to the demo tape that they sent me a few weeks ago. Since a little bit of that type of music goes a long way with me, I didn't listen to very much of the recording. I don't want them to feel discouraged or defeated by my personal rejection, because they'll get plenty of that if they stay in the business for any length of time. However, I don't want to bother with them. We should return their demo with a brief cover letter. Let's tell them that I listened to the recording with great interest, but I can't use their talent. Tell them I'm not taking on any new clients, because I'm planning on retiring in the near future. That should do it. Now, have you noticed anything else in this pile of letters that needs my immediate attention?"

"Yes. Your office lease expires in three months. There's a letter from the leasing agent asking if you would be interested in signing another five-year agreement."

"See if you can get them to extend my lease for six months. That should give me adequate time to wind things down and evaporate. Was there anything else of importance in this pile of letters?"

"Nothing I can't handle," she told him. "Good. I'll just ignore them and let you take care of the mess. Have you started looking for another job?"

"No," she said. "I don't believe you'll quit."

"Helen, Helen, I'll give it to you in writing if that's what you want. This time I'm serious. I don't need it anymore."

"We'll see," she told him. The phone rang, and Helen answered it. She looked at Stan and said, "It's Drew Daily. He wants to talk to you."

"I don't want to talk to him."

"What shall I tell him?" she asked.

"Tell him anything you'd like. Say I'm out of town on vacation or something. Tell him to go to hell. I don't care what you tell him, just get rid of him."

"I'm sorry Mr. Daily, Mr. Bernstein isn't available. No, Mr. Daily, that's not possible. Mr. Bernstein will be on vacation for a few weeks. Helen hung up the phone and asked, "What do you have against Drew Daily?"

"He's an ass. I'm sorry about the rough language, Helen, but Daily is one of the many people I won't miss when I get out of this business. If he calls again, tell him to get lost and don't bother being courteous about it. A few years before you came to work for me, Drew Daily was one of my clients. I put a lot of time and no small amount of money into pushing his career. When it started to soar, he went behind my back and dealt directly with entertainment buyers. For the most part, they were the same people I originally dealt with to find him work. After he became an established draw and found out he could book himself, he dropped me like a hot potato. Daily didn't want to pay anyone a commission to find him work. He thought it was an unnecessary expense and perhaps he was right. Those things happen in this business, but in Drew's case, he wouldn't even honor the last nine months of our contractual agreement."

"Why didn't you sue him for breach of contract?" She asked.

"It wouldn't have been worth the effort. At that time, Daily had so much money coming in he could've fought me in the courts until I went broke trying to prove a point. Now his career is in a slump, and he wants someone to help him rejuvenate it. Well, he's not going to get any assistance from me."

Stan spent the rest of the day going over loose ends with Helen and left the office promptly at 6 o'clock.

Chapter 2

The Irwin Booth Revue – 1946

Freddie Hayes had conducted the orchestra for the Irwin Booth Revue for many years. Now that he was 65, it was his only full-time work. The Revue toured for three months each summer, performing at state and county fairs. This work, plus full-time teaching throughout the rest of the year, gave him an adequate income. The first band rehearsal for this year's tour would start within the hour, and Freddie was looking forward to it.

Laura North, the choreographer for the Revue, had been rehearsing the girls for about 10 days. Her dance routines changed very little from year to year: the revisions were primarily cosmetic. However, each year she would choreograph one routine to a new pop song. The new music and new costumes helped con the audience into thinking they were seeing what was advertised, a brand-new show. At one time, Laura and Erwin Booth had a rather torrid love affair. When it cooled down, they remained friends.

Laura operated a school for dancers in the Chicago area. Each year, many of the girls in the Revue were students, or former students of the Laura North Dance Academy. As always, there were 12 girls in the line. They did some singing, but their primary function was dancing.

For the first time in years, all of the musicians and dancers showed up on time for the dress rehearsal. After the second break, Erwin Booth walked into the room. He watched from the back of the hall for a while, and then came forward to greet Laura. After a brief hug, he told her, "The girls look well rehearsed, and I like the new costumes. Laura, you did it again."

"Thanks! Do you see anything that you want me to revise?"

"No. Not really. I noticed that Joy Wells is with us again."

"Yes. Joy was one of my most gifted students," she said. "I'm delighted that she could be with us again this year."

"How many years has it been, Laura, about 14?"

"Probably," Laura replied.

"Well, I couldn't help noticing that she stood out from the rest of the girls. The others look so much younger. I believe this should be Joy's last year with us. Which one have you picked to be our dance captain for this year?"

"Claudia Fleming," she told him. "She's the sixth girl from the right on this routine. Claudia is a hard-working, talented, ambitious, bossy bitch. I know she'll keep the rest of the girls on their toes." During the next rehearsal break, Laura introduced him to the girls. When she came to Claudia Fleming, Erwin said, "Laura was just telling me about your many talents, and I want to congratulate you on being chosen dance captain. I'm sure you'll do a good job for us."

Erwin spent a few minutes informing Freddie about the various acts booked for the season. Freddie was familiar with many of them, because he had conducted their music on numerous occasions. Freddie jotted down the names, telephone numbers, and dates of appearances for all of the acts that were new to him. He would contact them during the following days and determine if their music was suitable for the limited instrumentation of his orchestra.

Freddie had hired eight musicians for the tour: two trumpets, three reeds, drums, piano and bass. At the smaller county fairs, this would be the entire instrumentation. At the state fairs, the band would be increased to comprise thirteen musicians. Freddie would hire the additional musicians from cities near the respective state fairs. He was thankful that Steve Post was working for him again. Three years ago, Steve played one season and wrote the special orchestrations. Looking at the numerous names of acts not known to him, Freddie knew that Steve would be busy writing throughout the tour. With the exception of two musicians, everyone in the band had worked for him at one time or another. The two new men were Mike Moore on second trumpet, and Stan Bernstein on third alto. Mike was one hell of a trumpet man. Freddie knew that he could take over the lead trumpet position if anything happened to Eddie Barnes. Stan did a satisfactory job, however, if it wasn't for the fact that Steve Post recommended him, Freddie probably would have hired someone else who had more experience.

Erwin Booth handed copies of the itinerary to Laura and Freddie. As they passed it out to the dancers and musicians, Erwin explained the travel arrangements. "As usual, we will travel by train," he told. "This Revue transports so much baggage, we get one private coach for free. There will only be four overnight train rides during the tour, so I know all of you will forgive me for not having a sleeper car. We will plan on having two musicians share a room and four girls share a room. To minimize your expenses, a bus will pick you up and take you to the fairgrounds. It will return after the last show and drop you off at your hotel. Now if anyone wants to provide their own transportation, or have a single room, let Freddie or Claudia know about it. We are flexible and want you to have a good time this summer. Also, if you have preferences as to those you want to room with, let us know. If you do not, Freddie or Claudia will match you up with roommates."

The only two who wanted to take their own personal cars were Freddie Hayes and Larry Steele. Larry was a drummer. Freddie was the only one requesting a single room. Erwin Booth told them he would drop in from time to time, thanked them for their attention, and then hurried back to his office. Two of his higher-priced acts, appearing only a specific state fairs, were giving him a lot of flack about their billings, order of appearance, and numerous other things that Erwin thought as being somewhat petty. He hoped to resolve these differences of opinion and smooth over their dissatisfactions. He was beginning to dislike entertainers.

During the second week on the road, Steve Post and Stan Bernstein found themselves sharing a bathroom with four of the girls. The bathroom was located between the rooms. On the other side of the bathroom were Claudia Fleming, Norma Anderson, Doris Rogers, and Janet Cooper. There were a few accidents, until everyone remembered to lock the bolt on the inside of the opposite door when they entered. Then there was a time that Stan forgot to unlatch the bolts when he left. A short time later Claudia was screaming, "You dirty son-of-a-bitch, unlock this door. I have to go." By the end of the week, they were somewhat familiar with the idiosyncrasies of each other's plumbing.

The first unpleasant situation occurred a short time later. Larry Steele put the make on Claudia. He was a good-looking guy with nice manners, and Claudia enjoyed the attention. One night, after the second show, Larry asked her if she would care to drive a short ways out of town and get something to eat. "I know where there is a fabulous all-night restaurant. It's only about 5 miles out of town, and we can be there in a matter of minutes."

Since it was a free meal and a chance to get away from the other girls, Claudia agreed. After the meal, Larry started to drive toward the city. At the top of the first hill, Larry drove to the side of the road and stopped on a turnout. He said, "Let's enjoy the view here for a few minutes." At first, they just talked, then Larry turned on the charm. After a few gentle advances, Claudia (much to her surprise) started to become sexually aroused. Thirty minutes later when Larry was begging for it, she was ready. Claudia lifted her skirt and started to remove her panties. At that moment, Larry reached across, opened the door and pushed her from the car. He shouted, "Walked back to town you damned slut," and drove off.

The following day, Claudia was still in the state of shock when the first show started. She couldn't keep her mind on the routines, and her confidence was gone. She wondered if anyone noticed. Steve Post noticed right away. When the last show was over and they were riding the bus back to the hotel, he got up from his seat, walked over to Claudia and asked, "Mind if I sit down?"

"Suit yourself," she told.

After a while, Steve said, "If you have something on your mind that you'd like to talk about, I'm a pretty good sounding board."

"I'll bet you are at that, you nosy bastard. If I should have something on my mind, it sure as hell isn't anything I want to discuss with a guy. Christ, I'm beginning to think all the males in this Revue are a bunch of perverts."

"Claudia, I suppose you know that Larry is spreading the word about how he made out with you last night."

"He's a liar," she said in a low voice.

"Well, whatever happened is none of my business, and I certainly don't care one way or the other. However, I know that Larry's head is all fouled up when it comes to women, and I suggest that you and the other girls stay away from him."

"No kidding!"

"No kidding," he replied. "I'm going to tell you a few things about Larry that you might find interesting. Let me ramble on for a while, and if what I'm saying doesn't mean anything to you, I'll stop.

"Larry was divorced a short time ago from a girl he met while stationed in England. He was nuts about her. But shortly after she arrived in this country, things started to fall apart. During this period, I was working with Larry at the Stevens Hotel. The band played dinner music, the ice show, and dance music: so Larry was confined to the hotel for about seven hours each evening. While he was working, so was his wife. She was selling herself as a call girl. When Larry found out about it, they separated for awhile. However, Larry really loved her, so they decided to forgive, forget, and try again. The final breakup came about two months later. She found a guy who wanted her to be his mistress. The way I heard it, she told Larry she only married him to become a citizen of the good old USA and find a rich man. I believe her last words to him were, 'You served my purpose, I found what I was looking for so it's over sucker and I don't intend to see you again.'"

By the following evening, Claudia had regained most of her self-confidence back and was feeling better. Eddie Barnes felt worse. He was backstage throwing up from food poisoning. Michael Moore moved over to the first trumpet chair and played the show. Mike didn't even put a feather on a note, let alone make any mistakes, and his phrasing was spectacular during the performance. Steve Post turned around and said, "When I hear a good lead man, I could follow him anywhere." Steve never gave direct compliments.

Mike Moore was a heavy drinking, hard living man, and he didn't try to hide his lifestyle. His only concession to health was lifting weights. Even on tour, he would visit the local YMCA or health club and work out three or four days a week. Since Mike and Stan were the only new musicians in the band, they had something in common and became casual friends. Once, Stan asked why he preferred weightlifting to other forms of exercise. Mike informed him that lifting weights was his second choice. "My first choice is sex. When you're having sex, you exercise every muscle in your body."

One night after the show was over, Mike asked Stan if he would care to go out and do a little drinking. Stan wasn't into having a few drinks after work, but that evening he agreed. He knew that Steve Post would be working throughout the night on a revised chart. Steve had a habit of humming some of the lines as he put them down on paper. The off and on humming would usually wake Stan up, so he decided to spend the night with Mike and sleep the following morning. They hailed a cab and asked the driver to recommend a place where they could hear some good music. The driver suggested a roadhouse about 3 miles out of town that supposedly had a good jazz combo. During the taxi ride, Mike had a few belts of whiskey from his hip flask.

The roadhouse was crowded, noisy and dimly lit. After they were seated and ordered drinks, Mike looked around the room and saw Norma Anderson and Doris Rogers. They were with two guys he did not know, probably locals. He pointed them out to Stan and waved a hand. The girls noticed and waved back their acknowledgment. Stan and Mike were enjoying listening to someone else's music and didn't pay much attention to what was going on around them. Suddenly, the girls appeared and sat down. Norma said that the boys they were with were becoming drunk and vulgar. She wanted to get away from them.

Mike asked, "Did you come out here as a foursome?"

"Hell no," Norma replied. "We met them about 30 minutes ago. They came over to our table and offered to buy us a drink. At the time, I thought they might be interesting, but now they seem to think that a few drinks entitle them to own us for the evening." Mike shrugged and said, "Okay Norma, I'll tell them to get lost."

The two locals came out of the men's room, noticed that the girls had left their table, looked around the room and started toward Stan and Mike. As they approached, Stan wished he had stayed at the hotel. The bigger one leaned on the table, faced Mike and snarled, "What do you think you're doing with my date?"

Mike looked at him for a moment before saying, "Shut up and get lost." When he started to reply, Mike jabbed him between the eyes and knocked him out. As he hit the floor, Mike was still sitting down and looking at the other one. Finally he asked, "Want me to help you get your friend's body outside for some fresh air?" The fellow nodded and they removed the body. It happened so fast, hardly anyone noticed the incident. The people around them just assume that someone passed out from too much booze. However, the owner knew better, having seen the whole thing from behind the elevated bar.

While Mike was on his way to the door, the owner came over and said to Stan, "Your friend handled that neatly. I've had trouble with those two before, so I'll just assume that they had it coming to them. However, they will probably return with some of their friends, so I believe you should finish your drinks and leave."

When they returned to the hotel, Norma wanted to eat something before turning in for the night. They found a place a few blocks away and three of them ordered food. Mike continued to drink. During the walk back to their hotel, Mike was a typical happy drunk. By the time they reached the hotel, he was hanging onto the streetlight pole to keep from falling down. They were talking and laughing when a police car pulled up to the curb. One of the officers asked if they were all right and Mike said, "Sure. I'm just holding on to this poll to keep from falling off the face of the earth." The officer shook his head and asked him to get off the street.

Since they didn't want to press their luck, they moved inside and made sure that Mike found his room. Stan was certain that Steve would still be writing and humming, so he told the girls he was going back to the lobby and read for a few hours. They said good night and parted. Stan found a newspaper and finished the front page when his reading was interrupted. Doris came bounding down the stairs saying, "I'm so excited I can't sleep. This is the first time in my life that I have been thrown out of a club and ordered off the street." The desk clerk looked up from his work for a brief moment.

They sat in the lobby and talked until the sun came up. Then Doris said, "Let's go out and take a look at the sunrise." As they went outside, she asked, "Did you know that Norma's real last name is Abrams?"

"No. I didn't know she used a stage name," Stan replied.

"Norma told me that Laura North suggested the change. Did you know that Laura's real last name was Goldstein?"

"No. I didn't know that either," he told her.

"What do you think about people who change their names?"

"I've never thought about it. But if it makes them more comfortable, I don't see anything wrong with it."

"Have you ever thought about changing your name?" She asked.

"I don't feel a need for it. Besides, if I changed my name, I'd have to change my face or nobody would believe me. I don't feel like changing my face, so I think I'll continue to be Bernstein. It has a good ring, and I like it. Have you ever thought about changing your last name?"

"What's the matter with Rogers? I like it."

"That makes us even," he told her. "I feel the same way about Bernstein. You sure do ask a lot of questions. If I give the right answers, do I get a prize?"

"Don't be silly," she said. "What could I offer? Did I ask a question you don't want to answer?"

"Which question?"

"About traveling," she replied.

"Oh, that one. For a moment you had me slightly rattled. I don't mind traveling. It's a way to make a buck, but if I had my choice, I'd prefer to stay in one place. I probably got my fill of traveling in the service. Why do you ask?"

"I was just wondering if you enjoyed it as much as I do. I grew up in Wilmington, Illinois and this is the first time I've been out of the state. I think it's really exciting."

Stan felt comfortable with Doris, and they continue to talk until exhaustion started to overwhelm them. When they returned through the door, his arm brushed against her face and her glasses fell to the floor and broke. He felt awful, but Doris assured him that it wasn't a problem, because she had another pair of glasses in her room. Stan offered to pay for having the lenses replaced, but she replied, "It was just as much my fault as it was yours."

Stan stated, "For whatever it's worth, I'm sorry." He looked so serious that Doris felt sorry for him. She smiled and hurried across the lobby saying, "This party is getting rough. I'm going to pull up my pants and go home." And she again started up the steps, the desk clerk glanced at her and then stared at Stan. Stan just shrugged and returned to his room.

The season came to a close in Jackson, Mississippi. Erwin Booth made arrangements for a farewell party at the local country club. Even though Jackson was located in a dry county, Erwin made sure that the banquet included a well-stocked bar. When someone asked him how he managed to obtain the liquor, his only response was, "The good people of the South are resourceful."

It was a great party, and many of the people exchanged addresses and telephone numbers. When they finished their meal, Erwin made a speech. He thanked everyone for a successful tour and hoped they would return next year. Erwin mentioned that the bar would remain open until 6 AM, so there wasn't any reason for anyone to hurry away. A short time later he concluded his speech by saying, "Now I have one final message for the members of our orchestra. Gentlemen, you have spent three months traveling with 12 attractive girls. They worked hard for us, and I believe we owe them a debt for doing such outstanding work. Outside this door is a large golf course that is completely deserted at this time of night. I believe it is your responsibility to make sure that not one of these girls has to go home and admit to her friends that she is still a virgin. I'd handle this matter myself, but at my age, all I can do is think about it."

Chapter 3

The Nick Gray Orchestra — 1950

For over a decade, the big bands dominated the live performance field. Although their Era had peaked in 1950, their rapid decline in popularity was still a few years away. Some of the bands were superb: outstanding musicianship; great charts; and good-looking vocalists who sang in tune with poise and intelligence. Others were just awful, but these differences meant very little to the majority of people who considered dancing a national pastime. If a band played dance-able music and was affiliated with a good booking agency, it worked and made money.

Nick Gray's 12 piece band was strictly middle-of-the-road. He didn't want a band that musicians, but only musicians, praised. By the same token, his musical ability would not permit him to stand in front of a *corn band* that played stylized, gimmickry music. Nick was a bandleader because it provided him with a good income. If the band business started to dry up, Nick simply assumed that he would go into a different line of work. When it came to music, he could take it or leave it. What fascinated him was making a fast buck.

Years before, Nick had stopped entertaining thoughts of having a top name band. His early recordings did not generate significant sales, and he detested the rigorous, exhausting schedule of playing one night stands. Therefore, he directed his efforts toward becoming a successful hotel and ballroom orchestra. By the late 40s, he had achieved his goal.

In Nick's case, this did not happen by chance, it was a result of careful planning. His charts were musical but easy to play. This enabled him to maintain a consistent professional sound with average caliber musicians. He did not feature individual instrumentalists to any extent. Solos were limited, because he was selling a danceable sound, not specific musicians. When a solo passage occurred in his arrangements, it was restricted to eight or twelve measures, and the musicians were not permitted to improvise freely. Nick knew that his kind of audience wanted to hear the melody, and that was what they were hearing tonight at the Aragon Ballroom in Chicago.

After the last set, Nick reminded the musicians that there would be a rehearsal the following afternoon at 2 o'clock. He went to his dressing room, changed his clothes, and wondered how many musicians he would have to replace after this three-week engagement. Nick paid scale wages to his musicians. The only exception was Dick Weber. Dick played piano, was road manager for the band, and his wife (Fran) was the girl vocalist. Nick left the ballroom and walked the two blocks to his hotel. He went into the coffee shop, saw Dick Weber and Fran, and decided to join them.

After ordering a light meal, he told Dick, "If I'm late for rehearsal tomorrow, start auditioning the new musicians without me. Tomorrow morning I will be at the MCA office signing contracts, and I may get tied up with Bryce Zeller. He has booked three one-nighters on our way to the Peabody Hotel in Memphis, so now we don't have any days off between the Aragon and Peabody engagements. When you charter the bus, I believe you should leave Chicago at 10:00 AM or before. This will allow you plenty of time to get the musicians checked into a hotel, and let them rest for a few hours before the first one-night stand. Do you know if any of the musicians are planning on giving their two week notice during this engagement?"

"Red Potter is considering it," Dick said. "He told me that he was offered the third trumpet chair at the Chicago Theater. The salary is excellent. After playing the first trumpet for you, it may hurt his pride to play in the section, but I believe he will take the job. His wife is expecting their second child and wants him to get off the road. I think he will go to work at the theater to appease her."

"So be it. Tomorrow, we will try out the trumpet men first. You know of anyone else who is considering leaving us?"

"No."

"That's good", Nick replied. "Oh, one more thing, I expect two or three girl vocalists to show up at the rehearsal. Fran, you'll have a job with me for as long as you want it, you know that. I'm just trying out the girls to protect myself in the event that you get sick or decide to quit the road. Dick, don't audition the girls. I'll take care of that chore."

Dick was not surprised. Whenever they played at a place that provided a private dressing room for the bandleader, Nick would try out the girl vocalists. Fran had been with the orchestra for three years, and they had been married almost that long. During this period, Fran had never missed a performance, but Nick had auditioned about 100 girls.

Nick Gray woke up at 9:30 AM, hurried through a shower, shaved, dressed and went to the elevator. While waiting for it to arrive, he noticed the maid going into Billy Baker's room. Billy played bass in his orchestra, and he was the type of musician that Nick liked having on the stand; young, good-looking, single, always on time, and he didn't break any of the rules. Nick had a list of 20 rules ranging from drinking on the job to wearing the wrong color socks. When a musician broke one of the rules, he was fined in accordance with the infraction magnitude. The money was placed in a 'kitty'. When a significant amount was accumulated, it was used to throw a party for the orchestra.

Nick ordered breakfast and looked around the room for Billy. He didn't see him. The past couple of evenings, Billy appeared to be preoccupied, and Nick hoped he wasn't thinking about turning in his notice. Driving down to the MCA office on Michigan Avenue, Nick continued to think about Billy.

Bryce Zeller had the three contracts ready for his signature. Bryce also discussed four other possible one night stands between the Memphis and New Orleans engagements. When Nick agreed to these tentative contracts, Bryce was able to contact two the ballroom managers and obtain their verbal approval. While his secretary typed up the two new contracts, they discussed advertising posters for the orchestra, a possible recording date, and the feasibility of a West Coast tour in the fall. With the numerous phone calls and other interruptions that made up Bryce's typical day, time slipped by.

Finally, Nick stood up and said, "Thanks for everything, Bryce. I have a rehearsal that starts in a few minutes, so I'd better be on my way."

"Nick, you trying out girl vocalists today?"

"Maybe," Nick said. "Why do you ask?"

"Well, after your rehearsal last month, one of the girls showed up here and raised a lot of hell. She said you tried to seduce her in your dressing room, and she wondered what kind of a referral service we were running."

"That's nonsense," Nick told them.

"If you say so, but I wish you'd use a little more discretion in your dealings with the opposite sex. I mean it, Nick. Sordid rumors can hurt your career, and if you don't make money, I don't make money."

"Yeah, that's the bottom line. Okay, I'll cool it for a while."

During the drive back to the Aragon Ballroom, Nick was glad that he hadn't lost his temper with Bryce. If anyone else talked to him that way, he would've told him to shove it. After all, easy access to young girls was a fringe benefit of his job.

The rehearsal was well underway when he arrived. As Nick walked across the large dance floor, the band was playing his theme song, and it never sounded better. He noticed that the lead trumpet part was being played by one of the new musicians. It looked like eight new musicians showed up along with one probable girl vocalist. Nick introduced himself to the new people and took over the rehearsal. It didn't take him long to conclude that all of the new musicians were capable of playing his book: however, one trumpet man was outstanding. Nick turned his attention to the girl vocalist and found out that her comfortable vocal range was slightly lower than Fran's range. She was straining to get out some of the high notes. He told the band to take a break, and asked the girl into his dressing room.

Nick closed the door, and noticed the girl watching him like a frightened rabbit. He decided it would be wise not to make a pass at her and got right down to business. "Lois, you're singing range is not suitable for my charts, and it would cost a lot of dollars to have them transposed into your range. If anything should happen to Fran, I would look for a girl who sings in the same keys. Your voice sounded good to me, but it's the wrong pitch for my orchestra. Even though I can't use you, I may hear of someone else who can, so why don't you give me your address and phone number." They talked for a few minutes, said goodbye, and Nick resumed the rehearsal.

They ran down charts for another hour, and the new men were tried out at various chairs. The other girl vocalists didn't show up, so Nick concluded the rehearsal and dismissed his regular musicians. One by one, the new musicians were called into his dressing room. The last one was Mike Moore. Nick told Mike, "I may need a lead trumpet man to replace Red Potter. If this happens, will you be available to join the band in about two weeks?"

Mike said, "I have a few casual engagements booked, but I can get out of them if it is necessary. The guys will understand if I tell them I found steady work."

"Good! We are booked solid for the next five months, and most of the engagements have a duration of two or three weeks." Nick continued to explain his schedule, what he was willing to pay, and the conduct he expected on the bandstand. Mike agreed to the conditions, and Nick told him he would call him within the next few days and let him know one way or the other.

That evening, Billy Baker was not doing his usual good job. During one of the intermissions, Nick asked him, "Do you have something on your mind beside music?"

"Yes. I'm getting married," Billy said.

"Is the thought of it so awful that you can't keep a beat with your bass? Cheer up, lots of people do it and continue to function. While you're playing for me, don't think about it. Right now, lots of magic is associated with the idea, but you'll probably live to regret it. Most people do."

"Thanks for all the encouraging words," Billy replied. "You're probably right about living to regret it, because I don't think I want to get married."

"If that's the case, why are you even considering it? Tell the girl you've changed your mind. Hell, girls change their minds all the time, she'll understand."

"It's not that simple, Nick. I got her pregnant, and now she says we have to get married."

"Billy, I don't want to pry into your personal life, but I wish you would fill me in on some of the details that led up to this blissful event."

"There isn't much to tell," Billy said. "When we closed in Milwaukee last month, right after the job we packed up and drove to Chicago. It was about 4 AM when I checked into my room. Before unpacking, I decided to stretch out on top of the bed for a few minutes and dozed off. When I woke up it was around nine and a girl was leaning over me. The girl turned out to be the maid. The door was unlocked from the inside so she assumed the room was vacant. I still had all my clothes on. She asked me, 'If you're not going to mess up the bed or use the bathroom, how am I my going to earn my money?' Then she asked, 'How long are you staying here?' I told her I'd be there about four or five days this trip. Then she asked me what time I usually got up, and I told her, around 10. She volunteered to wake me up each morning, and at the time, it sounded great. To make a long story short, she stopped by my room each morning. After the first day, I started having sex with her. When came back to the city a few days ago, she told me she was pregnant."

"What's her name?" Nick asked.

"Barbara Black."

"When do you think you'll see her again?"

"Tomorrow morning," Billy said. "Barbara will stop by my room around 10. When she gets off of work at two, we're going to take our blood tests and start making plans for the wedding."

"Before the wedding, I'd like to meet the bride-to-be. Perhaps you can introduce me sometime tomorrow, would that be okay?"

"Sure, whenever," Billy told him.

The following morning, Nick was at Billy's door at twenty minutes before ten o'clock. Billy was surprised to see him, but let him in and then got dressed. A short time later, Barbara tapped on the door and let herself into the room. She looked at Billy and said, "Hi, honey. What are you doing dressed?"

"Barbara, I'd like to introduce you to my boss, Nick Gray."

She turned her head and saw Nick in a chair at the end of the room. Her eyes opened wide.

Before she could speak, Nick said, "Barbara and I have met before. When was the last time Barbara, about a month ago? Tell me, how come you're giving it away to Billy? Each time we got it on, you charged me twenty dollars. I'll bet you laid at least sixty guys last month. If you're pregnant, and I doubt it, what makes you think you can pin it on this dumb kid? If I had twenty dollars for every guy that pumped away between your legs, I would consider myself to be a wealthy man. What are you trying to do, become the richest whore in Chicago and have Billy be your legal pimp?"

Barbara threw an ashtray at him and yelled, "You bastard, you ruined it for me." As she stormed out of the room her last words were, "I'll never take care of you again."

They were silent for a few minutes before Billy spoke. "How can I ever thank you. I feel like the world's biggest jerk."

"Don't give me your notice for a while," Nick told him. "I like the way you play bass when you're not in love. See you tonight kid.   Right now, I'm going back to bed and get some sleep."

When the Chicago engagement ended, the charter bus arrived promptly at ten o'clock AM to pick up the musicians. Within ten minutes, everyone and everything was loaded and ready to go. They left Chicago with Nick leading the way in his new Lincoln.

During the first one-night stand, Nick had his eyes on one of the young ladies. Apparently, she came to the dance with a girlfriend, but she was busy dancing with various boys. The third time she requested a song, the band was playing a forte passage. Nick leaned down so he could hear what she wanted them to play. Then he put his face near her ear and said, "I'd like to lick you all over." She just smiled at him and didn't say another word.

Nick was late getting back to the stand after the last intermission, so Dick Weber picked out the set and started the orchestra. Nick showed up for the closing number. When they played the final chord, Nick thanked the audience and hurried out the back door with the young lady. While the musicians were packing up their equipment, the ballroom owner approached Dick and asked, "Where's Nick Gray? I have his money in my office."

"I believe he stepped outside," Dick said. "I'll take a look and be right back." When Dick when outside, he noticed that Nick had moved his Lincoln to the back of the parking lot. He started to walk toward it, but noticed two bodies thrashing around in the back seat. He returned and told the ballroom owner, "Nick isn't feeling well. He's lying down in the backseat of his car. I'll sign for the money."

The following evening, Fran had an appendicitis attack and was rushed to the local hospital. Dick Weber went with her, and Nick finished the job playing the piano. He called Bryce Zeller around three AM and told him, "Fran had her appendix removed. It will be a few weeks before she recovers, and I need another girl vocalist for the Peabody job."

"Why call me in the middle of the night?" Bryce asked. "You must have at least a hundred names."

"Don't be funny; I've been making calls for the past two hours. The girls I reached are working steady jobs, and they won't quit them for a few weeks work with me. I have five more names of girls in the Chicago area. Their phones ring, but no one answers. Let me give you their names and phone numbers, so you can try to reach them in the morning. If none of them are available, find someone else. I'm counting on you Bryce, so don't let me down."

Nick went to bed as the sun was coming up, but his sleep was interrupted by the ringing of his phone. "What is it?" He asked.

"This is the police department. Do you have a musician in your orchestra by the name of Mike Moore?"

"Yes," Nick replied. "What happened to him?"

"We have him locked up. If you want him back you have to pay a $50 fine."

"What for?" Nick asked.

"For sleeping off a hangover in the city park."

"That costs fifty dollars?"

"It does when you're nude. Early this morning this clown decided to take a swim in the river. He didn't bother to get dressed after he got out of the water. Our Girl Scout Troop saw him that way and reported it."

Although this situation was not covered in Nick Gray's list of 20 rules, Mike was given the maximum fine. That evening, when they were midway through the dance, Nick received a phone call from Bryce Zeller.

"I finally found a girl vocalist for you, and she will arrive in Memphis tomorrow afternoon. I don't believe you know her, but she is good."

"What's her name?" Nick asked.

"Norma Anderson. She's worked a few times with my band on weekend jobs, and Norma has always been well received by the country club crowds. I would use her more frequently, but she is usually working steady jobs. For the past two months, she was in the musical production show at the Shubert Theater. They closed last week, and I feel fortunate to find her available. Rather than have her stay across the street with the musicians, I made reservations for her at the Peabody. Since she is not familiar with your library, you will probably be reviewing vocal charts during the afternoons. I thought it would save time and work out best if the two of you were staying at the same hotel."

"Good thinking, Bryce. As always, I appreciate your help."

They finished the dance, packed up and drove to Memphis. After four or five hours sleep, they were playing luncheon music. The brass section had cup mutes in their horns, because the luncheon customers didn't want their conversations drowned out by music. Everyone was playing a constant mezzo piano, so there were no dynamics. Nick looked intent as he stared at his music stand while conducting the orchestra. Only the musicians knew that Nick's stand didn't hold any music. He was reading the Wall Street Journal.

At 2 o'clock, they concluded the noon session. Eleven of the musicians went back to their rooms to get a little more sleep. Dick Weber stayed behind, because he had to get the music and stands moved upstairs to the Skyroom for the evening performance. Nick Gray went to the desk to find out if Norma Anderson had checked in. She had not, so he left a note asking her to call him as soon as she arrived. He went to his room, got out one of his navy blue suits, put on his most flattering leisure clothes, and unpacked the vocal lead sheet book.

Norma arrived about 3 PM, had her luggage sent to her room, called Nick and went to his room to review the lead sheets. They picked out 10 songs she was familiar with. Nick called Dick Weber and told him, "Round up as many of the musicians as you can find for a special rehearsal in 30 minutes. I want our new vocalist to hear the background music before she has to perform. We only have about 45 minutes to rehearse before they start seating people for dinner."

Norma unpacked, hung up her gowns to get the wrinkles out, then went to the top floor with the lead sheets. Dick Weber was at the piano when she walked into the Skyroom. He started running over the songs with her as the other musicians straggled into the room. Nick arrived a few minutes later and started the full band rehearsal. There was only enough time to run down each chart once. During the third song, Norma had trouble finding the starting note after the modulation into the final eight measures. Nick stopped the band and said, "We won't do this one tonight."

Normal replied, "I'm sure I can do it now. May I try it again?"

"No," Nick told her. "I know you'll be able to sing it tomorrow night after you rehearse it tomorrow afternoon with Dick, but right now, I'm thinking of tonight. I don't want you to sing anything that you're not comfortable with. Let's try the next number: one, two, three, four..."

When the room opened for dinner customers, the rehearsal ended. Nick decided that Norma could safely sing seven songs that evening. There wasn't time to eat, everyone hurried to their rooms and got dressed. In less than an hour, they would be performing.

During the initial fifty minutes, Norma sang all seven songs. There was one instrumental, one vocal, one instrumental, one vocal, etc. Nick wasn't trying to be a slave driver. He only wanted Norma to be comfortable with the room and music before the 30 minute coast-to-coast broadcast. When they took their first intermission, and went backstage into the musicians' room, everyone was pleasantly surprised. Nick had ordered a buffet. He told them, "I paid for it out of the Kitty. Of course, our major contributor for this spread is Mike Moore."

At the mention of Mike's name, Norma swung around, recognized him and said, "I know you."

"Hi Norma," he repeated. "I was wondering if you were going blind or just trying to ignore me."

Nick spoke, "Have you two worked together before?"

"Yes," Mike told him. "Norma and I worked with the Erwin Booth Revue about four years ago".

Nick threw up his hands and said, "Well why in the hell didn't you tell me she was a great vocalist? I was half sick worrying about how she would sound on stage."

"To be completely truthful, I couldn't recall how she sang," Mike replied. "All I remembered about Norma was her dancing. That impressed me, because she had a fine pair of legs."

That comment broke Norma's nervous tension, and the rest of the evening went by as smooth as silk. After the final song was played, Nick said to Norma, "Let's go out in the world, and I'll buy you a decent meal."

"Thanks Nick, perhaps some other time. Tonight, I'm going to talk over old times with Mike."

In Chicago, Bryce Zeller had just finished playing a dance at one of the country clubs. In addition to booking 20 road bands for MCA, Bryce booked his own band for casual engagements throughout the Chicago area. He had a philosophy; you have to make it while you can. When he returned home, he poured a drink, called Nick and told him, "I booked two more one-nighters for you. They will fill up your open dates between the Memphis and New Orleans engagements. The contracts are in the mail. How's the new girl working out?"

"Terrific," Nick told him. "She's doing me right now."

Bryce wondered if he had completely misjudged Norma. He doubted it. Nick was probably indulging himself in another one of his fantasies, he thought. Actually, Nick was steaming mad about being turned down on his offer to buy Norma a meal. He was thinking, 'that dumb broad is probably across the street going Dutch treat with Mike,' and he was right.

The all-night restaurant was crowded. After all, where else could you get a good meal at 1:30 AM in Memphis? Norma was drinking her second cup of coffee. So was Mike, but he was spiking his with booze. Norma asked him if he ever ran into any of the guys from the Erwin Booth Revue.

"Not recently, but about six months ago, I did play a casual engagement with Stan Bernstein. He finished his undergraduate work at the University of Chicago and started his law school studies. He was concerned about his grades. I guess he felt that he wouldn't be able to complete his graduate work. Stan has been booking various types of entertainment on campus and in the surrounding area. As a musician, he is capable but not outstanding: however, he sure knows how to make a dollar. He told me that Larry Steele got into drugs. Larry took the cure once, but went right back on the hard stuff. When he was fired from his network job, he went home, put a pistol to his head and blew his brains out."

"How awful," Norma replied.

"Yes, he had everything going for him, what a waste of talent. On a lighter note, Steve Post moved to Los Angeles. I heard from him last year. Steve said he was making a good living playing in the studios. Do you remember Eddie Barnes?"

"He played trumpet, didn't he?"

"Yes, that's him," Mike said. "At the time we were with the Revue, I didn't know that he was going to dental school. The following year, I received a notice that he was working with another dentist. I saved the notice. About a year after it arrived, I had a tooth broken in a fight. So, I went over to Eddie's office and had him fix it. He told me that his partner liked to ski. Every winter, his partner takes two or three months off and goes West to hit the slopes. Eddie still likes to play the trumpet, so he took the previous summer off and played with the Erwin Booth Revue. Some people get their kicks in strange ways, but Eddie felt it was a good arrangement. They can cover for each other when they take off to do their thing, and still keep the practice open all year. And he told me that playing in the Revue Orchestra is like a tonic. I guess he plans to continue doing it for as long as Freddie Hayes will have him. It sounded like a lifetime agreement. I haven't seen Eddie in almost two years. Apparently, alcohol consumption is good for me. It kills the germs in my mouth and keeps my teeth healthy."

"Mike, I'm exhausted. It just hit me, and I want to sleep."

"I'll walk you back to your room," Mike said. "Have you stayed in touch with any of the girls?"

"I just finished working with Claudia Fleming at the Shubert Theater. Claudia got me the job. It was a road show version of a Broadway musical. The principles were brought in from New York, but the other members of the cast were from Chicago. Claudia contracted the girl dancers. She's a real hustler. If there's a job opening for a dancer in Chicago, she'll find it. When she called, I was surprised and delighted. It had been almost a year since I had seen her. When I walked into the theater for our first rehearsal, I hardly recognized Claudia. She had caps on her teeth, and her nose was shorter. She told me the nose job cost her two months work, because it wouldn't stop bleeding. If I had Claudia's guts, I would go to New York and try to get into the Broadway musicals. Those two months at the Shubert were the high point of my career so far. They even gave me the chance to do some of the dialogue."

"Don't sell yourself short," said Mike. "Do it."

"Well, someday I might try it, but not right away. I guess I'm intimidated by that city: even the name, New York, scares me. Speaking of scare, I saw Doris Rogers a few weeks ago. She's skating in the ice show at the Stevens hotel. I didn't know she could skate, and I guess she couldn't until a short time ago. Doris told me that she had been dancing at the club on Rush Street. At the time, it was the only work she could find. Between the drunks and the pimps, she said she was afraid every minute of every day. I believe Doris was even considering getting a straight job, like a clerk or typist. Well, her roommate was skating in the ice show, so Doris bought skates and the two of them practiced afternoons. After a month, Doris had learned the routines. When one of the girls quit because of her chronic back problems, Doris was hired as the replacement. She told me that she hopes the show runs forever."

They got in the elevator and went up to the fifth floor. As they were walking down the hallway, Norma started to talk about Janet Cooper. She stopped when they heard angry voices coming from Nick's room. A woman's voice said, "This is only fifteen dollars. We agreed on thirty."

"Fifteen is all you were worth, now get out," Nick shouted.

Suddenly, his door opened and a woman charged out saying, "I'm going back to Kansas City where a girl can make a decent living and not have to put up with chiseling shit heads. At this rate, I'm not even taking care of my expenses."

They walked on in silence until they reach Norma's room. Then they laughed and said good night. Mike continued down the hall until he reached the room assigned to the musicians. It was a place where they could warm up their instruments before performing. The hotel didn't permit them to warm up in the entertainment areas, because the noise might offend some of the customers. Mike hadn't been in the room before, because he didn't bother with warming up or practicing when he was working. He saved those things for times when he was unemployed. Mike unlocked the door, walked in and looked around. It was a typical hotel room: a bed, chest of drawers, nightstands, chairs, and bathroom. He noted that a few of the musicians had left their instruments. The extra uniforms hung from a rack on the window wall. He locked the door and returned to his room at the Hotel Tennessee.

Norma enjoyed the luxury of a long sleep. She didn't sing afternoon sessions. The hotel's contract specified that only soft instrumental music would be performed during the luncheon. After breakfast, she studied lead sheets. At 3 o'clock, she was upstairs in the Skyroom with Dick Weber. They rehearsed until Nick arrived.

"How's Fran doing today?" Nick asked.

"Just fine! She thinks they will discharge her in two more days. I would like to go to the hospital and pick her up, but I don't see how I can do it without missing a noon session."

"That's no problem," Nick said. "I will cover for you at the piano. Take my car and go get her. Now, how's rehearsal coming along?"

"I believe I can do the three songs you discarded yesterday plus three more," Norma told him.

"Good. Let's hear them."

Norma and Dick ran down the songs, and Nick was satisfied. He told Norma that they would use them tonight, but not during the broadcast. He wanted her to sing them a few times with a full band background before she sang them over the radio network. Nick picked out a few more songs that he wanted Norma to memorize by the following day and said, "Tomorrow we will have a full band rehearsal after the noon session. I received three new arrangements today. We will rehearse them along with the songs that will be new to Norma. Now Norma, if you need help memorizing the songs, I'll be glad to spend some time with you after we finished the evening session."

"Thanks Nick," she said. "I'll study them during the next hour. If it looks like I need help, I'll let you know." Norma went to her room, laid down and looked at the lead sheets. She thought, 'that old fox is pretty clever'. Somehow, someway, she wanted to stop his advances but avoid a direct confrontation. She called room service and had a meal sent to her room. This gave her another forty-five minutes to go over the lead sheets. Norma was still studying them as she dressed.

During the second intermission, Nick asked, "How are you doing with your new songs?"

"No problem, it will be easy to learn. Thanks for offering to help, but I won't need it."

Nick walked away, and Norma started looking for Mike Moore. When she found him she blurted, "Mike, will you spend some time with me tonight?"

"Of course, Norma, that's the best offer I've had all week."

"No damn it, I don't mean it that way. I want to talk with you." Mike laughed and said, "Sure, we can do that. Let's go to the same place we were at last night. I like to watch the people and hear the noise."

After the dance, Norma and Mike walked together to the elevator. While they were waiting for it to arrive, Nick joined them. Norma put her arm around the back of Mike's waist and hugged him. Mike tried to hide his surprise. After they crossed the street and sat down, he asked, "Is the old man trying to seduce you?"

"I think so, and I believe he'll trap me if I'm not careful. Don't get me wrong, I won't sleep with him. That's not the problem. It's just that I want to avoid telling him something like, 'I won't lay you.' I don't want to be put in that position if there's another way out. Anyway, he would probably make my life a living hell during the next two weeks if I out and out turned him down. God knows, I don't feel very well right now. And he keeps saying, 'Norma I don't want you to be uncomfortable' - bull shit! He's a tricky guy. I'll bet he knows a hundred ways that no one else has ever dreamed of to be alone with a girl! I don't know how to handle this mess. I wish he'd stay away from me and just let me sing my songs."

The waitress came to their table and Mike ordered a cheese sandwich and coffee. Norma said, "Just coffee, I think I'm going to throw up." Then the waitress left, Norma started to sob into her paper napkin.

Mike watched her for a few moments before saying, "So Nick has the hots for you, and he's giving you a good chase. What's so awful about that? You should feel flattered, not frightened. This is nature's way of saying you've grown up, and sometimes human nature plays dirty tricks. It tells the girls to lock their legs together, and then it tells the boys to look for ways to unlock all those legs."

She giggled and said, "Must you be so crude?"

"Are you feeling better now?" Mike asked.

"Yes! Let's get the waitress, I'm hungry. Mike would you mind pretending that we are lovers? It might discourage Nick. You wouldn't have to overdo it, just pick me up at my room before the evening session, and walk me out of the Skyroom after we finish."

"What you're suggesting would probably make me look like a big man to the other musicians," he told her. "I suppose I could arrive at your room a few minutes early each evening. You could let me inside, and sooner or later, Nick will see us walking out together. That should fool him, or at least give him something to think about."

"Well, will you do it?"

"If I help you with your problem, will you help me with mine?" After a short pause, Norma asked, "What's your problem?"

"One of my girlfriends is coming down here on Wednesday to spend four days with me. Unfortunately, I received a letter today from another girlfriend. She will be arriving on Saturday. That means they will both be here during Saturday. I don't want them to know about each other, and with your help, I think I can handle it."

"I'm beginning to think that you boys are all alike," she said. "What do you want me to do?"

"Here's my plan," Mike told her. "I'll put the first girl up at the Hotel Tennessee. When Patty arrives, she'll stay with you Saturday evening. I'll tell her all the rooms at both hotels are taken, and I've got another musician for a roommate. Then on Sunday, I'll move her to the Hotel Tennessee. You'll only have Patty for one night. With the girls in different hotels, there shouldn't be any problems. However, if Patty leaves you and comes looking for me, I'll expect you to give me a warning call."

"Jesus, Mike, you're not a very nice person."

"Those two girls don't feel that way about me, and all's fair in love and war. What's your answer?" Mike asked.

"Yes! I'll help you. After all, what choice do I have?"

When they arrived at Norma's door, Nick was getting off one of the elevators. They greeted him and disappeared inside Norma's room. Mike picked up a magazine and said, "I wonder what Nick thinks about our exit into your room? Among other things, he's probably considering firing me."

Norma started to go over the lead sheets. She had trouble singing the intervals in one song that she wasn't familiar with. Mike sang the difficult intervals for her, and then with her, until she had it down pat. He wondered why most of the vocalists never bothered to learn how to sight read music. After he left, Norma stayed up most of the night until all of the songs were memorized.

The full band rehearsals started with Norma's songs. Nick was satisfied and excused her. He was very businesslike. Rehearsal continued with the orchestra playing one of the new instrumental arrangements.

That evening, Norma asked Dick Weber, "Are you still planning on picking-up Fran tomorrow?"

"Yes," he replied. "I'm leaving at six in the morning. It's about 200 miles, one way, to Cape Girardeau. We should be back in Memphis shortly before three. That should give me plenty of time to get Fran settled and still make the evening session."

"I'll be glad to go with you," Norma told him. "If nothing else, I can help her in and out of the girls' room."

"I appreciate your offer, and I'll take you up on it."

"Good! I'll tell Nick."

During the last intermission, Norma told Nick that she wanted to ride along with Dick Weber and help him with Fran. She asked if he had any objections.

"That's very thoughtful of you," Nick said. "What you do with your free time is none of my business. All I ask is that you continue to be on time for the job and rehearsals." Norma went over to Mike Moore, put her arms around him and whispered, "I think it worked."

When Dick and a nurse wheeled Fran to the car, Norma introduced herself and asked, "I hope you don't mind my coming up here with Dick?"

"Of course not, it will be nice to have a girl to talk with. For the most part, all I ever see are male musicians. What a bore! The only subjects they want to discuss are music and women."

During the drive back to Memphis, the girls talked incessantly. After two hours, Nick spoke his first words, "Let's stop at this restaurant and take a breather." After a short break, he wheeled Fran back to the car. While Dick was putting the rented wheelchair in the trunk, he heard Fran saying, "I don't know why I got into this nutty business." Dick raised his voice and shouted back, "Sure you do, you wanted to meet me."

"Shut up. I was talking to Norma. This life isn't the way I thought it would be. I'm twenty-seven, and in the business almost ten years. When I started, I had dreams of being a famous recording star or something. Lots of money. Fame. Interesting people. Champagne dinners. That's what I thought it would be like. So what happened, I'm a girl vocalist in a second rate band."

"Now honey," Dick said, "Stop feeling sorry for yourself. We have money in the bank, and in a few more years, we'll get off the road."

"I'm sorry Dick; I'm just having another one of my bad days." She turned to Norma and said, "I'm not always this bitchy, please excuse me."

"What's there to excuse?" Norma replied. "I can't think of anything more depressing than being alone in a hospital for five days. If it were me, I would probably be screaming and clawing the walls."

"God, it's nice to talk with someone who understands. You're just like me."

Dick shook his head, but remained silent.

Fran continue to talk. "While I was in the hospital, I had plenty of time to think. I know I'll never be the world's greatest vocalist, or the second-best, or the third best, or the fourth best, and it doesn't bother me anymore. The initial excitement of this business wore off a few years ago, and that bothers me. I used to look forward to singing, now I feel trapped. It's a grinding drudgery to sing the same crap night after night. I'm tired of the whole scene, living in hotel rooms, traveling in a bus with a bunch of guys. I want to get off the road and have a place of my own. Dick, can we have children?"

"Sure," he said. "Do you feel well enough to start trying tonight?"

"Smart ass. I can't even talk with you. Just keep driving. Norma, why did you get into this business?"

"Probably for the same reasons as you did, but I still like to sing, dance, act and travel. I grew up in a small town in northern Indiana. Singing with the glee club and performing in student plays were the only things that I excelled at. It's a wonder they gave me a diploma. I was a shy, timid dummy. I always liked to dance, and during the last two years of high school, my folks sent me to Chicago for dance lessons. I guess they thought it would build up my self-confidence. Every Saturday, I got on a bus and went to the Laura North Dance Academy. After graduation from high school, I had no idea of how I might make a living. Laura North found a job for me as a dancer in a revue, and it turned out to be a fun summer. By the time our tour ended, I was hooked on show business. My folks have helped a lot. When I'm out of work, they send money for dancing and acting lessons. So I keep busy one way or another. This job showed me how little I know about music, perhaps I should take some singing lessons."

Dick interrupted by saying, "Don't bother. You have a good natural voice. Singing lessons would probably do more harm than good."

"But I can hardly read music," Norma replied. "If it wasn't for your help, and Mike's, I would not have been able to handle the singing job."

"Now you're talking about music, not singing," Dick told. "If you want to take music lessons, that's a different story. Can you play the piano?"

"No!"

"That's where you should start," Dick said. "Since you can't read intervals very well, you could pick them out at the piano and learn them that way. You have a good ear for music, so that's no problem. After you hear someone else sing or play the intervals, you don't have any trouble singing them. It's just a question of identification, or in other words, learning the nomenclature of music. With a little practice, you'll be able to sight read music."

"You make it sound easy," Norma replied.

"It is! I'll tell you what, in five or six days, Fran will start getting her voice back in shape. Since she knows all the songs in Nick's library, you two can practice scales and intervals while I play them on the piano. We'll handle the intervals as broken chords. It may sound complex, but it isn't. This will give you a good introduction to music nomenclature and sight singing. It will not make a musician out of you, but it will be a start."

"That's nice of you, Dick, but how can I pay you back for all the help?"

"Just being with Fran is enough. As you can tell, she needs the companionship of another woman."

Fran had been sleeping soundly during the discussion of music. Norma joined her a short time later, and the two girls slept the rest of the way to Memphis. The following day, after the noon session, Nick asked everyone to go downstairs to the radio station complex. Their nightly air shots had been taped by the station. Throughout the week, Nick had been listening to playbacks, and he didn't like some of the things he heard.

As the first tape rolled, Nick said, "Listen to the reeds during the next passage. Someone in the section isn't using the proper vibrato. It's too slow. Do you hear it? Now, listen to the next brass figure. The entire brass section holds the last note in the following measure. My God, there is a chord change on the first beat of that measure. Isn't that awful?"

Nick continued to criticize the orchestra and Norma listened intently to his comments, but everything sounded good to her. This was the first time she heard her voice recorded with professional sound equipment. It was a pleasant surprise to her, because her voice sounded so confident on the tape. Nick didn't say anything about her vocals, but he continued to find fault with the orchestra. Without calling out specific names of individual musicians, the criticism continued. He referred to instruments or sections, not the people playing them. After they listen to three tapes, Nick excused the orchestra. He went over to Norma and asked, "What did you think of yourself?"

"It didn't sound the way I thought it would," she said. "I think it sounded better, but what do I know. Nick, why didn't you criticize me?"

"Because there wasn't anything to criticize. Your voice records beautifully and you didn't do anything wrong. The slight huskiness in your voice almost disappears when it is recorded or projected over a sound system. The minor problems you have with intonation aren't offensive. If anything, they enhance your vocal style. Anytime you need a recommendation for a singing job, use my name."

That evening the orchestra sounded wonderful. Nick was proud to be standing in front of it. All of the musicians were careful of their phrasing, and even Norma could tell the difference. It was one of those rare evenings when everyone on stage took a great deal of pride in what they were doing. When it was over, Norma looked at Nick and wondered if she liked him or hated him. One thing was certain; she respected his musical ability more than anyone she had known.

A few days later, Mike introduced Patty to Norma and suggested the three of them have a late dinner in Norma's room. Then he hurried across the street to have an early meal with Suzy. After they finished, he told Suzy that he had to leave early to talk over the broadcast before the evening performance. He told her there was something special about tonight's air shot, but he didn't know what it was. Also, he would be late returning after the evening session, because Nick wanted them to listen to the taped broadcast. Then he hurried back across the street to have a second meal with Patty and Norma.

When the orchestra started playing, Mike was so stuffed that he couldn't blow his trumpet in his usual forceful manner. No one paid much attention. The volume of the orchestra automatically dropped down to what he was doing. After they finished the job, he took Patty downstairs for a snack. Then they went to the musicians' room where they could be alone. Sure enough, it was empty. All of the musicians had left the hotel and they had the room to themselves. Mike took her to bed and jumped up and down on her bones until they were both exhausted. They returned to Norma's room to say good night. He told Patty he would pick her up shortly after two the following afternoon and transfer her across the street.

"Can you make it sooner?" She asked.

"I'm sorry Patty, but this has been a hectic day. I'd better sleep in tomorrow. He hurried across the street and had a cup of coffee while Suzy ate something solid. When they got back to her room, Suzy wanted Mike to prove his love one more time.

Mike could get it up, but he couldn't get it off. After a while he faked a massive orgasm, and Suzy was satisfied. They slept for a few hours, and then Suzy had to pack her things. Mike said goodbye to her around eleven o'clock. He took a taxi from the train station back to the Peabody and just made it back in time for the noon session. Then he picked up Patty at Norma's room and moved her across the street into the room that Suzy had. When she was unpacked she asked, "Can we do it again before you go back to work?" Mike threw himself into the act, but wondered what in the hell he was trying to prove.

When they started the evening session, Mike could hardly hold his trumpet, let alone blow it. After they finally finished playing for the dancers, and as he was walking out of the room with Norma, she asked, "How's it going, stud?"

"Fantastic! However, if you ever worried about my making a pass at you, tonight you can relax. The animal in me has been temporarily tamed."

Norma woke up the following morning and acknowledged the fact that she had only a few more days' work with Nick Gray's orchestra. She dressed, had breakfast, and started making phone calls. Her third call was to Bryce Zeller. When she asked if he knew of any openings for girl vocalists, he told her, "No, I'm sorry, but I don't know of a thing at the moment. When will you be back in the city?"

"I'll be there in four days," she told him.

"Okay. If anything turns up, I'll keep you in mind. Take care of yourself and stay in touch."

Norma continued making calls until she ran out of names. During her last day with the orchestra, the phone rang mid-afternoon. She picked it up and heard a voice from the past.

"Hi Norma. This is Stan Bernstein. Do you remember me?"

"Of course," she replied. "How have you been?"

"With the exception of not being able to make it through law school, I've been fine. Right now, I'm working at the Stevens. They have a lot of conventions booked next month, and I'm responsible for getting the entertainment. I guess you could call it a temporary entertainment director's job. I called Bruce Zeller earlier today and hired a couple of his bands. I still need a trio and a girl vocalist for the cocktail hours and some of the smaller gatherings. I won't have any trouble finding a suitable trio, but I haven't been able to find a suitable girl vocalist. Bryce recommended you. Are you interested and still available?"

"Yes I'm interested and yes I'm available," she said.

"Good. Consider yourself hired. When you get back to Chicago, give me a call and we'll discuss the details."

The following morning, Norma was on a train bound for Chicago. The Nick Gray Orchestra was traveling south for a one night stand on their way to New Orleans. As usual, Nick was leading the way in his Lincoln and looking for new conquests.

Chapter 4

Transition - 1955

The American public decided it was tired of dancing away its evenings, and the big band era was over. The transition started ten years before when vocalists became the stars, not the instrumentalists. It seemed that everyone wanted to hear the words, and the music became secondary. The adults stayed home and watched their new toy, TV, and the teenagers looked for a new music they could call their own. They found it and called it Rock 'n Roll.

In its early stages, background music for the rock singers remained acoustic, with the exception of the electric guitar. The big difference was the use of wind instruments. Rather than have sections of brass and reeds, rock groups usually had one or two wind instruments. Some of them didn't use any wind instruments. With these small groups, backup musicians didn't have to be proficient at reading music. The musicians could just *fake it*, so to speak. Many of the instrumentalists from the big band era complained that the amateurs were taking over the music business. Those who stayed in the business migrated to the film industry, Broadway shows, or symphony orchestras where sight reading skills were still required.

The initial success of rock music was propelled by the new financial opportunities it opened for the promoters. In the recording industry, it was no longer necessary to have special arrangements and ten to twenty musicians in the studio. They could record the vocalist with head arrangements and use three to six musicians. In many instances, recording companies didn't pay scale wages, because they could get by with nonunion musicians. With the new wave music, non-union musicians sometimes did a better job than the union musicians.

They weren't inhabited by the so-called rules taught to the schooled musician, and they had an enthusiasm for the new music that their predecessors lacked.

Many of the promoters and personal managers had a field day. They could sign up teenage performers to contractional agreements that were previously unheard of. No longer were they required to limit their fees to those specified by various professional unions, because they weren't promoting established professionals. If their properties decided they wanted a more desirable percentage of their earnings, they could always be replaced by another new talent that was hungry for fame. The primary market became the adolescent girl, to be more specific, twelve to eighteen year olds. The philosophy was, if you can reach the young girls, you automatically get most of the young boys.

Most of the promoters and record producers weren't unscrupulous, but it was a new era. They usually took care of the initial investment of producing and promoting new talent. If their initial investments were paid off, and the downstream profits showed a good potential, equitable contractual agreements were usually reached, and everyone involved made money for a few years.

The problem that many of the new entertainers faced was a short career. They grew older, but the market for their talents remained in the same age bracket - twelve to eighteen year olds.

Some of the entertainers were able to age and still get a good response from the youth market, but most of them watched their audience decline and fade away. A few of them tried to hang on to their own age group, but the period between twenty-five to thirty-five years old usually turned out to be a disaster. Most of their contemporaries did not have a significant amount of money to spend on entertainment. They were in debt for house payments and busy raising their families. Only a few performers were able to survive this period, and Jerry Ross was one of the survivors.

Chapter 5

The Survivor - 1970

Jerry Ross lived in his fantasyland that fame and money provided. By the time he was eighteen, Jerry had a successful career. His first modestly budgeted record earned back its cost during the first month it was released. Two more record dates followed in rapid succession, and with the release of his third record, Jerry became big business. For ten years, everything he did made money. His live performances were usually sold out. His records made money, and his songs were recorded by other artists. Then overnight it ended.

Unlike many people in the business, Jerry knew it wouldn't last forever. He had invested his money wisely, and his total worth exceeded a hundred million. He didn't have a worry in the world: good health, lots of interests, and a beautiful considerate wife who let him indulge himself in various pleasures. For a year, he relaxed and enjoyed not having any commitments. Then in 1970, at the age of 29, he made a discovery. He missed being Jerry Ross – "The *Celebrity.*"

If money could buy it back, Jerry could make the grade. He realized that making records would not be the immediate solution, because nobody had contacted him for record dates in over two years. Many of his previous recordings had been reissued, and Jerry could tell from his residuals that there wasn't a large record buying public waiting for a new release. The current rock concert scene didn't look promising. He was never into the drug culture and always maintained a clean-cut, well-dressed, wholesome image. Jerry decided to forget the kids and leapfrog into the adult market. The over thirty-five group was the audience he wanted to capture. He looked forward to the challenge and started developing a nightclub act.

His first step was to find a personal manager familiar with the nightclub circuits. He looked for someone who could give him guidance as well as find him bookings. He finally decided on Teddy Goldstein. Teddy had a good track record of booking adult vocalists.

Jerry told him, "I will be available for work in about four months, and I would like to be booked for three months of continuous work. Let's avoid the major cities; just book me into moderate sized rooms. If audience response is not satisfactory, I'll withdraw for awhile and think about it. If I get a good response, we will write up a new agreement and proceed with additional bookings. I'm very open on money, get what you can, but don't price me out of the market. I want to work."

Teddy Goldstein got on the phone and started contacting clubs. Within three weeks, they had another conference. Jerry was satisfied with the money and places which were tentatively lined up. Teddy made the suggestion to Jerry that he have all of his charts re-orchestrated to uniform instrumentation. Teddy knew the type of house bands used in the rooms which he had in mind. He thought Jerry's instrumentation should consist of drums, keyboard, bass, guitar, three trumpets, one trombone and three reeds. Teddy gave him the names of five arrangers who did this type of work for some of his other artists. He also suggested a few monologue writers.

Jerry dug out his old charts and records. He listened to the records and pencil marked the piano parts where he wanted sequences revised for his new nightclub act. Then he started picking out new pop songs recently recorded by other pop artists. Jerry located one of his former keyboard players, Neal Becker, and hired him as rehearsal pianist. They worked eight to ten hours a day. Neal noted all the sequences and important instrumental figures that Jerry desired, then Jerry would get the layouts to other people to be orchestrated. Neal offered to do some of the orchestration work, but Jerry didn't want his help in this area. Jerry went to three of the biggest name arrangers in the live performance field. He considered himself a big name, and he wanted big names stated on his charts and acknowledgments. After all, whoever heard of Neal Baker, he was just another unknown. However, Neal was hired to play piano and conduct the orchestra.

Two weeks before his first engagement, Jerry had Neal hire musicians and start full band rehearsals of the new arrangements. The rehearsals were taped so Jerry could listen to the charts during the evening. Throughout the rehearsals, Jerry wanted to make changes. Since he was not capable of actually revising the background music, Neal dealt with the revisions as best he could. The musicians took a ten minute break each hour, but during these breaks, Neal was busy sketching revisions on their parts. After five days of rehearsing, Jerry dismissed the musicians and reviewed the tapes with Neal.

During the discussions, Neal suggested that a permanent rhythm section be hired for the tour. They would pick up the other musicians, or use house band personnel, from the various cities they would be playing. Jerry didn't think it was necessary to carry three more musicians, but he approved it. During the day, Neal rehearsed the rhythm section. At night, he made permanent revisions in the scores and copied new parts for the individual instruments.

Jerry lined up the sequence of songs for his typical one hour and twenty minutes show. He had enough musical material for two shows, so he considered many options. Then he went to some of the monologue writers recommended by Teddy Goldstein. Jerry wasn't impressed with their initial thoughts, so he decided to write his own monologues.

They opened at Sut Miller's in Dayton, Ohio. Audience response was polite but not overwhelming. Jerry taped every show throughout the week. Material that died was removed immediately. Songs that consistently received a lukewarm response were replaced at the end of the week.

As the tour continued, numerous revisions were made. Neal was busy rewriting the background music, and Jerry kept revising his monologues and song sequences. Occasionally, the audience's response was enthusiastic, but Jerry noted that it only occurred when the majority of the people in the room were young adults. He wasn't getting any standing ovations from the over thirty-five crowd. After three months, he told Teddy Goldstein and Neal Becker, "The tour fell short of my expectations." They parted company, and Jerry went back to New York to think things over.

The ordinary person would have given up, but Jerry Ross was not ordinary. The disappointing tour only strengthened his desire to return as a superstar. He became a fanatic in his desire, and with fanatics anything is possible.

For a few weeks, Jerry listened to the tapes from his tour, but he didn't learn anything new from them. Then he decided to witness what was going on in the adult entertainment field. He and his wife attended most of the concert performances in New York. It was during a performance by Drew Daily that he heard something that set him on fire. The thirty piece orchestra was superb, but it was the rhythm section that grabbed him. He was sure no one could get a sound like that from five rhythm musicians on stage.

The following afternoon, Jerry started making telephone calls and eventually got through to Drew Daily. Drew was about six years younger than Jerry, and he was flattered by the call and praise. During his early years in the business, Jerry was one of Drew's idols.

When Jerry wanted something, he could be the most charming person on the face of the earth. After a few minutes of conversation, Jerry asked, "How do you get your rhythm section sound?"

"It isn't a big secret," Drew told him. "Quite a few of the pop recording artists are using it in their nightclub acts and concert performances." He invited Jerry backstage that evening to talk with his soundman and see the show from the wings.

Jerry arrived about thirty minutes before show time, and the security guard took him to Drew Daily's dressing room. They talked briefly and then Drew introduced him to Pete Harper. As Drew dressed for the show, Jerry and Pete went to the sound equipment area, located just off stage. Jerry saw the usual sound counsel, but beside it were two tape players.

Pete explained that the two reel to reel tape players contained identical tapes which were synchronized. In the event of a mechanical or electrical failure in one machine, the other tape would continue to play. He told Jerry, "It's just a backup feature. Each machine contains the rhythm sounds from Drew's actual recordings. Since you can't duplicate live what is done in a recording studio, we've taken the rhythm sounds from the original 24 track recordings. This approach allows us to get all of the echo, fuzz, reverberation, and other special effects particular to a recording studio during a live performance. The musicians on stage play along with the recorded tracks and make still more sound. One of the hazards that goes along with this sound reproduction technique is the balance of volume. If the musicians play louder than the sounds coming from the tape machines, they might lose the beat coming from the rhythm tracks, and we could have a musical train wreck. To help prevent this from happening, I'm busy mixing sounds throughout the performance. Do you see the large monitor speakers on each side of the stage?"

"Yes," Jerry replied. "I was wondering why they were directly opposite the orchestra."

"There's a reason for it," he told him. "I pipe the sound from the tape machines through those speakers so the musicians on stage can hear the recorded sounds, just like the audience is hearing them out front. There is a mike for every instrument on the stage, and I mix the actual sounds from the musicians at a slightly lower volume level and feed them through with the recorded sound. The monitor speakers reproduce sound at a level higher than the musician's actual sounds, so they only hear themselves through the speakers, and the recorded rhythm tracks are always slightly louder than anything coming from the actual musical instruments. When we get to the final vamp of the song, rather than fade out like the record, Drew's conductor has written actual endings for the orchestra. I watch the conductor, because I can't see Drew when he is out front on stage. When Drew wants to get out of the vamp and conclude a song, his conductor signals me, and I start fading out the tape and bringing up the volume of the orchestra. The wind and string instruments are orchestrated to build and become more predominant. As the orchestra goes totally live, the audience doesn't notice the fadeout of the rhythm tape. There are many other tricks, and you'll see and hear most of them during the performance."

During the first performance of the evening, Jerry was fascinated by the electronic wizardry. After Drew Daily returned to his dressing room, a group of people started to gather outside his door. Those whom Drew wanted to see were eventually admitted. As Jerry watched the activity backstage, he thought he saw Buddy Israel among the group waiting to see Drew. A few years ago, Buddy and Jerry had co-written three songs.

Pete Harper rewound the tapes and excused himself by saying, "I hang around for a while after every performance. If Drew heard something during the show that he didn't like, he chews me out and I try to fix it. Since he doesn't like to be kept waiting, I'd better get in the line and see if I'm wanted." Pete joined the conductor outside Drew's door.

Jerry recorded the names and model numbers of Drew's equipment. He also made notes of what he saw, heard and the placement of the various sound devices. When he finished, the people in front of Drew's door had disappeared. Jerry walked over to the security guard and told him he wanted to thank Drew and say goodbye. In a few minutes, Pete Harper walked out and Jerry was admitted by Drew's secretary, Lois Martin.

Drew was changing his clothing in the inner room. Lois started to introduce Jerry to Buddy Israel, but Buddy rose from his chair and came toward Jerry saying, "Don't bother, Lois, we're old friends."

Buddy's breath smelled like he had been on a continuous drunk. They sat down beside each other, and Buddy lit a new cigarette from the one he had been smoking. He told Jerry, "I'm working on some new songs for Drew's next recording date. One song is finalized. I've been trying to finish two more, but Drew doesn't care for the words. I guess the chord changes and melodic lines are satisfactory, because he hasn't complained about them. I've written so many different words, it seems I can't even remember what I wrote yesterday or the day before. I don't know what Drew is looking for, but it certainly isn't what I'm writing. If he doesn't like my latest concept, I guess I'll throw in the towel."

"Why discard the music if the words are the only problem?" Jerry asked him. "Find someone else to write the lyrics, and stop sweating it."

"Would you be interested in giving it a try?" Buddy asked.

"Sure! I'm very available and would enjoy making a stab at it."

Drew came out of his room and took the lead sheets Buddy handed him. He looked at them for a few minutes and said, "I'm sorry Buddy, but this is the same old crap. Can't you think of anything new to say?"

Buddy's voice was shaking as he spoke, "Jerry offered to collaborate with me and write new lyrics. Is that okay with you?"

"If he doesn't mind working with a no talent drunk, it's all right with me," Drew replied. "I don't know if I even like your music, so I've been considering material from other songwriters. If you two want to give it a last-minute try, you can use the piano in here." He walked out of the room and slammed the door.

They went to the piano, and Buddy started playing one of his songs. Jerry took a few sheets of manuscript paper from the top of the piano and listened. He liked what he heard and wished he had Buddy's talent for writing original music. As Jerry tried to find some appropriate words for the music, Lois started cleaning up the room. The half-filled glasses and dirty ashtrays from the previous guests were emptied and washed. The room would be spotless when Drew returned to get ready for the last show.

One hour later, Drew walked through the lounge area and went into his dressing room. He didn't say a word. When the orchestra started to play his overture, he called for Lois and she applied stage makeup to his face and made sure there wasn't any lint on his clothing. He departed for the stage with Lois behind. She carried a tray with a pitcher of water, two glasses, towels and extra makeup. When they reached the wings, Drew took a final drink of water and charged on the stage. As the audience cheered and applauded his entrance, Lois placed the tray on a stand and returned to the dressing room. She would be back in the wings in thirty minutes when Drew made his first brief exit. The orchestra would be playing bow music from one of his biggest hits.

Jerry and Buddy continue to work as the show proceeded. Maybe it was a long layoff, perhaps it was the joy of working with the talent you respect, probably it was just luck, but Jerry wasn't having any trouble writing new lyrics to Buddy's songs.

After the show, Drew burst into the room with Lois. He had received four standing ovations during the show and was high from the applause. He asked to see the new lyrics, Jerry handed him the words for the first song. Drew looked at them for a while and then asked Jerry for his pencil. He started circling words while he told Jerry, "I like this. It's very good, but a few of the words have been overused. See if you can come up with some substitutes. How is the other song coming along?"

Jerry handed it to him and said, "I only completed the lyrics through the bridge." Drew looked it over and said, "Damn, you did it again, but I think you should try to move this statement from the bridge into the final phase of the song. Those words could be the hook that gets them. Let's keep them guessing until just before the song ends. You think you can complete them in a day or two?" "Probably," Jerry replied.

"Good. When they are finished, get them to me. Lois will give you a number where I can be reached while I'm in the city. You guys had better get out of here and go to work. Lois, hold off the mob until I have a chance to relieve myself and wash up."

As Jerry and Buddy left the room, Lois smiled at the people outside and said, "Mr. Daily is taking care of an emergency call. He will be with you in a moment." She closed the door so they wouldn't hear the toilet flush.

Jerry told Buddy, "I'll call you as soon as I get all of the words worked out." Buddy went home and crashed. Jerry returned to his home and went to work.

Jerry's wife, Peggy, woke up the following morning around nine o'clock. She dressed and started walking toward the kitchen. As she passed the living room, she noticed that the door to Jerry's study was closed. Peggy was relieved to know that he had come home. Sometimes Jerry would be gone for a few days at a time without letting her know where he was at. She continued to the kitchen and made breakfast for herself. Afterwards, she made a tray for Jerry with a pot of coffee, juice, and one piece of toast. Jerry had been trying to lose a few pounds. Peggy tapped lightly on his door, went in, placed the tray on the edge of his desk and asked, "Will this be enough?"

Jerry did not look at the tray or his wife. He continued to work and said, "That's fine, thanks dear." By mid-afternoon, he had finished the job. Jerry slept for a couple of hours, showered and dressed. After checking over the words to the new songs, he made a few minor revisions. Then he called Buddy Israel to let him know the new lyrics were finished.

An hour later, Buddy let Jerry into his apartment. It had a shabby feel, and the lingering odor of stale tobacco was everywhere. They went to the piano and started revising Buddy's melodic lines to fit with the new lyrics. After a few hours, they completed the songs. Buddy said he would make new lyric sheets and get them to Drew Daily. Then he told Jerry, "You'll have sole credits to the words."

"No! That would not be fair," Jerry said. "Many of the words and thoughts were lifted directly from your previous lead sheets."

"Shut up Jerry, I don't want to argue with you. If Drew likes these things and records them, I'll probably make a nice piece of change from the music credits. Before you came into the picture, it didn't look like I would make a dime. Now get your butt out of here and let me go to work on the lead sheets."

Two days later, Jerry received a call from Lois Martin. She said, "Mr. Daily liked the lyrics you did on those two songs. He has decided to use them in his new record album. A few changes have been made in the music, so Mr. Daily will be sharing the music credits with Buddy Israel. You will still retain sole credit for the lyrics. I just finished making out new applications for copyright registration. Mr. Daily would like to have you review your new lead sheets to make sure the lyrics are right before you sign the copyright applications."

"I'll be glad to do it," Jerry told her. "Where can I find you, or would you prefer to bring the material over to my home?"

"Would it be possible for you to meet me at World Wide Recording Studios?" Lois asked. "I believe they are located a short drive from your home. Mr. Daily is at the studio supervising some of the rhythm track recordings for his album. If you find anything you don't like in the lead sheets, the two of you could then resolve any errors. I have some correspondence for him to sign, so I'll be at World Wide in about one hour. May I meet you there?"

"Of course," Jerry said. "I'd like to see how Drew operates in a recording studio, and this will give me an excuse to watch for a while. I'll see you there in an hour or so, and thanks for calling."

When Jerry arrived at the recording studio, he noticed that the red light over the door was dark, so he went right into the console control room. He recognized the sound technician, and they exchanged greetings. Jerry sat down in one of the numerous chairs and look through the glass into the soundproof recording area. Drew Daily had five musicians gathered around him. They were marking up their master rhythm parts as Drew explained what he desired.

In a few moments, Drew burst through the soundproof door and said, "Hi Jerry, thanks for coming over. Lois should be here in a few moments." He sat down next to the sound technician and told him, "Turn on the two-way speakers." Then he shouted, "Okay guys, whenever you're ready."

His conductor kicked off the tempo, and the musicians started playing. Drew turned to the technician and said, "I want more treble on the electric guitar." The sound technician replied, "I would prefer to add it when we mix the tracks."

"I don't give a damn what you prefer to do. Put more treble on the guitar, and do it now."

The technician advanced the treble control on the guitar and Drew barked, "Not that much; back it off a bit. Good, hold it there. That's what I want." Then he shouted, "Chris, put in a big drum fill at the end of this phrase."

Jerry thought the drummer vigorously hit everything that surrounded him, but Drew yelled, "Louder when we do the take; make it build."

Lois Martin walked into the room as Drew continued to shout orders at everyone. She sat down, opened her briefcase, and handed Jerry the lead sheets and applications for copyright. Lois also removed the correspondence that was ready for Drew's signature, but held onto it and waited until he was ready for her.

Jerry looked over the lead sheets and didn't find any errors in the lyrics. Since the musicians were still playing, he examined the chord changes and the melodic lines. The chord changes were identical to the previous version. The five revisions in Buddy's melodic lines were minor and didn't affect the lyrics in either song. He picked up the applications for copyright and noted that Buddy and Drew had signed the forms as co-writers of the music. As he signed his name, he thought that Drew Daily was something of an opportunist. The music stopped and Drew said, "Let's do a take; cut our sound to the musicians." The red lights glowed over the doors, and the musicians started playing. Drew held out his hand, and Lois gave the correspondence to him. He glanced at the letters, signed them and handed them back to her.

When the musicians finished and came into the control room, everyone listened to the playback. After it ended, Drew spoke, "I'm satisfied. Is anyone unhappy with what they did?" The musicians uttered the usual, "I guess it's all right", and "I could've done better, but I'll fix it up on one of the additional takes."

Drew turned to his conductor and told him, "I want to add the acoustic guitar after the first eight measures. Write something in sixteenth note patterns and keep him in the upper register." As the conductor sat down to write, Drew was with the keyboard player saying, "I want you to work out some sustained things on the organ for the last twelve measures. That's the next thing we will tape, so get back in there and see what you can come up with." Drew came over to Jerry and told him, "I have some thoughts for new songs. Why don't we get together sometime and knock them around?"

"Sure," Jerry replied. "Give me a call when you're ready." As Jerry left the studio, he felt sorry for Buddy. He hoped that he never found himself in a similar situation where he needed the money.

Jerry contacted the various recording companies that owned the master tapes of his old hit records, and had them run off four copies each of all rhythm tracks still in their vaults. As they arrived, he listened to them and was somewhat disappointed. They were bland in comparison with the ones Drew Daily used. However, he knew that a lot of people had bought his old records, and some of those record buyers would be coming to see his next nightclub act. Although he wasn't sure how the tapes would be used, he felt certain they could be utilized. If nothing else, they would appeal to the people who wanted to remember yesterday.

Jerry puzzled over his new nightclub act for a few months, and then two things happened that helped him rebuild his career. First, Drew Daily's latest record became a big seller, and the hit single from the album was one of the songs with lyrics by Jerry Ross. Second, he received a call from Buddy Israel.

"How would you like to collaborate with me on a few songs?" Buddy asked. "It sounds interesting, but do you have anything specific in mind?" Jerry asked.

"I sure have," Buddy told him. "It's a Broadway musical. This thing has been on the back burner for almost two years. Now it's in rehearsal, and I'm writing most of the original music and lyrics. The director is Irving Hill. He is also responsible for the staging and choreography. Irving is a bastard to work for, but he sure knows how to pull a show together. As far as I know, all of the music is completed except for two songs. I know Irving's premise for the words, but I can't get anything down on paper that makes any sense. Will you do the lyrics?"

"Sure," Jerry replied. "When do you want to get together?"

"Right now, if that's possible."

They worked incessantly for a few days, and Jerry went to the rehearsals with Buddy. As the dialogue on stage was revised, it sometimes necessitated minor changes in the lyrics of previously completed songs. If Buddy couldn't find the right combination of words, Jerry would help out. During this period, Jerry realized that Irving Hill was a knowledgeable tyrant. If he didn't like what the dancers were doing, Irving would jump on the stage and show them exactly what he wanted them to do.

Jerry believed that old Irving could dance better than anyone in the cast. However, because of his age, he couldn't keep up for any great length of time. When it came to staging, he was a master of the art. His sense of timing, visual and audible, was uncanny. The mockup sets were rebuilt, modified and repainted continuously. The cast responded to his directives without hesitation or argument, and that included the principals, Jim Jones and Norma Anderson.

The experience of seeing a Broadway musical in rehearsal was brand-new to Jerry Ross. When his career was at its peak, staging was incidental. Sometimes, thousands of kids turned out to see him on a portable stage that was almost bare. And with the exception of a few gestures, all he did was stand on the stage and sing. Jerry was witnessing and learning the skills of a different facet of show business that was directed at a specific audience: adults. When people went out to see this medium of entertainment, they expected professionalism throughout the show: lighting, sound, staging, music, and performance.

Buddy Israel and Jerry Ross attended the musical's first dress rehearsal. As they found seats in the Lunt- Fontaine Theater, they were relieved that their work was over. Irving Hill was on stage and telling the cast, "I hope to have you out of here in four hours. Don't stop for any reason, unless there's a foul up - or I tell you to stop. Now let's get down to business."

Irving walked to the middle of the theater and took a seat between his prime dance choreographer and music arranger. Then he picked up a portable microphone and watched the curtains close. The house lights went totally dark, stage and exit lights flashed on, and the orchestra started playing the overture. After the second tempo change, a voice came out of the darkness, "A little faster, George." The conductor picked up the tempo.

When the overture concluded, the musicians made a direct segue into the opening number. Members of the cast came down three staircases singing the title song of the show. When they reached the stage, Jim James entered from the wings on the left side and Norma Anderson entered from the right. Norma was carrying two canes. When they met at the center stage, Norma handed one of the canes to Jim and a voice boomed from the darkness, "Stop!"

"Norma, don't poke that cane at Jim. Slowly hand it to him with a circular motion. Try it!" She did and it looked better.

"That's good Norma," Irving said. "Let's start the opening number again with the entrance of Norma and Jim. No girls, don't go back up the staircase. You're supposed to be on stage. We'll start at measure thirty-three. George, isn't that about where the cast reaches the floor?"

The conductor replied "Yes".

"All right then, that's where we will start. Let's go!"

Then Norma handed the cane to Jim. The voice in the darkness said, "That's better, but do it slower. Keep going!" They concluded the opening number and the stage went dark. As the cast left the stage, unnoticed in the darkness, the orchestra started playing the next song.

The stage still appeared to be dark, and Jerry could not see any light coming from the music stands. He wondered if the musicians had memorized their music for this segment. It didn't seem likely, and he puzzled over how it was done.

Midway through the next number, the drummer omitted the initial rim shots as the dancers started their kicks. Irving Hill didn't say anything, but he nudged the music arranger on the right. The arranger had been watching the stage and noticed the omission. He looked at his score and realized he had neglected to put in any rim shots. He admired him for being so alert and made a mental note to pencil in the five rim shots on the drum part and cue them on the conductor's part. As the number progressed, Irving leaned to his left and told his choreographer, "Get with those dancers and cleanup their turns as soon as they conclude this number. While you're with them, find out why Kate and Billy were a little late making their entrance."

The choreographer hurried through the side door entrance to the stage and waited in the wings for the dancers to make their exit.

The next segment featured Norma Anderson on a vocal. As she made her entrance, singing and walking down the center staircase, Irving's voice drowned out her vocal. "Norma, if you're going to wear your hair that full, wear more makeup. Your facial features just disappear with all that beautiful fluffy blonde hair. Make your eyebrows much darker." She nodded and continued her song.

In a few moments, Irving turned to his arranger and said, "The background music is too heavy and loud. It's covering some of Norma's lyrics, and it detracts from the sensitivity I want in this scene. Lighten it up." As Norma continued to sing, the two men discussed specifics. When the vocal segment ended, Irving said, "Hold it right there. I'm sending Chico up to make some changes in the music."

Chico told George, "We will have the arrangement end with just the piano, bass and drums. Have them start running down the last eight measures and we'll see what they come up with. Reeds, mark your parts tacit. Brass, use cup mutes throughout the arrangements, and circle out the following measures…"

As the musicians did their thing, Irving walked to the side of the stage. He caught Norma's eye and motioned for her to come over to him. When she arrived at the edge of the stage, Irving told her, "You must move to the right earlier in your song. You were six feet away from the end of the curtain when you're vocal ended. I want you to disappear behind the curtain as your last syllable fades. Can you do it, or should I have the curtains advanced?"

"I can do it," she told him.

"Good, now one more thing. When you come down the staircase, try not to look at your feet. I know this is the first time you've been down the actual staircase, but when you look down, it detracts from your magnificent stately pose. If the stairs are too steep, I'll have them rebuilt."

"No, they're just fine," Norma said. "By the time the show opens, I'll be comfortable on them."

They ran down the segment again and continued. The stage filled with people hurrying back and forth. Two boys and two girls were carrying on a conversation as they moved with the choreography. The voices were picked up loud and clear by the sound system.

Jerry asked Buddy, "Do you know how they get such a uniform voice pickup from the stage mikes? With all of that movement, I would've expected them to be using cordless microphones."

"They're using transistorized sound units, hung on their bodies," Buddy replied. "The units are flat and positioned in the small of their backs. They transfer an electrical signal directly to the sound console, and then it is projected through the speaker system." "But where are the mikes?" Jerry asked.

"Look below their throats. The microphones are small and can be concealed by ornamental pins or clasps. See that guy on the left? He has his pickup device attached to his shirt and hasn't tried to hide it. The cord runs inside his shirt from the sound unit to the mike. I believe those things cost about $3,500 apiece."

The number ended, and Irving's voice came from the darkness one more time. "Percussionist, I didn't like the way you played your timpani part. When the runners touch their hands on the floor, you should start your timpani roll. When they start to run, you stop your role and strike the timpani, hard! Make it sound like an explosion, brrrrrr-bom! It must be done precisely with their actions. Also, during that portion when you're playing the timbales, give me a heavier backbeat."

The percussionist marked his part, and the rehearsal continued. After ten minutes more, the musical conductor announced that it was time for the musicians to take a break. Irving replied, "All right, take your break, but be back promptly in ten minutes. We're running behind schedule, and that bothers me."

Jerry Ross went backstage and found one of the musicians smoking a cigarette. He asked him if they memorized their music for the stage blackouts.

"No, we haven't had the time to memorize a thing. I know it looks dark from out front, but our music stand lights are still on. They are dimmed during stage blackouts and glow with a faint blue hue. I guess that it's an ultraviolet blue, because you sure as hell can't see anything under the light that's not treated. Our music is sprayed with a special coating of something that breaks up the color spectrum. The whole thing is kind of strange. When our lights are dimmed, you can put a sheet of regular music under the light and not be able to read a note. When the music is sprayed, you can read it. It's faint but readable. If you want to know more about it, talk to Phil Rizzo. That's him standing next to Chico. My break is just about over, so if you will excuse me I'll get back to the sweatshop and pump out more notes on my horn."

A few of the girls were late getting back on stage and Irving roared over his microphone, "Come on girls, move it or I'll have it." With the exception of Norma and Jim, the segment started with the entire cast on stage. It was a busy number and Irving was yelling at the cast, complaining about the lighting, and most unhappy with the percussionist. When it concluded, he burst on the stage with his arranger and choreographer.

Irving started showing the performers how he wanted them to exit and return to the stage. The choreographer was going over the dance steps with the male dancers, and Chico was working with the rhythm section - trying to get different musical effects from the various percussive instruments. Everyone was nervous and tempers were beginning to get raw. With everyone on stage, Irving said, "Let's try it with the boy dancers. George, where did they start their routine?" George replied, "Measure 121."

"Go!" was all Irving said and they were underway. When they started their kicks, the dancers were forward and near the edge of the stage. The band was playing a double forte, and everything fell apart. The dancers complained that they couldn't hear the drummer's rim shots on the fourth beat of the measure and the first beat of the following measure. This figure repeated itself several times until the kicks ended. Irving looked at Chico and said, "Fix it."

Since the drummer was playing as loud as he could, Chico decided to reinforce his rim shots with the percussionist. He took the percussion part and tacited out the bongos. Then he marked in a timpani part that started on the fifth of the chord and went to the tonic. These two notes occurred simultaneously with the drummer's rim shots. They tried it, and it worked perfectly.

Irving had them start once more at the beginning of the routine. They were barely into it when he stopped everyone and shouted, "Percussionist, I don't like the sound of the bells, try something else; and I don't think you're playing your part correctly. The notes you were playing were not precise with the beat, and it's confusing the dancers. What's the problem back there?"

"I'm playing everything just the way it's written," Felix replied. "What you want isn't on my music. The big problem back here is that my parts are all fucked up..."

Chico exploded. "You're saying I didn't do my job right? There isn't anything the matter with my arrangements. If all of your taste wasn't in your mouth, we wouldn't be having these problems."

The silence on stage was unbearable. After a long pause, Chico said, "I'm sorry Felix. Let's take a look at your part and see what we can come up with." Chico and Felix decided to replace the bells with the triangle. The triangle made less noise but would be heard more precisely. Everyone got back to work and forgot about the outburst, everyone except Irving Hill. When they were ready to try it again, Irving told Chico, "I want you to stay with the orchestra for a few numbers and work with Felix."

Irving and his choreographer left the stage and went back to their seats. With all of the delays, the rehearsal was taking longer than he thought it would. Irving continued to try hurrying things along, but he slowed things down again when he decided to reverse two segments of the show. The first segment went through without a hitch, but when the second segment started, the last girl dancer to come on stage didn't have her costume on. She was dressed in high heels, bra and tights.

Irving hollered, "Sue, what the hell do you think this is, burlesque?"

Sue said, "I didn't have enough time to get into my costume." She had appeared in a skit during the latter part of the proceeding segment, and when the segments were reversed, no one realized that there wasn't enough time for her to change costumes. Irving spoke, "For God's sake Sue, go get dressed. We'll work something out to allow you a little more time. Cast, take a break. George, Chico, figure out a way to extend the instrumental music thirty or forty seconds between those segments. I don't want the show to feature half naked girls."

Chico did a quick mental calculation and concluded they could go back to the bridge after the last chord and then play it out. This would give them almost forty seconds of additional music. He asked George to have the musicians mark the parts with repeat signs at the bridge and two measures before the end. After the break, Chico rejoined Irving in the theater. During a lull in the show, Irving asked, "What's the matter up there? Is it you, the music copyist, or the percussionist?"

"I only saw two copy errors," Chico told him. "That's not bad for nearly thirty minutes of music. Perhaps I could have used better judgment in places with my choice of percussive instruments. I may have been thinking too much about musical effects and not enough about the needs of the cast. The percussion parts are in reasonably good shape, I would say that 95% of the notes, symbols, and cues we desire are on them. Sometimes things work out better when they are left open for the individual initiative of the musician. In this case, that approach leaves something to be desired. Felix is not very resourceful, but I believe he will do a satisfactory job by the time the show opens."

When they took their next break, Irving motioned for his conductor to join him. "George, when today's rehearsal is over, fire Felix. I want to see someone else playing the percussion book at tomorrow's rehearsal, and I'm counting on you to find the musician who will do a better job."

After nine hours, five more than anticipated, the rehearsal finally ended. Four days later, the show opened and received good reviews. Although it wasn't sold out for every performance, ticket sales were adequate to ensure a profit over the long haul. After a few months, response was solid enough to warrant a recording of the show's music by its cast. Three months later, the album was released on RCA records and tapes, and this was about the time that Jerry Ross decided to move to Las Vegas.

Jerry and Peggy flew out West and went house hunting. Eventually, they were shown something that they both felt would be adequate for their temporary residence. The realtor told them that the house had belonged to a comedian who had been appearing regularly on the Strip until his drinking got out of hand. He was taking the cure and wanted to stay away from the city for a while.

Jerry signed a six month lease, and they moved in. During the evenings, they frequented the showrooms. When Jerry would see or hear something that impressed him, he would jot it down. If it was something technical, such as lighting, sound, sets or music arrangements, he would try and find out the name or names of the people responsible for the work. At that time, ten hotels had a continuous star policy. Every week or two, a different group of superstars were brought into the showrooms.

As Jerry's presence in the city became known, he was invited to appear on the various TV programs which were taped in the showrooms during the afternoon. He did not turn down any interviews, because he wanted to keep his name alive and known. If they wanted him to sing, he would do something from one of his old hit records. One or two songs would always receive a warm audience response. If a TV host asked him what he had been doing the past five years, his reply would be, "I've been writing songs." Then he would refer to the lyrics he wrote for Drew Daily's latest record and the Broadway musical. He never mentioned the unsatisfactory three-month tour during the previous year.

Besides rebuilding his image, his stay in Las Vegas opened his eyes to what the hotels expected from their entertainment. Plain and simple, it was to increase *the drop* in their casino. Jerry made an effort to meet the entertainment buyers at the major hotels, and he tried to establish cordial relationships with them. Out of the group, Ben Fox was the one who leveled with him and got him thinking in the right direction. It occurred late one evening at Jerry's house. Ben had been doing some concentrated drinking and was trying to get drunk. With all the nervous tension he was encountering at his hotel, Ben was working up to the point where he couldn't even get a buzz on. However, he was in a talkative mood.

Their wives were off doing the things wives do when their husbands want to discuss business, when Ben said, "Jerry, I know you've been trying to get me to make you an offer to work at my hotel. You have the national recognition necessary to be a headliner in the city, but it's not that simple. I'm sure your name would bring people into our showroom, but they may not be the right kind of people. If it is a younger audience and they fail to gamble, I could not bring you back. That would not help you rebuild your career, and it would spoil our friendship. You'd think it's how many asses you put in the seats that counts. That's the way it was when you were doing your concert tours and appearing at places that held upward to 20,000 people, but it doesn't mean a thing out here."

"Now Ben, you're not trying to tell me that having a show room full of people doesn't mean anything, are you?"

"Jerry, be still for a moment and let me make my point," Ben said. "Figure it out. I only have a nine-hundred seat showroom. If you filled it twice a night, what must I charge the customers to break even? Between your salary, the culinary workers, musicians, stagehands and other fixed overhead - admission prices would become astronomical. The Las Vegas showrooms have never paid their own way. They are a diversion to get people into the hotel and keep them near the casino."

"If you're trying to tell me that entertainers can't make a living in the city, I know you're wrong," Jerry replied. "Some people are being paid around $200,000 a week to appear in Vegas."

"Sure, but those are the ones who have a proven track record. They fill up the showrooms with people who spend big bucks in the casinos, but you don't know if you'll draw all those kind of people and neither does anyone else. Since you're trying to get back in the business, I don't think you should start out by taking a chance on this place. If you open in Vegas and don't draw well, every trade paper in the country will print it and your career will be over before it gets underway. If you do draw well, but the people don't gamble, every entertainment buyer in the state will know that, and you won't be hired anyplace on the Silver Circuit. It is almost a no-win situation. Don't try to rebuild your career in this city. The odds are against it."

"Are you suggesting that I quit before I get started?" Jerry asked.

"No, but I believe you should stay away from Vegas until you have a lot more going for you."

"Are you trying to tell me, go out and play the cow towns for a while?"

"Hell no! What good would that do? It wouldn't mean a thing. First of all, let me tell you what draws people into our showrooms. Recent recording success is the biggest thing that makes a star draw for us. When was the last time you had a hit record? I'll bet it was at least four years ago."

"Yes something like that," Jerry said.

"Well get back in the recording studio and put something new on the market. The next thing that brings people into our showrooms is exposure on television and movies. I realize you been making TV appearances, but it has been primarily on daytime TV. Forget about daytime TV, because it doesn't count. People who watch daytime TV don't go out at night to the clubs. Think about getting some film exposure and a new hit record. When you've got those things going for you, then try Las Vegas. At the very least, you will be sure of doing a good job of drawing people. If they don't spend money in the casinos, you'll still get good press reviews on the attendance. Being a good draw in Las Vegas will help you get bookings somewhere else. Then you will at least be able to start playing places where money can be made from ticket sales."

Ben's concept was vividly pointed out to Jerry the following evening. He was in Bobby Brown's dressing room. The last show was over, and it was the final night of his current engagement. Bobby had been working at the same hotel for eight years. He was a Las Vegas fixture and one of the fortunate vocalists that had found a home. Bobby was about fifty years old and had maintained a constant career for almost three decades. During this engagement, he was the opening act for a hot new comedian that had a TV series, Ed Ricky.

Jerry was congratulating Bobby Brown on his performance and remarking about the attendance. "I have to hand it to you Bobby; a 90% filled showroom on a Wednesday night is almost unheard of. What are you doing right that everyone else is doing wrong?" "It's not me," Bobby told him. "Ed's the one that's filling up the room."

"Don't be so modest. If you weren't a good draw, you wouldn't be offered multiple engagement contracts year after year. I heard the applause tonight, and your audience is loyal and responsive. When Ed Ricky is forgotten, you'll still be appearing at his hotel."

"I wish you were right, Jerry, but thanks anyway for the kind words. Tonight I needed them."

"Hey, what gives, it sounds like something is bothering you. Would you care to talk about it?"

"Sure," Bobby said. "It might help me get over the shock. The hotel isn't bringing me back next year. I guess the bulk of my audience consists of little old ladies who play the nickel slots, so the powers that be said that they couldn't afford to keep me around anymore."

"I'm sorry to hear that," Jerry told him. "I'm also surprised, but you'll find another place on The Strip that wants your talent."

"I doubt it. This hotel has been good to me, and there isn't any animosity in the parting. Two years ago, when the showroom head-counts started to drop during my engagements, they decided to stop using me as a headliner. We talked it over, and I didn't have any objections to being moved from headliner to opening act. After all, you can't expect to stay on top forever. This year, they only used me as a substitute. If one of the acts couldn't perform because of sickness or something, they would bring me in to plug the hole. My contract states that I'm committed to do three more engagements this year. Tonight they paid me off in full. This is the first time I been paid for not performing, and I can assure you of one thing, it doesn't do much for the ego."

"Do you have any plans," Jerry asked.

"Nothing definite as yet, but I'll probably move back to New York. My agent keeps telling me the East Coast is my strongest region. That's where the bulk of my old recordings are still being sold. So I'll probably go back there and sing to the little old ladies from time to time."

The following day, Jerry and his wife drove to Los Angeles. Peggy started looking for a house, and Jerry started looking for an agent. When he discussed his plans with Stan Bernstein, Jerry felt certain he had found the right man.

Stan listened to Jerry as he outlined his goals, and then he advised him, "I wouldn't rush out and put a new record album on the market without a specific plan. As I recall, your biggest sellers were the songs you composed."

"Almost without exception, you're right," Jerry replied

"Sure, your trademark was singer, composer, Jerry Ross. I think we should stick to that identification. If you can't write eight or nine new songs in a reasonable length of time, why not consider co-writing them with someone associated with the major recording company. If you still don't come up with enough new material for an album, fill it out with the things you did for the Broadway musical. If you're willing to make yourself available for promotion tours, we won't have a problem finding a recording company with national distribution. That's the only sensible way to get a record on the market these days. The small independent labels don't have the clout to launch a nationwide campaign. When they get a hit it's a fluke, so let's stack the odds in our favor and plan on tying up with some of the big boys."

"Your approach sounds good to me," Jerry told him.

"Thanks, Jerry. I know it's a pain in the butt to do promotional tours, but it will assure us that you'll receive airplay in the cities where you appear. You will have to greet the people, sign autographs, talk to the disc jockeys, and appear on local TV shows: but it should make your name a household word again, and that's our first goal in reestablishing your career."

During the next two months, Jerry was busy writing and co-writing new songs. By the time he had enough new material for an album, Stan Bernstein had negotiated a recording contract with a major label. The contract included options for additional recordings if the initial album made money. Jerry went into the recording studios and sang the songs against basic rhythm tracks. When he was satisfied with his vocals, the recording company brought in arrangers and musicians to do additional rhythm tracks plus sweeten the songs with strings, brass, and reeds. These sounds were mixed and the master tape was made.

When they finally started producing records, six months had been spent on the project.

During this time, Stan Bernstein worked with people who designed album covers, posters, and miscellaneous items that go along with recording promotion. Mainly, he approved or rejected cost quotations and proposals. He also made some of the arrangements for radio and TV interviews. Most of the costs were billed to Jerry Ross Productions, but this was anticipated and he could afford it.

Jerry spent a lot of money and energy during the four-month promotional tour, but it paid off. Record sales were hyped by his personal appearances. When the tour ended, total record sales were significant. The recording company exercised their option, and Jerry started writing more songs for his next album.

While Jerry was working on new music, Stan Bernstein was looking into the nightclub market and presenting various proposals to him. Jerry was not impressed with any of the proposals. After many false starts, Stan finally asked, "What the hell are you looking for in the live performance field?"

"I'm looking for a room where I can exercise complete control," Jerry told him. "It's beginning to look like I have to lease a room if I want to control it. Why not? Get on the phone and see if anything is available on the Las Vegas Strip."

"Jerry, you're talking about a four-wall agreement, and I think it would be a serious mistake. You don't need that kind of grief."

"Do as you're told," Jerry said. "When I get back into the live performance field, I don't want anything to go wrong."

"But Jerry, do you really want control over every person that works in the room? If that's the case, you'll have to hire, and sometimes fire, the maître d', waiters, waitresses, musicians, stage hands, and comply with all of the union contracts. If you try to handle all of those problems, I don't think you're going to have any time left to perform. Do you want to compromise your show business career by getting into the hotel business?"

"Perhaps you're right, Stan. I guess I was overreacting to some of the asshole entertainment buyers I worked for in the past. I'm sure you know the type. I call them the know-it-all-would-be performers if they had any talent, but of course, they never do. I don't want any of those characters telling me how I should do my act or exercising control over my performance. I also want some type of control over the people working in the show room. Most of all, I want something to say about the audience. If the room doesn't fill up with paying customers, I want to be in a position to see that it's filled by other methods. I don't want to perform in a half filled room. Do you have any suggestions?"

"Sure," Stan replied. "Coming up with the inventive contracts is what I do best. I'll start looking for a showroom in Las Vegas with which we can reach a partnership agreement. The way your recording career is going, I might be able to find a hotel that will pick up all of the costs, split the gate, and still give you considerable control over the room. When do you want to start working?"

"Let's say six months," Jerry told him. "That will give me time to complete my next record album and get a new nightclub act together. Yes, six months should be perfect."

Jerry found it difficult to come up with nine more songs, so he co-wrote with three other people. His input was usually small but honest. He didn't steal credits without adding something of significance to his songs.

For his nightclub act, he wanted a very impressive orchestra. He decided to use three trumpets, three trombones, two reeds, percussion, drums, guitar, bass, keyboard and three backup vocalists. In addition to the basic orchestra, the arrangers would also write optional string parts for violin, viola and cello.

Jerry worked with quite a few rehearsal pianists in his effort to put together a new nightclub act, but he wasn't satisfied with any of them. He needed someone who was willing to work at odd hours and on short notice. He also needed someone capable of working out and noting sequences, important instrumental lines, introductions and endings. Out of desperation, he called his previous conductor, Neal Becker.

"Neal, this is Jerry Ross. How is your family? What are you doing these days?"

"My family is just fine, and I'm doing a single at a cocktail lounge. What's up Jerry, why are you calling?"

"I need you," Jerry told him. "How much money are you making it the cocktail lounge?"

"With benefits, it's almost $600 a week."

"I'll pay you $1000 to come back and work for me. You have to move to the West Coast, but I'll guarantee you at least eight months of continuous work. What do you say?"

"That's a very tempting offer, but I'll have to say no," replied Neal. "My wife has a good job here in New York. I know she won't quit, because she'll be vested in a retirement plan in three more years. No Jerry, I can't do it."

"All right, if that's the case, I'll pay you $1500 a week."

"When do you want me to start?" Neal asked.

"Just as soon as you can get here. How about tomorrow?"

"Jerry, that's out of the question. It can't be done. I'll have to give two week's notice at the cocktail lounge. It will be 15 or 16 days before I can get to the West Coast."

"Try to make it sooner. When you arrive in Los Angeles, call me. I'll expect you to be available 24 hours a day, seven days a week."

"I understand," Neal replied.

While Jerry was waiting for Neal to arrive, he obtained the rhythm tracks from his last album. The recording company also gave him copies of the basic master rhythm parts. With this data, he was able to call in two arrangers and get them started on stage band arrangements. They had to come up with actual endings instead of using the fadeout endings on the recorded versions. Then they orchestrated Jerry's nightclub instrumentation over the existing tracks. Jerry had each arranger do charts for all nine of the recorded songs. This way, he would have a choice. If one arrangement didn't grab the audience, the other one might. If neither of them did the job, he would have Neal make composites using the best phrases from each arrangement.

When Neal arrived in Los Angeles, he went to work on the songs from Jerry's old hit records. Jerry decided to put them into medleys. The first medley was the important one, and it would be used during every performance. It contained the songs that received good audience response during his previous tour. The second medley contained recorded songs that received mixed audience responses. The second medley would only be used if the audience gave overwhelming applause to the first medley and acted like they wanted more of the same. If the second medley was used, Jerry decided he would introduce it as *"some of my hits that missed."*

Rather than do a full course on each song, they used short phrases of 8 to 16 measures. After each song, they worked out short instrumental interludes. If the audience wished to applaud, it would happen while the orchestra played;

not during Jerry's vocals. When a proceeding song was followed by a song in another key, Neal would include a modulation in the interlude. When Neal came up with the interludes that were comfortable for Jerry, he would notate the chord changes and melodic lines on manuscript paper. Then they were recopied on vellums so reproductions could be made for rhythm section musicians and the arrangers. Neal hired musicians that played bass, drums, guitar - and the four of them went into the studio and recorded the inserts. While Neal was supervising the cutting and splicing of Jerry's old tracks and the new inserts, he received a phone call. "Knock it off and be at the international airport in three hours," Jerry told him. "We're flying to Las Vegas."

Neal left the studio and drove to his apartment. As always, the freeways were sheer torment. Jerry hadn't mentioned how long they would be gone, so he packed enough clothes for a week.

When they boarded the plane, Jerry told him, "I think Stan has found a special room. He's been talking directly with the president of the hotel, because the entertainment director was fired last week. I guess they've tried everything: stars, production shows, musicals, but nothing seems to work for them. Right now, they're back using a star policy. Before Stan does anymore negotiating, I will look the place over and make sure it's right for me."

The flight took less than an hour, and the hotel's limousine was waiting for them at McCarran Airport. During the drive to the hotel, Jerry told Neal, "We'll see both shows tonight. Tomorrow they change headliners, and there will be a rehearsal at noon. I want you to attend it and check out the musicians in the house band. I'll try to find out what has been going on in the way of attendance figures and see how much freedom they're willing to give me."

At 7:15PM, Jerry and Neal left their rooms and went to the casino. There was a line of about 400 people waiting to be seated for the dinner show. They ignored the line and walked to the entrance. The maître d' had been notified that they were invited guests of the hotel, so they were immediately seated in one of the booths. The waiter was pleasant, and the meal was more than just adequate. Shortly before the show started, Jerry estimated that the room was about 70% filled. With the exception of one loudmouth drunk, the people were orderly and appeared to be in a good mood. Fortunately, the drunk passed out before the line of chorus girls opened the show.

The girls performed for about twenty minutes, and they were well received by the audience. Then the star of the show came on stage and did one hour and twenty minutes of bombastic dancing and singing. Sonja Hart was a real worker.

Jerry thought she was a super talent, but he didn't enjoy her show. The sound was too hot and, at times, the intense volume hurt his eardrums. The male backup singers were all over the stage, and just watching them wore Jerry out. He told Neal, "Their choreographer must not believe in heart attacks." Every imaginable lighting effect was used, and Jerry didn't know if it was the lights, volume, or both, that caused his splitting headache. It was almost a relief when the show ended.

Jerry told Neal, "I'm going backstage to meet Sonja. Would you care to come along?"

"If you don't mind, I'd prefer to go to the musicians' room. I think I know one of the guys in the house band."

"Suit yourself," Jerry said, "but be sure you're back in the show room before the second show." They walked through the stage exit and headed toward the stage. A security guard stopped them at the end of the hallway, so Jerry introduced himself and Neal. The security guard said, "I'm sorry Mr. Ross, but you'll have to wait a few minutes until little miss super bitch cools down."

As they stood and waited, he could hear Sonja screaming at her sidemen. "You lousy bastards, can't you do anything exciting? I'm dying out there and you keep playing the same old shit. If you assholes don't get something going during the cocktail show, your all fired. Now get the hell out of my sight."

After the sidemen walked out of Sonja's dressing room, the security guard said, "Thank you for waiting Mr. Ross, please follow me."

As Neal walked up the stairs to the musicians' room, he could hear Sonja cooing, "How nice of you to come backstage to see me. I can't begin to tell you how pleased I am to finally be meeting you."

Neal reached the top of the stairs, opened the door marked "Musicians", and saw Mike Moore wiping the perspiration off his trumpet. He walked over and said, "Have you slammed any car doors on your trumpet recently?"

Mike turned, looked at him and said, "Neal, what are you doing in sin city? Are you single again or just looking for a piano that's been tuned recently?" He finished putting his trumpet away and asked, "Care for a drink?"

"Sure," Neal replied, "Where's your flask?"

"It's in my trumpet case, but these days I save it for emergencies. Let's go over to the Musicians' Union and do our drinking there."

"I'd like to Mike, but I have to be back for the second show."

"So do I," Mike said. "I work here. It will only take us a few minutes to get there, and then we will have over an hour to drink and tell lies."

They got into Mike's car and headed south down The Strip. When they reached Tropicana, Mike made a left turn and then a right at the next street. They went inside and ordered drinks at the bar. A seventeen piece jazz band was playing at the opposite end of the room, and Neal asked, "Does this go on all the time?"

"It goes on five nights a week from ten until six. Two bands split it up each evening. There are ten bands that play here on a regular basis. It gives the unemployed and the under-employed musicians a chance to keep their chops up. This rehearsal hall is also open during the day from noon until four. The bands that rehearsed during the day only go at it for two hours, so once in a while I'll play with one of them. It's a nice change from the showbiz crap we usually play at the hotel."

"How long have you been working in the Las Vegas showrooms?" Neal asked.

"Some days it feels like forever, but I guess it has only been about three years. At least I can relate to the working girl these days. Most evenings, when the last show is over, I feel like a damned whore. With all the prostitution of the art that's going on these days, I sometimes wonder: Whatever happened to good music?"

The rehearsal band took a break and one of the trumpet men joined them at the bar. Mike shook hands with him and said, "Neal this is Gino Rizzo, one of the best unemployed trumpet men in Vegas. Gino, this is Neal Becker. I'm going to the men's room for a moment and make room for another drink."

"Hi Neal, what's your instrument?"

"Keyboards," Neal told him.

"You're lucky. There is more demand for it. At least you can play a single. How long have you known Mike?"

"We met about eight years ago. Actually, until tonight, I haven't seen him since then. For two months, we worked the East Coast with the James Orchestra, and it was a blast. Good music, good booze, and good fun all of the time. Mike made a lasting impression on me, and it wasn't just his playing. No matter what happened, he never seemed to lose his cool."

"Yeah, if you don't have cool, you don't have anything," Gino said.

"At the time Mike and I were working together, he carried his trumpet in a cloth gig bag. One evening before the job, three of us went out for a sandwich. It was cloudy but pleasant, so we walked about four blocks to a restaurant. We had our uniforms on and Mike was carrying his trumpet. While we were eating, it started to rain. Since we didn't want our uniforms to get wet, I called a cab. When it arrived, the drummer and I made a dash for the closest door. Mike ran around the cab, jumped in the other door and slammed it. He still had his trumpet under his arm and the door flattened the bell. Mike thought it was funny and laughed all the way back to the hotel. I thought it was tragic, but it didn't faze him. When we walked into the ballroom and got on the stand, he asked the drummer for one of his sticks, rolled the bell out, and played the job like nothing had happened. It sounded just the same."

Mike returned, heard the last sentence and said, "I thought it sounded better. I should've kept that horn. It was the freest playing trumpet I ever owned. Let's have one more round before we return to the dungeon."

They ordered, and while they were drinking, Gino asked, "How's Dave playing his trumpet these days?"

"Just fabulous, as always," Mike replied.

"I'm surprised. I heard he was hitting the booze pretty hard."

"That's a fact," Mike said. "But he still plays fabulous. It's just that he doesn't do it as frequently as he used to."

"Well, if you ever need an add, or fourth trumpet man, or if someone gets sick, please keep me in mind."

"You can count on it, Gino. Don't get discouraged man; you know how fast things can change in this business. Tomorrow may be your lucky day."

They left Gino, went to the parking lot, and Mike headed his car toward the hotel. On the way back, Neal asked, "Who's Dave?"

"He's our third trumpet man. Last year when they had the production show at the hotel, Dave was playing lead and split his lip. It broke on both sides of his mouthpiece and tore all the way up to his nose. That was when I got my first steady job in the city. At the time Bill hired me, he said the job would only last until Dave healed up and was ready to go back to work. I could buy that, because Dave played with Bill's groups for about twenty years. Hell, they'd been working together from the time Bill Davidson had a semi-name band. Bill is a good guy. If a musician works hard and does the job, he won't let him go unless he does something that jeopardizes Bill's job. When Dave returned, he didn't have the endurance to play lead. He knows music and he knows his trumpet, but those scars won't let him play the screaming high notes for any length of time. Anyway, Bill found a job down the street for his third trumpet man and put Dave in his chair. Everyone was happy, including me."

"Being that kind of a leader, Bill can probably hire just about any musician in town," Neal said. "That probably explains why the house band sounds so good."

"Sure, all of the guys know their instruments," Mike told him. "We have a few *prima donnas*, but that's Bill's fault. If a musician constantly cuts the shows, Bill will close his eyes to a lot of things that should not be going on. One thing he couldn't ignore forever was the drinking. That really got out of hand. You could hardly walk behind the music stands without tripping over bottles and partially filled glasses of booze. Don't get me wrong, some of the guys never touch the stuff. It's just that a few of the musicians abused the privilege. The whole mess hit the fan a few months ago. During an instrumental interlude, the headliner's conductor was waving his arms in a grandiose manner. I guess he was trying to impress the audience. Anyway, one of our reed men, Ed Foy, was half tight and took offense at all of the hand-waving. He stood up behind his music stand and started mimicking the conductor. A few people in the audience thought it was funny, but no one else did. Because of that incident, the hotel initiated a policy that musicians cannot be served a drink until after the last show. That's why we did our drinking tonight at the Musicians' Union."

Mike parked his car, and they walked in silence across the lot. As they went through the stage entrance, Neal said, "Sonja's backup musicians sure make a lot of noise. I could barely hear the wind instruments over the electronic rhythm section. Is Sonja Hart the exception, or do most of your headliners have their sound level that hot?"

"Most of them want it loud, but Sonja is the worst offender," Mike replied. "I have to wear earplugs during her show to keep from going deaf. Her background music has always been loud: and her staging, songs and dancing have been aimed at the frustrated male. A year or two ago, I thought she had a very exciting show, then the whole goddamned thing started to get out of hand."

"What you mean by out of hand?" Neal asked.

"Each time she returned to the hotel, she wanted the sound technician to keep cranking up the sound still more. I'm sure Sonja has suffered a hearing loss during the past year; otherwise she couldn't stand all of the amplified distortion. The electronic gadgetry used to enhance her background music, but now, everything is buried by earsplitting sounds and a relentless beat."

"I felt the same way when I heard her at the dinner show," Neal replied.

"Between the strobe lights, smoke machines, grotesque costumes and the thundering sound effects, I got the feeling we were accompanying something from a comic book," Mike told him. "Being from the pre-rock era may make me prejudiced, but I think you have to be a kid, or a kid at heart, to relate to her kind of pseudo neo-modern fantasy. I am certain of one thing though, if her background music gets any louder, we will have to pass out ear plugs to the customers."

As they approached the dressing room for the chorus girls, two of the girls were hurrying inside. They watched them go through the door and saw another girl, naked from the waist up, putting makeup on her face. They walked a few more steps and Neal asked, "Did you see that?"

"Shhh - quiet, I'm having her now."

Neal found Jerry Ross in the showroom. When the orchestra started playing, Jerry said, "I thought they had three trumpets." Before Neal could reply, he saw the third trumpet man hurry out of the wings and join the rest of the musicians.

The following day, Neal left his room shortly before noon to attend the rehearsal. Carl Kay, a country singer, was the new headliner. As Neal entered the showroom, Carl's conductor was passing out the books.

"Gentlemen, my name is Pat Anderson and I'm Carl Kay's conductor. I know all of you cats can sight read our simple charts, but we're going to run them down anyway. It should only take us about two hours. Carl probably won't attend today's rehearsal, but if he should drop in, please watch your language. He's a born-again Christian, and we don't want to offend him. One more thing, Carl sometimes flips meter. It's a totally unpredictable thing, so watch me at all times. I'll be at the piano throughout the show. When Carl skips a beat or two, I'll wave you out and catch up with him. When we're together again, I'll call out a bar number where I want you to come back in. When we reach the bar, I'll give you a downbeat with my right hand to bring you back in. The books are all lined up, so let's start with the first number, *Release Me*."

As the band started to play, Bill Davidson walked into the room and saw Neal. Bill came over, introduced himself, and sat down. The house band wasn't having any trouble with the charts. It was once through and then on to the next arrangement. Neal told Bill, "I think every guy in your band is an outstanding musician."

"Yes, I know," Bill said. "I'm proud of all of them." When the band took a break, one of the musicians came over and asked, "Bill, do we have to play that shit?"

"Now Tom, it's not that bad."

The musician said, "Carl's music is so simple it could be played by high school kids. The chords are nothing but triads and sevenths. The wind instruments don't have anything to play but footballs. Man, out of boredom, we'll all go to sleep during the show."

"Well, after playing the Sonja Hart show for two weeks, you deserve a rest," Bill told him. "Just relax and enjoy it, because we have some tough challenging shows coming up next month."

Shortly after the rehearsal resumed, Carl Kay walked onto the stage. He nodded to Pat and listen to the band run down three of his charts. Then he spoke, "I think the last chorus on that arrangement should be played much more softly." One of the musicians said, "Hey Carl, let's make a deal. You take care the singing, and we will handle the music."

Without hesitation, Pat Anderson addressed the band, "I want to do that arrangement again from the top. And this time, we will hold down the volume on the last chorus."

While the rehearsal continued, Jerry Ross was with Sam Gold. They had just finished reviewing the showroom attendance figures, and Jerry told him, "It's not fabulous Sam, but it isn't as bad as I thought it would be. When I heard your entertainment director was fired, I thought these figures would look like a disaster area."

"We didn't fire Tony because of the showroom counts," Sam said. "He was fired because he became greedy and dishonest. It first came to my attention when my chief accountant asked me to look at the musicians' payroll. Once in a while, our basic house band is enlarged for specific entertainers. Sometimes we have strings. On other occasions, we add one more reed, trombone, trumpet or percussionist. Tony would approve these additional expenditures. Bill Davidson would hire the musicians and supply Tony with the names, instruments and W-4 forms. When the payroll department made out the checks for showroom personnel, all of the checks were delivered to Tony. He would review the checks and transmit them to the department heads, such as Bill Davidson. Well, from time to time, Tony was putting himself on the musicians' payroll as a fourth trumpet man."

"That's ridiculous," Jerry told him.

"Yes, I know, but it was only the tip of the iceberg. We did some more checking up on Tony and found a few items I prefer not to mention. That guy was even taking kickbacks from some of our headliners. When I found that out, his employment with us was terminated."

"It sounds like a mess."

"Amen, and I'm ashamed that it happened at my hotel. Is there any more information I can get for you?"

"No, but I do have a question," Jerry said. "Over the next five months, how does your convention business look?"

"It looks constant. We usually book our conventions one to three years in advance. If you're wondering if our hotel rooms will be filled during your planned engagement, I would estimate that we'll average about 85% occupancy. That's what it has been during the past year, and I don't see anything that would cause a radical fluctuation."

"What are your feelings about giving me complete control over showroom personnel?" Jerry asked.

"I thought you wanted some type of a two-wall partnership agreement. Stan didn't tell me you are interested in leasing the room for three months."

"I'm not interested in a straight lease agreement. However, if employees are not doing their jobs, I want to be in a position to fire and replace them."

"Could you be a bit more specific?" Sam asked.

"Sure. If a musician shows up drunk, or a waitress is rude to a customer, will you let me fire them?"

"Jerry, I don't have anything to say about it, because those employees are covered by union contracts. In the case of a drunk musician, our agreement with the Musicians' Union clearly states that he or she can be fired. Of course, if they file a grievance and say they weren't drunk, representatives from this hotel would probably have to appear before the Board at Local 369 with affidavits from eyewitnesses to prove our case. The situation with the waitresses is a little more complex, but in any event, we honor the union contracts. I know you can't get by with nonunion musicians, and I doubt you could get by without using culinary union members. Does that answer your question?"

"I guess so," Jerry replied. "From what I saw last night, I don't have any objection to your maître d', stagehands, or culinary workers. However, I do want to bring in my own soundman, and perhaps, all new musicians."

"I'm agreeable to those conditions," Sam told him. "When you let me know the exact date you'll start working, appropriate notices will be given to the people you don't want to use. Would you mind telling us why you don't like our sound engineer or musicians?"

"It's not that I don't like them. They seem to be capable employees, but I have unique requirements. I will be bringing in my own sound console and rhythm track tapes. The tapes won't displace musicians, so there shouldn't be any problem with the union. I need a sound engineer who is intimately familiar with all of my arrangements, and he must be able to react immediately to on stage directives from my conductor. Since I won't be using your sound console, and mine requires specialized training, I need my own man. As for the musicians; my instrumentation will be different from your house band. You had four reeds on the stand last night. I only need two, but they must double on all of the reed instruments for color effects. Because of the taped rhythm tracks, I believe I need my own rhythm section people. Perhaps we can use some of your musicians, but I'd like to have my conductor make that decision."

"I don't like to fire employees," Sam said, "but I can see that you have specialized requirements. I'll see to it that the appropriate people are put on notice when the time comes. Everyone you don't need or want will be terminated, everyone except for Bill Davidson. The hotel can keep him partially busy handling the musical needs for special events and conventions. If you can use any of our musicians, I'm sure they will appreciate the work, and I know it will please Bill. After you've opened and closed, Bill Davidson will still be working for us. I don't want to offend him any more than necessary, because I consider him to be a good musician and a friend. Would you be interested in using our chorus girls as your opening act?"

"No," Jerry told him. "They do a marvelous job, but they don't bring people into the show room. I want someone or something with a name value that will help me pull people into the room. I've been considering using comedians who have had recent TV exposure. Is that agreeable to you?"

"It sounds like a good idea, Jerry. We are always pleased when our showroom is filled, and I believe you're going to do it. At the present time, we have headliners booked for eight more weeks. Does that give you enough time to get your nightclub act ready, or should we extend our current bookings?"

"I wasn't planning on opening that soon," Jerry said. "But after talking with you, I'm enthused and anxious to get started. I'll simply accelerate things and be ready in eight weeks. Now, I have one more favor to ask you before I leave. During the initial week or two of my engagement, I want the room to be full. Since I don't know how well I'll draw, will you give free comps to employees of the hotel to ensure that the room fills up?"

"I'll be glad to do that," Sam told him. "And if it becomes necessary, I'll give free comps to their friends."

"Good. I'll have Stan get in touch with you and work out the details of our contract."

Jerry and Neal saw the first show that evening, and afterwards, they discussed some of the musical requirements for Jerry's show. During the conversation, Jerry told Neal, "We don't have as much time as I thought we would have to get my show ready. Sam Gold would like to have me open in eight weeks, and I've agreed to do it. Since I'm planning on doing an all new act, and it requires new music, we probably should start rehearsals in the near future. Do you want to hire musicians from Los Angeles, or would you rather use musicians from the house band plus our special men?"

"From my standpoint, the easiest thing to do would be to hire Los Angeles musicians. We could rehearse them, find all of the mistakes in the new music, make any modifications you desire and bring a completely rehearsed group to Las Vegas. It's also the most expensive way of getting the job done. If we bring in out of town musicians, someone will have to pay an additional 10% above scale wages to the Las Vegas Musician's Union. The musicians would also have to receive a per diem to cover expenses for rooms and meals. I think we should hire musicians from Los Angeles to play bass, guitar and drums. That way, we can start rehearsing the new music with you as soon as it becomes available. It will give us a chance to make sure the chord changes and song sequences are satisfactory. I believe the rest of the musicians should be Las Vegas based."

"That sounds reasonable. You want to use the house band musicians for the other chairs? Sam Gold would appreciate it if we did."

"I'd rather not hire them as a unit," Neal said. "It's not that they couldn't play the music. They are all outstanding musicians, but I don't believe I could control their behavior on stage. If Bill Davidson is around, I know I'd lose control. He's like a big daddy indulging his children. Some of those guys think they can get away with anything as long as they play all the notes in the show music. I don't want any musician to say or do anything on stage that might embarrass you or detract from your performance.... Jerry, that was difficult for me to say. I don't enjoy being put in that position or making those decisions."

"I'm not paying you to win popularity contests. As my conductor, I expect you to offer that kind of advice. Why do you think I brought you with me? This is a business trip, not a vacation so you can visit with old friends and have a good time. Do you know enough musicians in Las Vegas to contract your own band?"

"No, I don't, but I know someone who does. His name is Mike Moore, and he plays lead trumpet in the house band. I would trust Mike's judgment, both musically and otherwise when it comes to musicians. I don't know if he would be interested in being our musical contractor, but I'd like to approach him on the subject. It might jeopardize his job with Bill Davidson if he works for us, but that's his decision. Do you have any objections to my discussing it with him?"

"No! Go ahead and feel him out."

After the second show, Neal and Mike went to the cocktail lounge in the hotel. They watched the gambling in the casino until the waitress brought their drinks. After the first sip, Neal asked, "Would you be interested in working for me as a contractor?" Then he explained the details.

"It sounds like a foul ball situation," Mike told him. "If I don't take the job, I'll be out of work for three months. If I take the job, I have three months work but that will probably be it. I doubt if Bill would rehire me, because you're asking me to break up his band."

"Not really," Neal replied. "The entire band will be put on notice before we open. You'll be free to hire anyone you want, just as long as you avoid the troublemakers. It's as simple as that. I don't want some of the characters in Bill Davidson's band, because Jerry has a big ego and a bad temper. The last thing I need is a riot, and that's what will happen if one of the musicians shoots his mouth off at Jerry. One big ego on stage is enough."

"I'd like to think about it for a while," Mike said. "How much time can you give me before I have to say yes or no?"

"If you don't say yes within four weeks, I'll find someone else - or bring in musicians from Los Angeles."

They were silent as they watched an impeccably groomed woman walk into the lounge. She was alone and seated herself at the opposite side of the room. Finally Neal spoke, "You certainly have a lot of beautiful women in this city."

"Yeah, that's a fact."

"If I weren't married, I'd probably make a fool out of myself chasing after that gal."

"We all have our weaknesses, but I don't think it would be that hard to catch her," Mike said. "One hundred dollars would probably end the chase."

"Are you trying to tell me you think she's a prostitute?"

"I'd bet on it," Mike replied.

"You must be getting callous and feebleminded from being in the city too long. I've got twenty dollars that says she isn't."

"I'll take that bet," Mike replied.

"You're on, but how will we find out for sure?" Neal asked.

"That's easy. I'll go over and ask her. If she slaps my face, tries to get me thrown out, or gets up in a huff and walks out, you're the winner. Order me another drink. I may need it."

Neal signaled for the waitress to bring two more drinks and watched Mike approach the woman. Mike stood by her table for a moment and said something to her. She smiled at him, and he sat down in a chair next to her. They smiled and talked and smiled and talked, and after about five minutes, they got up and walked out of the lounge.

Neal hurried after them. When the three of them got on the elevator, Mike acted as if he didn't know Neal. The elevator stopped at the fifth floor, and they got off. When Mike and the woman went to the right, Neal went to the left and walked slowly. He had only taken a few steps when he heard a woman's voice say, "This is my room." Neal took a few more steps, turned around, and saw that the hallway was empty.

Neal knew Mike well enough to suspect his actions with the woman. In any event, he was out twenty dollars. Not knowing if he had been set up or not, Neal felt frustrated. He decided to go down to the casino and work out his frustrations at the blackjack table. After about 40 minutes of gambling, he became bored. Since he was still wide awake, Neal decided to go back to the cocktail lounge and have one more drink before he called it a night. As he puzzled over the incident of the previous hour, in walked Mike and the woman. They went to the opposite side of the room, and the woman sat down. Mike remained standing as they talked and smiled for a few moments, then he turned and walked away.

On his way out of the lounge, Mike noticed Neal. He walked over to him, sat in one of the empty chairs and asked, "Where's my drink?"

"Here's the twenty I owe ya, buy your own drink."

"Neal, I didn't know you were a sore loser."

"I'm not, but I don't know if I lost or you suckered me in."

"If anyone is a sucker, it's me," Mike said. "You won't believe it, but I'm going to tell it like it was."

"Good. I would enjoy a good bedtime story this time of night. Lead on... I'm all ears."

"When I walked over to her table and asked if she was a prostitute, she smiled and said 'Yes I am.' I asked her if she enjoyed her work and she replied, ' I certainly do. The only thing I enjoy more than sex is traveling.' She was so charming, and her frankness so refreshing, I had to stay and hear more. She told me she only worked a city for one or two weeks. That way she could see all of the sights and avoid being hassled by the police. She was so enthused about her lifestyle, I found myself becoming fascinated with her. I was hooked when she told me, 'It simply thrills me and sets me on fire to know that almost every night I'll fall in love with another man.' She was so convincing, I had to try her out."

"How was she?" Neal asked.

"Hey, there's no substitute for talent and enthusiasm. She's a real professional. I think she even drained my sinus. Christ, that's the first time in my life that I paid for a piece of tail, but it was worth it."

The following day, Jerry and Neal returned to Los Angeles. Jerry hired a sound engineer, and they purchased the new equipment. Then he worked with Neal to finalize the song sequences for his nightclub show. Jerry got the sequence sketches out to various arrangers and then turned his thoughts to his new record. He and his co-writers went to work and finalized enough songs to complete the album.

When the new sound equipment arrived, Neal hired musicians for the rhythm section chairs. The four of them started rehearsing with the sound engineer and the taped rhythm tracks. The new arrangements were being completed on time, and everything was falling into place. As time permitted, Jerry would drop in on rehearsals. He would sing with the group and work out signals with Neal when he wanted to omit arrangements or make other changes.

About five weeks before they were scheduled to open in Vegas, Mike Moore called Neal and told him, "I'll be your musical contractor if you still want me. Is the job still open?"

"Yes! Consider yourself hired. We'll have six days of rehearsals before Jerry opens. The hotel has given us one of the convention rooms for five days, and then we'll move to the showroom for the sixth day. Rehearsals are scheduled from noon until four, but they may run a little late if we are having problems. Since many of them, including you, will be playing two shows in the evening, I know it will be a lot of blowing each day. If you think it will be necessary, we will accept substitutes during the first few days of our rehearsals. I will leave that up to you."

"That sounds like an excessive amount of rehearsal time," Mike said. "What gives?"

"All of the arrangements will be brand-new, and there will be two arrangements on most of the songs. During the first two days of rehearsals, we will probably spend most of our time looking for mistakes in the music. I doubt if Jerry will be able to attend all of the rehearsals, because he is still working on the new album. Jerry wants all of the arrangements taped so he can listen to them. He hasn't heard most of the lines written for the reeds and brass, so I'm sure there will be a lot of last-minute revisions. Can you get permission from the Musicians' Union to allow us to tape the new charts for review purposes only?"

"I'll see what has to be done," Mike said. "I'm sure they will want one of their business Agents present during the tapings, and we may have to use tapes with prerecorded bleeps. Somehow, the union will want to be sure that the tapes can't be used for commercial recordings. When I have the answers, I'll call you back."

"Good! Now start looking for musicians to play the following chairs: percussion, three trumpets, three trombones, two reeds, and make sure the reeds bring all of their instruments. Between the two of them, we must have an oboe and an English horn. I'll see you in a few weeks, and remember, I don't want any egotistic characters in the band."

During one of his conferences with Jerry, Neal asked if he could take a few days off and go back and see his wife.

"No," Jerry told him. "I need you here. Besides, there isn't anyone else I can trust with this work. Why don't you have your wife come to Los Angeles?"

That evening, Neal called his wife and asked her to take some time off from work and fly out to Los Angeles. "I can't Neal. I'm not eligible for any vacation time until next month. After you open in Las Vegas, I'll take two weeks' vacation, and you can show me the city."

"That sounds good," Neal told her. "But in the meantime, why don't you fly out here for the weekend."

"I'm awfully busy, Neal. I don't see how I could pull it off."

"Joan, tomorrow is Friday. Why don't you see if you can catch a flight out of LaGuardia Airport? If you leave right after work, we could be together for two days."

"That's a wonderful idea, but I won't do it," she told him. "You are busy and I'm busy. It would not be too much of a reunion under those circumstances. Just be patient, and I'll see you in about five weeks. I miss you very much. Please call me when you can."

After the telephone conversation with his wife, Neal felt exhausted and went to bed early. He had just dozed off when his phone rang. He hoped it was Joan and she changed her mind about flying to Los Angeles. When he picked up the phone, he heard Jerry's voice.

"I just hired three backup girl vocalists and they're fantastic. They've been doing most of the sweetening track vocals for my new album. These kids told me they dance up a storm, so I'm going to find a choreographer and have him work out some routines for them. What are your plans for tomorrow?"

"I was going to rehearse the five new arrangements that arrived late today."

"Call the musicians and delay their rehearsals for a few days," Jerry told him. "Here's what I want you to do tomorrow. First thing in the morning, get a second set of tapes made of all of my stage band arrangements. I want to get them to a choreographer. Then get the vocal group lead sheets together for the girls. I'll bring them by the rehearsal room about noon. I'll drop the girls off to rehearse with you when I pick up the tapes."

"Jerry, I don't think I can get dupes runoff in that length of time. Besides, we don't have tapes for all of your stage band arrangements. Hell, some of the arrangements haven't been completed yet."

"Get everything you can," Jerry said. "I'll see you at noon."

Neal called the musicians and told them they were off until Monday. He went back to bed but couldn't sleep. So around 1:00 AM he got up and started calling recording studios. He found one studio with high-speed reproduction equipment that could work him in at 5 o'clock. He got dressed, gathered up all of the tapes, and loaded everything into the trunk of his car. Then he went through the arrangements that were sacked around his apartment and pulled out the vocal group parts. He put the vocal group parts on top of his piano conductor book and carried them to his car. On the way to the studio, he stopped at an all-night diner and gulped down coffee as he watched the clock. When Neal arrived at the recording studio, a technician was ready for him and they went to work. At eight, he was back in his apartment setting the alarm on his clock for loud - and ready to get a couple of hours sleep.

At noon, Jerry arrived at the rehearsal room with the girls. "Ladies, this is your new boss, Neal Becker. Neal, these talented girls are Connie Scott, Lorie Leach, and Jean Storm." They shook hands as Jerry continued to talk. "I want the girls to memorize all of their music, and next week, we will start working with them on dance routines."

"Jerry, there's a lot of music for them, and some of it is rather complex," Neal said. "I don't think it is possible for them to memorize all of this stuff in less than four weeks."

"Don't tell me it's not possible," Jerry said. "It is possible, and I want it done. If their parts are too complex, simplify them. Do you have the second set of tapes I asked for?"

"Yes, copies of everything are in this box."

"Okay, I'm on my way to drop these tapes off with a choreographer recommended by Stan Bernstein. Now girls, Neal is always available. If there is anything in your music that you're not sure about, or if you're having problems with some of the harmonies, don't hesitate to call him."

Jerry left and Neal started rehearsing the girls. He was tired and felt like he was impersonating himself, but it didn't take him long to realize the girls didn't sight read very well. Lorie and Jean were having a lot of trouble with the harmony parts. Connie was singing lead, and she was the best sight reader in the group. Fortunately, all of the girls had good memories and good ears for music. When Neal played their lines on the piano, they could hear their parts and eventually be able to sing most of them.

Jerry didn't have a specific backup vocal group in mind when he got the original musical sketches out to various arrangers. Therefore, the arrangers just assumed vocal ranges. As the rehearsal proceeded, Neal realized that many of the parts would require revoicing. All of the girls sang within an alto range. When Connie's part would extend into the soprano range, Neal had to invert their three way chord voicings. If the girls couldn't hear some of the non-chordal voicings for passing tones, he would have them sing the top line in unison or octtava. On busy lines with hard to hear accidentals, Neal had to simplify their parts. They rehearsed until the girl's voices started to get hoarse. By that time, Neal knew what Connie, Jean and Lorie were capable of doing. They had run down about twenty percent of the charts, so Neal told them he would take the remaining arrangements home and rework their parts that evening.

While they were gathering up their belongings, Connie told him, "We sure appreciate your help. Actually, we're not singers, we're dancers. If you weren't so understanding and considerate, I doubt it that we could handle this job."

"Thanks, but rewriting music is part of my job," Neal said. "We'll continue to revise these parts until we come up with passages that are comfortable for your voices. Let's plan on rehearsing tomorrow and Sunday. I'll see you here at noon and we'll go at it until we get tired."

Neal went back to his apartment and reviewed the rest of the vocal group parts. It was around 5:00 AM when he put the last arrangement down and went to bed. The rehearsals on Saturday and Sunday went smoothly, and they got through the rest of the arrangements. Neal enjoyed working with the girls. Unlike Jerry, they had a great sense of humor and could laugh at themselves when things went wrong. Jerry was becoming an arrogant driven perfectionist, and most of the time, Neal considered him a real pain in the ass.

When the Sunday rehearsal was over, Connie asked, "Do you want us to rehearse again tomorrow?"

"Yes! We still have a lot to do, so be here at eleven o'clock. Tomorrow, the entire rhythm section will be here, and I want you to start singing your parts against their sounds. Damn it, I forgot about the five new charts that came in a few days ago. They're at my apartment. Tomorrow, I was going to pass them out to the men. My apartment is three blocks away, so it will only take me a few minutes to dash over there and get your parts. I'd like to go over them with you before we get together with the rhythm section. Wait here. I'll be right back."

Lorie said, "I'm hungry. Can't we knock it off for a while and get something to eat?"

"Sure," Neal told her. "There's a fast food restaurant at the end of this block. Here's twenty dollars, get something for all of us."

Jean decided she would go with Lorie and get some fresh air. Connie didn't want to stay alone in the studio, so she asked Neal, "Would you mind if I go with you to your apartment?"

"Not at all," Neal replied. "We'll take my car and save a few minutes."

When they walked into Neal's apartment, Connie saw music scattered in piles throughout the rooms and said, "I don't mean to offend you, but this place is a cluttered mess. Do you like having wall-to-wall music around you, or are you considering starting a music publishing business from this warehouse?"

Neal told her, "I suspected it all along and now you've confirmed it. You're a woman! A man would not complain about seeing a few piles of music on the floor, piano, and chairs. You probably won't believe it, but I have all of the scores arranged in some sort of alphabetical order throughout this place."

"You're right," she said, "I don't believe it. Why don't you put everything in one place?"

"Because I'm working on most of them, and it's easier for me to find things just the way they are. Besides, one of these days when I have some time, I'll start pulling the parts out of the scores and start making up books for the wind instruments."

While they were talking, Neal found the new arrangements. After he removed the piano conductor and vocal group parts from the folded scores, he said, "I've got the new stuff. Let's go."

Connie was on her knees looking at one of the stacks of music. As she bent over and placed the music on the floor, she gave him a good glimpse of her breasts.

The girls ate dinner snacks as Neal looked over their parts and drank coffee. He was glad the new parts were simple and repetitious. After a few minor revisions, the rehearsal resumed with Neal eating food with his left hand as he played the vocal group parts with his right hand. When the girls were comfortable with their parts, Neal thanked them for working late and went back to his apartment.

He called Joan and told her, "You made a good decision when you refused to fly out here for the weekend. The only thing I've had time for his work." They filled each other in on their busy schedules and after they said goodbye, Neal made a martini. Before he could take the first sip, the doorbell rang. He opened the door and saw Connie Scott.

"I forgot my purse," Connie said. "I didn't realize it until Jean dropped me off at my apartment. Aren't you going to invite me in?"

"I'm sorry, Connie, of course you can come in. You surprised me. I don't know what I expected to see outside my door, perhaps it was Jerry, but it certainly wasn't you."

Connie went over to the stack of the music she had been looking at earlier and found her purse beside it. She picked it up looked at Neal and asked, "Is that drink in your hand a martini?

"Yes it is. Would you care for one?"

"You'd better believe it. Make it a double. I've done some dumb things lately, but this takes the cake. I was lucky enough to find someone at the office. After they let me into my place, I tried to call you. Your line was busy, so I took my extra set of keys and drove over here. That wasn't too bright either, because my driver's license is in this purse. I think I'm losing my marbles, what do you think?"

Neal was thinking they'd probably end up sleeping together, but he said, "I think you're tired out. We've been going at it pretty hard and heavy the past few days. At least Jerry hasn't bothered us for a while. By the way, how's his new album coming along?"

"Don't ask me, because I'd be the last to know. We sang some aahs and oohs on a few songs, and that's about it. When he asked us if we would be interested in appearing in his nightclub act, it came as a complete surprise. Of course we jumped at the chance. Appearing on stage with Jerry Ross is bound to help our careers. The last few months have been damned slow, so we can use the work. We have done some TV jingles and that's all. Jean's dad has money in the studio where Jerry is recording, and that's the same place where we get most of our jingle work. How long have you known Jerry Ross?"

"I don't really know him," Neal said, "but I've worked for him on and off for about nine years. Why do you ask?"

"Well, everything happened so fast, I don't know what to expect from this gig. Jerry told us he wanted us on stage with him throughout the show. That's why we have to memorize all of the music. Do you really think he will feature us that way?"

"He might, but I wouldn't count on it. Jerry is selling himself and doesn't like to share the spotlight. I think your presence down front will depend on the dance routines. If your dancing enhances his performance, but isn't too distracting, you'll get a lot of exposure."

Connie thought about his statements and said, "In a nice way, I think you're trying to tell me he lied to us."

"I didn't say that, it's just- how can I say it - he has been known to change his mind."

"The few times I've seen him, he has always been friendly and gracious. Is he always like that?"

"No! When things don't *go his way*, Jerry can be as sour as they come."

"Are there ever any hassles over money?"

"Jerry always pays his bills," Neal told her.

"Would you like to go to bed with me?"

"Yes!"

It didn't take long for Neal to pop, and a short time later he said, "It's been a long time since I've had sex. The pressure was beginning to build up to the point where I thought my ears might fly off. How can I thank you?"

"Do you think we could do it again?" Connie asked. "I don't mean to complain, but a few fast thrusts and hearing' oh baby, oh baby', isn't just enough to get me off. You hosed me down before I had a chance to even get excited."

They went at it again and after they recovered, Neal told Connie he was married.

"That's interesting but not surprising," she said. "You're not the first married man I've slept with, and you probably won't be the last. I think people should go to bed with people they like, and I like you, Neal."

"I like you too, but I feel guilty. I should have told you about Joan before we got involved."

"Don't feel guilty," she told him. "We're both consenting adults, and we have our needs and desires. This is no big deal; after all, you did not seduce me. I was ready and it happened." Then she laughed and told him, "Look at it this way, all you did was perform a service and we both enjoyed it. If it hadn't been you, it would've been someone else."

The following day, they rehearsed the new arrangements. Midway through the rehearsal, Jerry showed up. He listened for a while and as usual, he was not satisfied with everything he heard. Jerry specified revisions, and when he didn't like what the girls were doing, he would sing the lines he wanted to hear. They responded without difficulty, because they were accustomed to working that way in the studios. After Jerry had everyone doing what he desired, they would tape the arrangement. It was Neal's responsibility to see that the scores and the parts were revised to be in agreement with the tape. When the rehearsal ended, Jerry thanked everyone for their attentive responses. Then he told Neal, "I have to go back to the recording studio - and you are going with me."

They got into Jerry's car and drove off. On the way, he managed to break most of the California driving laws. As they sped through a red light, Jerry asked, "What do you think of the girls? "

"I like them."

"Good, so do I. They should add a lot to my act. Do you think they will have trouble memorizing their music?"

"Jerry, you're asking a lot from them. Is it really necessary?"

"Probably not, but don't tell them that it's not necessary. Here is a list of songs, take it. Most of them are ballads, and I doubt if I want the girls out front with me on these things. If it looks like they can't memorize everything, these are the ones you should omit. In a few days, you'll get a call from Jim Kessler. He's the choreographer I've hired. When he's ready to work with the girls, tell the musicians to take a few days off. There isn't any point in paying them to sit around and watch the dance routines being worked out. Of course, I want you to stick around and accompany them on the piano. After the routines are set, call the musicians back and keep things moving. Tomorrow, I'll have to be in New York, so don't bother trying to reach me at home if anything comes up."

"How long will you be out of slot?" Neal asked

"I should be back in three or four days. I'm signing a contract with a new publishing firm. They have exclusive rights to all of the songs on my new album. I want them to get cracking on the sheet music so it will be on the shelves shortly after my record is released. Also, I've documented proof that my old publisher has been cheating me out of royalties. They have been sticking it to me and now I'm going to do it to them. If they don't agree to a fast settlement, I'm going to bankrupt them with legal fees and bad publicity."

They skidded to a stop at the recording studio and went inside. Jerry told Neal, "I don't like the keyboard work on one of my new songs. The piano man can't seem to come up with what I want, so I'm going to give you a shot at it."

They listen to what had been recorded as Jerry explained what he didn't like and the effects he desired. After hearing the tape three times, Neal sat down at the Rhodes piano and started playing out new lines. They worked together until it was time for Jerry to catch his flight.

A few days later, Jim Kessler had his first rehearsal with the girls. He had dreamed up some ambitious routines, and some of them were beyond the physical capabilities of the girls. During the first break, Connie told Jim, "I'm sorry we can't do all of the wonderful things you worked out for us, but we're singers, not dancers."

"I can see that," Jim replied. "Oh well, I'll just have to simplify some of the routines until we come up with the things you're capable of doing."

The days passed quickly, and before they were completely ready, it was time for the first full band rehearsal. Everyone was there, except Jerry. As anticipated, it took two days to find and correct errors in the music. During the third day, they recorded all of the arrangements. That evening, Neal took the tapes to the airport and got them on a flight to Los Angeles. He called Jerry's new secretary and gave her the flight number and arrival time. Early the following morning, Jerry called Neal and specified numerous revisions in the music. Neal, the musicians, and the girls spent the afternoon incorporating some of the revisions. When the rehearsal ended, Neal asked Michael Moore to find him an orchestrator and three music copyists. Neal stayed in the room and revise music. When the orchestrator and copyists arrived, he put them to work. At 4:00 AM Neal left and went to bed, but the other four men continue to work.

Jerry showed up for the next rehearsal. As he sang his songs and did his monologue, Jerry specified a few more minor revisions.

The final rehearsal was held in the show room. Jerry didn't make any additional changes in music. Instead, he concentrated on the lighting, sound, and staging. A platform was constructed for the girls. They would be sitting behind the reeds when they weren't out front with Jerry. As they went through the entire show for the last time, Jerry was the only one who didn't appear to be tired. After the third number into his show, he told the girls, "I don't think it's necessary for you to stay down front with me during the next song, so make your exit when the house lights dim. As a matter of fact, I believe you can sing your parts from the platform during the next five songs. I'll bring you down front again for the Show Stopper Medley." Then he shouted at the stage manager, "Bill, make sure you have three stools on that platform before tomorrow night. I want the girls to be able to sit down and get some rest between their dance routines."

Opening night had arrived. The first show would be for the press and invited guests only.

Mike Moore parked his car and took a long last drink from his flask. During the walk to the showroom, he sucked on an ice cube to try and reduce the swelling in his lips.

The sound engineer was getting a low-frequency hum from his equipment and couldn't isolate the source. Out of desperation, he and the stage crews were checking for loose connections and replacing microphones.

The girls had finished dressing and Connie was saying, "This is the most thrilling thing I've done in my life." Jean had her head over the toilet bowl and was throwing up. Lorie was applying her makeup for the second time and said, "Damn it Jean, if you don't stop doing that, you're going to make me sick."

The musicians took their places and played before the comedian. He didn't use any background music in his act and liked to perform in front of the curtain. Since the musicians couldn't be seen by the audience, some of them left the stand for a final smoke. Neal headed toward Jerry's dressing room to see if there were any last-minute instructions. His knees were shaking from a combination of nerves and fatigue. He wondered if anyone noticed.

Jerry felt good and could hardly wait to get on stage. Tonight, he was going to prove he was the best of them all. When Neal walked in, Jerry told him, "I've decided to change the lineup. Pull *Love Affair* and replace it with *Dolly*. Reverse the third and fourth numbers, and I don't like the clarinet obbligato on my opening number. Have it played on the flute."

"Those instruments are in different keys," Neal said. "The parts will have to be transposed. Can't you live with it the way it is during the first show? I'll rewrite it between shows and then we won't be taking any unnecessary chances."

"I'm getting tired of hearing you tell me why you can't do what I ask. I thought your friend hired some of the best musicians in the business? Isn't that what you told me? Well, did he or didn't he? Haven't you got someone out there who can transpose, or do I have to pull that number from the first show?"

"Leave it in," Neal said. "I'm sure Tom can transpose it. I didn't want to upset him with last minute changes and make him nervous. Is there anything else?"

"No. I think that's all."

Neal left the room and informed the sound engineer of the changes. He took his place on the podium and waited until all the musicians returned. Then he explained the changes to them and rearranged his own book. As he listened to the comedian wind down his act and get ready to introduce Jerry, Neal noticed a small torn piece of manuscript paper taped to the inside cover of his book. While he was with Jerry, Mike had written: Last Will and Testament... I, JERRY ROSS, being of sound mind and body, hereby will all of my worldly goods to my good friend and conductor, Neal Becker. It was signed, JERRY ROSS, SUPERSTAR.

Neal smiled, forgot about his nervousness, and gave the downbeat to the musicians. They cooked on a scorching up-tempo introduction. As the curtains parted, the audience saw the girls doing a dance routine. They looked charming and vibrant. Jerry's voice was heard, but he was not on stage. As the audience watched both sides of the stage for his entrance, a spotlight flashed on at the rear of the room. Jerry came through the middle of the room singing, smiling, and shaking hands. By the time he reached the stage. Most of the people in the audience were captivated and on his side.

The pacing of the show was excellent, and Jerry's singing and monologues received enthusiastic responses. He gave a flawless performance until midway through the show.

Jerry was doing his Old Hit Medley and was back with the audience. This time he was working his way around the perimeter of the showroom. As he sang his songs and stopped at about every fifth table, some of the people were trying to talk with him, and a few of the women were hugging and kissing him. Just before the medley ended, he found himself 40 feet from the stage. The stroll through the showroom had taken much longer than he had anticipated. Jerry had one arm around a girl, and as he smiled at her he spoken into the mike and said, "Keep it going, Neal."

With his left hand, Neal waved out the wind instruments before they went into the ending. His right hand played a vamp on the piano and the rhythm section followed him. His left hand was flipping back pages of his piano conductor part until he found another song segment in the same key. He covered his microphone with his left hand and called out the bar number to the musicians. As he stopped his vamp and gave the downbeat to the musicians, he yelled at Mike, "Play Jerry's part." The band came back in as one, and Mike's trumpet soared over the ensemble. It could not have sounded better.

Since all eyes were on Jerry, no one noticed the fast page turns and momentary confusion on the stage. Jerry detached himself from the girl and leisurely moved toward the stage. He continued to smile and shake hands. When he recognized where the band was at in his medley, he started to sing and Mike's trumpet faded away.

The audience gave him a standing ovation when the show was over. Jerry took three curtain calls before he left for his dressing room. He believed he could've done four, but since no one in the showroom had paid a dime to see him perform, he hesitated in pressing his luck with invited guests.

Before the members of the press arrived, Jerry washed off the perspiration and changed his clothes. He was relaxed and congenial as he answered their questions. Jerry acted like he had all the time in the world and gave them his undivided attention throughout the interviews. When it was time for him to dress for the second show, his secretary continued to offer drinks to anyone who was interested. As the comedian opened the show, the last of Jerry's guests departed.

Neal came to the dressing room and asked, "Will there be any changes in the second show?"

"Yes," Jerry replied. "But before we get into them, I want to be sure you straighten out the girls. They were getting pretty cute during the latter part of my show. I heard Connie bending those notes, and I didn't like it. I'm the singing star of the show, and I want the girls to sing their parts straight. And another thing, during my New Hit Medley, the trombone section sounded like a bunch of pigs rooting around in a sty. If they can't do a better job than that, fire them. Now about the changes..."

The following afternoon, Jerry had the three local papers delivered with his breakfast. As he drank juice and coffee, he read the show reviews. All the papers had nice things to say about him, and he could not have been more pleased. One of the columnists had written:

'Last night Jerry Ross made his Las Vegas debut and received an overwhelming response from the audience. Ross demonstrated that he is a mature entertainment pro and a major show-business personality. His act is spectacular. At age 32, Ross is at the peak of his powers as a performer, and if he is not, there is every reason to believe the best is yet to come. It is easy to see him remaining in Las Vegas showrooms for as long as he wants to continue working.'

Jerry cut the review from the paper and wrote a note to his secretary telling her to send copies to all of the trade publications.

To ensure that the showroom was filled, the hotel continued to give comps to the locals. Sometimes last-minute paying customers had to be turned away, but the ploy paid off. After the first month, it was not necessary to let people in for free. The word spread around the city that Jerry Ross put on a great show. Locals were recommending it to their out-of-town guests; taxi drivers were telling the tourists; and some of the other hotels were reserving blocks of seats for their conventioneers. The show was actually making money, and in the casino, the drop at the tables was up.

Trade publications started carrying articles about Jerry Ross. One of them stated he was an overnight success in his return to the showbiz scene. Jerry smiled as he read it, because it had been more than two years since he had made his first abortive attempt to get back into show business. They had been busy hard years, but well worth it. Once more, Jerry was a celebrity and he liked it. His new record was about to be released and his previous record was still selling well.

Jerry called Stan Bernstein and told him, "Now we're ready to make some real money. Start booking me with the highest bidders. I'll travel anyplace in the world if the price is right." Jerry knew that money was power, and he enjoyed the power almost as much as he enjoyed performing.

Sam Gold approached Jerry and asked him if he would care to extend his three month agreement with the hotel, but Jerry was not interested. A few days later, Sam wanted to work out a straight salary contract, but Jerry turned him down. Some of the more prestigious hotels in the city were interested in having him appear in their showrooms, and Jerry had Stan Bernstein negotiating with them. Three weeks before he closed, Stan had lined up an interesting four-month tour.

That night, after the second show, Jerry called Neal into his dressing room and told him, "I'd like to have you stay on as my conductor, but you have to take a $600 a week cut in pay."

"Jerry, my marriage is going on the rocks. When we close, I'm going back to New York and see if Joan is willing to give it another try. Even if you offered me a raise in pay, I'd have to say no."

Since Jerry's ego would not allow him to have someone quit, he told him, "I don't need you; you're fired. Of course, I'll expect you to work out your two week's notice."

Jerry had anticipated Neal's decision and had been talking with other conductors. During the final week of his engagement, a new man conducted the band. Neal had served his purpose. Jerry had enough music to do three completely different nightclub acts. Neal had even worked out stage band arrangements for the songs on his new album. Jerry had enough music to keep his act fresh for at least two years. If he wanted to add a few new charts, Jerry knew *someone* who was always available.

Mike Moore was hired for the tour. Jerry believed a considerable amount of rehearsal time and money would be saved if he carried a lead trumpet man, and he was right. Jerry was able to get Mike for less money than he had anticipated, because Bill Davidson would not rehire him.

When Jerry closed at the hotel, he kept the girls on until the novelty of having them around wore off. Besides, the girls were beginning to feel secure in their jobs, so he hired another group that expressed awe at his presence. Jerry knew the change would not mean a thing to the audience, because no one came to his concerts to see a specific backup vocal group, musician, or sound engineer. They came to see Jerry Ross. No matter what it took, even if he had to work twenty hours a day, he would not let fame slip away again. Being a celebrity, and playing cat and mouse with people, was more fun than anything else.

Chapter 6

Steve Post: Musician - 1980

Today, Steve Post would be discharged from the sanitarium. This was his second nervous breakdown in as many years, and he decided it was time to get out of the music business and do something else. He had been confined for three months, and this time, they would not let him have anything to do with music. That was alright, he did not miss it. Since there wasn't a radio in his room, he spent most of this evenings reading or watching TV. In four hours, Faye would pick him up and take him to the new apartment. It was just outside Oakland, California, and was only a few miles away from Faye and Jim's home.

Steve didn't like the idea of living so close to them, but he couldn't see an alternative. He had to go back to the sanitarium periodically for checkups, and the doctors were reluctant to release him to live in an area where he didn't have friends or relatives who would look in on him from time to time. Dan Daily lived a few blocks away from his apartment, and Dan had been a regular visitor after he was well enough to see people.

The first time Dan walked into his room, Steve couldn't have been more surprised or delighted. It had been ten years since they had seen each other. Shortly after Steve moved to Los Angeles in 1950, he met Dan on the recording stage at Paramount Studios. At the time, Steve was waiting out his LA card, so he couldn't work as a performing musician. However, he was working for a music preparation agency and had delivered the music to the studio. Since he didn't have anything else to do that afternoon, he asked if he could hang around and listen.

The conductor told him, "Sure thing. Just keep your mouth shut when we're recording so you won't screw up our session."

Steve was thrilled by the musicianship. Unlike most of the groups he had worked with, there was not one mediocre musician on the stage. Dan Daily was playing lead alto, and when the recordings were over, Steve went over to Dan and introduced himself. During the years that followed, they worked side-by-side at numerous recording sessions for the motion pictures. Each time they recorded, new music was played and the experience was always rewarding. The tension in the Studios never bothered Steve, if anything, it excited him. He was proficient on all of the reed instruments, and the picture industry gave him the opportunity to perform on them. The money was unbelievably good, and the work was satisfying.

When the motion picture industry hit the skids, some of the slack was taken up by TV soundtracks. However, working in the TV medium was not the same. Symphony size orchestras were gone, and costs became all-important. In many instances, music was contracted to the lowest bidder. As a result, the overall music quality decreased and nervous tension increased.

During the 50s, a considerable amount of time was spent trying to make the end product achieve a level that approached perfection. By the 60s, this attitude had changed. The prime consideration was to get the job done within the budget.

Music was played through once, and then it was usually recorded, unless the conductor heard something he didn't like. Steve still remembered the first incident that caused his enthusiasm for the music industry to decline. It occurred at a taping for a TV series. One of the musicians asked for a score check, because he thought he had a wrong note in his part. The conductor told him, "Fix it," and gave the downbeat.

As the orchestras declined in size, so did the amount of work available to musicians. What had been an outstanding livelihood became subsistence to many people who remained in the industry. In an effort to augment his income and keep busy, Steve started looking for arranging jobs. Unfortunately, most of the arranging work was being done by the conductors, and in many instances, the conductors were the music contractors.

Occasionally, Steve would get a call to do orchestration work. If one of the arrangers had an impossible due date and could not complete his work on time, he would call in people to write for him. In the trade, these orchestrators were known as *ghost writers*, because their names did not appear on the music credits. Steve did not resent the fact that he didn't receive credit for his work, because it helped keep him busy and added to his income. Most of these calls would come around midnight and before a recording session on the following day. Since there was never enough time to give the orchestrations much thought, there were many frustrations.

Monday through Friday of each week became pretty much the same. First thing in the morning, he would call the studios and music contractors to let them know he was available. Then he would sit by the phone and hope it would ring. If he left the house during the day, his calls were transferred to an answering service and he would check with the service throughout the day.

After many years of being busy with satisfying productive work, the shock of having too much time on his hands disturbed him. Sometimes, days turned into weeks without any calls for work. During these periods, he started taking antidepressant pills. If he received a call for an overnight orchestration job, he would take another pill to become alert enough to meet the due date.

After one of these all-night sessions, he delivered the music to the studio and ran into Dan Daily. Dan was playing on the date, and it was an industrial film for a corporation. Only a small portion of the music had been laid out to click tracks. It was a typical last-minute job, so Steve stayed at the studio to help with the patch up work. Many of the so-called *wild takes* had to be shortened or extended as they played them with the film and found the timing to be wrong. It was a hectic day, and when it was over, Dan told Steve, "This is my last day in the business."

"Congratulations," Steve said. "I always thought you still had the first dollar you earned. When it comes to being a miser, you're at the head of the list. I'll bet you owe me at least five drinks and a dozen reeds."

"You're probably right. Take this box of reeds, and we'll settle up on the drink business in a few minutes."

Dan sold his oboe to one of the other musicians on that day, said goodbye to everyone left in the studio, and packed up the rest of his instruments. Dan and Steve carted them to Dan's car and then settled in at the cocktail lounge across the street from the studio. After a few doubles and a lot of pleasant reminiscing, Steve asked, "Do you plan on staying in smogville?"

"Hell no! I won't even come back to pick up new-use checks at the union. If they won't forward them, they can keep them. I've had it with this city. I'm moving to a small community outside of San Francisco. If I should get lonesome for traffic, noise, and smog, it will only be a short drive away."

"Why did you pick that area?" Steve asked.

I didn't pick it. I'm moving there because they offered me a teaching job. For the past year I've been looking for something in the teaching profession. This was the first thing that turned up, so I took it. I'll be a bandmaster at a Class C School. What you think of that?"

"It surprises me," Steve said. "I was aware that you had been teaching summer clinics at some of the local colleges, but a high school? You'll never be able to stand it."

"What makes you think so?" Dan asked.

"Kids play a heap of bad notes. After playing with professionals for most of your life, I don't think you'll be able to stand the intonation let alone the bad notes. For every adequate musician in a high school band, there must be at least ten who can barely tune up their instruments. Those out of tune sounds will drive you nuts."

"I doubt it," Dan told him. "They couldn't sound as bad as some of the rock groups I've heard recently. The kids have to study music before they can get into a high school band. That puts them one step above some of the contemporary groups in the business. Last week, I did some sweetening track work on a record that should not be released … except as a joke. It was so bad, no amount of overdubbing could save it. There were six words in the lyrics, and the so-called vocal group shouted them about fifty times before they gave up out of boredom. I swear the group didn't even play the same chord changes. The bass man played the identical two measure phrase over and over - while the keyboards and guitars played whatever grabbed them at the moment. It was the most disgusting thing I have ever heard. I don't know how they can describe it as music."

"It's called pedal point in the bass and free form for everyone else," Steve said.

"You sound like an over-qualified arranger. After it happens, you guys can always dream up a name for it. If I didn't know better, I'd say you been *snowed* by the industry and the so-called 'today's sound'. I don't care what you call it, it stinks, and I don't intend to listen to any more of it. In comparison with some of the crap I've been hearing in the pop field, an out of tune high school band will be soothing to my ears. I can't relate to most of the music that's going on today, so it's time to get out of the business. And it's not just the music; I'm tired of wearing headphones and listening to click tracks. After four or five hours of listening to those things pop in my ears, I'm a nervous wreck."

"Dan, have you thought about all the demands that will be made on your time?"

"If you're referring to the PTA, Band Boosters Club, the concerts, marching at football games and parades, of course I've considered it. I've even thought about the overzealous students who will be calling me in the evenings when are having problems with their studies. Believe me buddy, I won't mind it. After putting up with some of the characters in this business, it will be a pleasure to deal with real people and real problems."

The gin had numbed Steve's lips, but he didn't feel drunk. When they got up to leave, they took a few steps and Steve fell down. Dan helped him to his feet and said, "I've seen you drink twice that amount and not fall down. What's the matter, are you getting old?"

"Probably, but I'm not that old," Steve said. "It must be the medication I've been taking."

"You're not getting old, you're getting senile. You can't mix booze with a controlled substance and expect your body to react in the same old way. Let me drive you home. Tomorrow you can come back and pick up your car."

"I'm all right now, but I'd appreciate it if you'd follow me home."

"Are you sure you can make it?" Dan asked.

"I think so, besides, I'd rather not try explaining to Faye why I left my car at the studio." They drove to Steve's house and said goodbye. It was the last time they saw each other in Los Angeles.

As Steve waited for Faye's arrival at the sanitarium, he remember the night Dan followed him home and what went on afterwards. Faye avoided him and later they fought because she didn't want to make love.

The marriage had started to fall apart a few years earlier when Steve started to do orchestration work again. Faye resented his irregular hours. She was a well organized woman and liked things to follow in a set routine. When he worked all night and the phone rang at odd hours because of his work, it bothered her. If they had to cancel out on engagements with friends because of last minute calls, they would be uneasy with each other's presence for a few days afterwards. Then there was the inconsistent income. For years, Steve had made a good living and Faye's jobs merely provided her with extra income. When Steve would have one of his slow periods and they had to pay some of the bills with her income, both of them became uncomfortable.

They were considering a separation when Steve was offered a job with Tony Sutherland. It was a five month worldwide tour and Steve would get back to LA three times before it ended. Since they would be separated most of the time for five months, they decided to tread water and think about their marriage until the tour was over. It seemed like the right job at the right time, so Steve went on tour and Faye found a new job at an advertising agency.

With the exception of a few appearances with symphony orchestras, Tony Sutherland traveled with a self-contained band. Many of his engagements were for one or two days, so there was not adequate time to rehearse musicians between engagements. There was a lot of unpacking, packing up, and traveling. After four weeks on the road, Steve had a few days off and returned to Los Angeles. Although there was still a considerable amount of tension between them, Steve and Faye had their new jobs to talk about. It wasn't pleasant being together again, but at least it was tolerable.

During the next phase of the tour, Steve developed a friendship with the conductor, Billy Baker. This was a result of mutual respect, and because they were the two oldest men in the orchestra. Billy was about ten years younger than Steve, but the rest of the musicians were in their twenties, just kids so to speak. Sometimes Steve thought Billy acted like he was twenty, but most of the time, he enjoyed his company. About the only time he didn't like being around Billy was during meals. If they had an attractive waitress, sometime during the meal Billy would ask if she was married. It didn't make any difference if the girl answered yes or no, because his next question would be, 'Do you fool around?' If the girl wasn't turned off by the question, Billy would be off and running in pursuit of his *wife* for the evening. If he was given a flat 'No', Billy's next question would be, 'What's the matter with you? Do you want to die stupid?' Sometimes this would get the conversation going again, and Billy had a philosophy, if you can keep them talking you got a chance to make out.

One evening after Billy asked the final question, the waitress wrote up the check, dropped it on the table and said, "Up yours fellah."

"Hey, is that any way to talk to a customer?" Billy asked. "You come back here and apologize or I'll ask to see the manager."

"If you want to see the manager, I'll get him," she said. "He happens to be my husband, and if you say one more word, I'll have him knock out some of the crap that's between your ears."

When she walked away, Billy turned to Steve and told him, "I guess I'm not her type."

They got up, paid the check, and hurried outside. On the way to their car, Steve asked, "Have you ever lucked out by selling yourself with that approach?"

"Sure, but I have to make a lot of calls before I get a sale." As they drove away from the restaurant, Billy laughed and said, "I guess we're damn lucky to be getting away in one piece."

"It sounds like wisdom may be replacing the crap in your upstairs," Steve replied. "If you don't back off from your routine, one of these days you're going to show up on stage with black eyes and a broken nose. When that happens, Tony Sutherland might have a few questions for his esteemed leader."

"Yeah, that might be kind of hard to explain, but I could pull it off. It wouldn't be a problem unless my bruises distracted the audience from his performance. If that happened, Tony might go into one of his black moods and fire me. On the other hand, he might go after the guilty party with his cannon. Since he became a regular cocaine sniffer, his behavior is rather unpredictable. If he should ever decide to fire that gun at anyone, I doubt if there would be enough pieces left for an identification. Have you seen that thing he carries around in his attach a case?"

"No, but I've heard a lot about it," Steve said. "Does he ever point it at anyone?"

"I'm afraid so. It happened again last night, but since he was straight at the time, it didn't scare the hell out of me."

"Would you care to tell me about it?" Steve asked.

"Why not? After the job, I rode back to the hotel with him. His car looks like it belongs on a race track and a couple of kids in their souped-up heap wanted to race with him. They had been drinking and they were feeling like big men. The kids would pull along side of us and say things like, 'Do you have anything under that chrome plated hood?' Then they would speed ahead but drop back beside us when Tony wouldn't join the race. They kept waving their hands and yelling at us. A few times, they blasted off and got a long ways ahead of us. When this happened, they would pull over to the curb and wait for us to catch up to them. After about five minutes of this sort of thing, we were stopped by a traffic light. The kids were still taunting him, and I could tell that Tony was fed up with them. He pulled out his gun, lowered the window and rested the barrel of his gun on the door ledge. It was pointed right at them, and their eyes got as big as golf balls. Tony told them, 'I just want you shits to know that I'm more than just a little tired of seeing you around here. You might say that I'm really pissed off at your presence. If you punks don't make a left turn when the light changes, I'm going to blow you away.'"

"That should have gotten their attention," Steve said.

"It certainly did. By the time the light turned green, those kids were completely sober. They made a left turn and floored their crate. It wouldn't surprise me if they're still speeding away from the place."

Billy parked the car, and they started toward the auditorium. Steve asked, "Does he have a permit to carry that gun?"

"You'd better believe it. When Tony is in his right mind, and that's most of the time, he doesn't take stupid chances with the law, press, or anything else. Let me modify that statement a bit by excluding broads with big boobs. As far as I know, he can carry that gun anyplace in the country."

"I wonder how he was able to get the permit?"

"I don't know, maybe Tony bribed the authorities with autographed pictures of himself. Pardon me for laughing, but sometimes he gets carried away by the special treatment that goes along with being a name. When we checked into the hotel in Reno last week, a bellhop cut him down to size and brought him back into the real world for a few minutes. Tony asked me to go with them to his room, and while he was filling me in on the European tour, a bellhop delivered his luggage. Instead of giving him a tip, Tony autographed one of his pictures and handed it to the bellhop. The guy said, 'Thank you Mr. Sutherland'. He walked out, closed the door, and slid the picture across the floor and back into the room. When Tony saw his picture come back under the door, his feelings were hurt. There isn't any doubt in my mind that Tony thought his autographed picture would mean more to the guy than a decent tip."

"That doesn't surprise me," Steve said. "When thousands of people applaud you every evening, and it goes on year after year, it's bound to warp your perspective. Getting back to the real world, I'd still like to know how he got the permit to carry the gun."

"I'm not sure, but Tony is an honorary member of quite a few law enforcement groups. He probably leaned on one of them, and they gave it to him for protection against theft. In addition to his jewelry, he carries about $10,000 in cash in his attaché case."

"He must be nuts or likes to press his luck. What has he got against banks and credit cards?"

"Nothing that I know of, but he likes to impress people with that bankroll. Also, he needs the cash to purchase drugs and other things."

When they parted, Steve assembled his instruments and got ready for the show. After a few more minutes, Billy gave the downbeat and another Tony Sutherland performance was underway. By now, Steve had all of his parts memorized and didn't bother to open his book. The music was simple and didn't require a lot of concentration. As he watched Tony sell himself to the audience, Steve tried to convince himself that things could be a lot worse.

Tony Sutherland had started out as a folk singer. After a few years of working in tea rooms and small clubs, he became very good at what he did. During the peak of the folk music craze, he received national recognition from his records and concerts. When the popularity of that form of music started to decline, Tony made a transition into country music and sustained his career. His singing style was easy and the bulk of his background music was transparent. Tony was always at ease in front of an audience, and his performance was never pretentious. On stage, he didn't appear to be high strung or pushy.

The lights dimmed and it was time for Billy's featured spot. As Tony made the announcement, Billy went behind the piano and picked up his acoustic bass. He carried it forward and started playing. Tony joined him and sang one of the hits from his folk song period. The only background music was Billy's bass. As always, it was well received by the audience. Billy returned his bass behind the piano, and the show continued.

Steve went through the motions and pumped out his parts. His indifference to the music and the show bothered him, because Tony Sutherland put on a truly professional show. Even though the music was somewhat bland, it was not distasteful. Steve felt he was making an honest living and didn't have to apologize to anyone for being associated with Sutherland, but he was bored and dissatisfied. It was a relief when the show was over, and he looked forward to getting off the road for a few days.

The reunion with Faye left a lot to be desired. She was working long hours at the advertising agency, and they saw very little of each other. On his last night at home, they had another argument. Before going to bed, they tried to smooth things over and make up, but neither of them slept very well that night.

Early the following morning, Steve had to catch a flight to Chicago. Faye drove him to the airport, and during the drive Steve said, "You don't like the way I make my living, do you?"

"No, not anymore, and I don't think you're satisfied with it, either."

"What would you rather have me do?" He asked.

"I don't know, most anything I guess. It would help if you did something more straightforward."

"But Faye, I'm trapped. I have no skills outside of the music business. What else could I do?"

"There are a lot of things you could do, if you wanted to."

"Is it the traveling?" He asked. "I'll quit the Sutherland job if that's what you want."

"I don't know what I want, but I think it's a normal life. If you worked regular hours it would help, but that's not the complete answer. I don't like most of your friends, and you don't like mine. We don't have a social life. I wish things were different between us, but we aren't good for each other anymore. Some couples grow closer as they get older. We haven't, and I believe we should consider a divorce."

"If that's what you want, I'll go along with it," Steve told her. "The tension between us is getting unbearable. But don't file any papers until I return next month. If we haven't changed our minds by then, we'll talk it over and work out an equitable settlement. Then we will see a lawyer and make the necessary arrangements."

"All right, I'll promise to wait it out until next month."

The traveling and playing gave Steve a purpose, and Billy's companionship helped fill the void during his leisure hours. When they were midway through the third phase of the tour, Billy asked, "Would you be interested in doing some orchestrating?"

"Sure, I could use the extra money, and the work would get me away from the barstools for a while. What do you have in mind?"

"Our two appearances with symphony orchestras," Billy told him. "Tony asked me to find someone to write the additional parts, and you're my first choice. You are familiar with his music and know he likes everything understated. When I see him tonight, I'll mention your name and see how he feels about it."

When the second show was over, Billy stopped by Steve's stand and said, "After you put your instruments away, meet me outside Tony's dressing room. He wants to discuss the orchestration job with you."

When Steve joined Billy, there were still a few people outside Tony's dressing room waiting for autographs. Billy and Steve were admitted with one of the autograph seekers, and Tony's secretary said, "Take a seat at the bar and help yourself. Mr. Sutherland will be with you in a few minutes."

While Billy fixed the drinks, Steve looked into the mirror above the bar and watched Tony deal with his fans. Tanya Allen was ushering them in and showing them out one at a time. Tony acted unhurried and relaxed with each admirer, so it was Tanya's responsibility to make sure that none of them stayed too long. Steve thought they made a good team. At the far side of the room, a TV set was showing the late-night movie. Its low-volume established a background noise and helped muffle the conversations.

When Billy put their drinks on the bar, Steve asked, "How long have you been with Tony?"

"My first tour with him was six years ago. At that time, I just played bass in the backup band. For a number of years before joining Tony, I tried to make it as a jazz bassist. The music was great, but the money left a lot to be desired. When I decided to stop indulging myself and go after the bucks, my choices were pretty limited. I've played the acoustic bass since I was a kid. It would've taken a considerable amount of practice to get familiar with the electric bass. Since I'm not big on practicing, that wiped out the rock music field. When the job with Tony came along, it was perfect for me. I'd still be playing bass for him, but two years ago he fired his previous conductor over a salary dispute. Since I had been with him longer than the other men, he offered me the conducting job. It was like a gift. Jesus, how lucky can you get. I never took a conducting lesson in my life. If Tony's music had a lot of tempo changes, I couldn't cut it. My conducting is nothing but down beats, but you know that."

"There isn't anything the matter with dictating everything," Steve said. "It's one way of getting the job done. I don't have any trouble following you, and neither does anyone else in the orchestra. It works… So why knock it?"

"I suppose you're right, but most of the time, I feel very silly standing in front of you guys. With all of that down, up, down, up movement, I must look like I'm driving nails. Oh well, sometimes life leads you into absurdities, but until Tony gets unhappy with me, I'm going to continue to take his money and keep moving my hands up, down, up, down. I'll bet I'm the only bass man in the business that's making a living as a conductor."

Tanya came over to the bar and turned on the radio. As the music volume slowly increased above the sound coming from the TV set, Steve wondered what was going on. Tanya left the radio, poured a cup of coffee and came over to them.

"Did he give you the high sign to get lost?" Billy asked.

"I felt it was coming on when I let the last one in the door. You should see the blooms on that gal."

Billy glanced in the mirror. All he said was "Wow" but he said it very softly.

Tanya sipped her coffee and said, "I think he's queer for those things. In every other way he acts like a grown man. He isn't disturbed by most things, but show him a couple of big globes and his normal personality disintegrates. He acts like a kid who has seen a new toy he can't wait to get his hands on. This may take some time. When he's chasing after a piece of tail, he shows real dedication and persistence. Can I fix you two another drink while you wait for Tony to see if he can bed her down?"

Steve declined, but Billy asked for another Manhattan. Tanya found the sweet vermouth and bourbon. While she fixed the drink, Billy said, "Don't get upset or jealous darling, I still love you even though you're not well endowed."

"Promises, that's all I ever get from you. Maybe I should start padding my bra and pushing everything up. I might meet a better class of people and get a little action. Who knows, Tony might notice that I'm around. He never pays any attention to me unless something goes wrong. Last week he really chewed me out when he had to fly the United Sky in the coach section. The way he carried on, you'd almost believe it was my fault that all of the first-class seats were taken."

As Tanya continued to tell Billy her problems, Steve looked in the mirror and saw Tony autographing one of his pictures. As he held onto the picture, it looked like he asked the girl a question. She got a shocked look on her face and her mouth started working. Tony didn't say anything as he reached for his attaché case. He opened it and took out a wad of bills. The girl continued talking as Tony counted out some of the money, close the case and locked it. He placed the bills on top of his picture and dropped a key on the bills. The girl stopped talking and Tony got up from his chair.

When Tanya saw Tony stand up, she started toward him, but he motioned her away. Tanya returned behind the bar and Steve thought he heard Tony say, "I'm a gambling man so I'll take a chance. I have some unfinished business here, but I'll be upstairs in about 30 minutes."

Tony left the girl sitting at the table and came over to the bar. He told Tanya, "Fix me a martini. I'm a little tense tonight and it might help me relax. How are you boys doing? Can Tanya get anything else for you?"

They declined and Tony continued to make small talk. After a few minutes, Steve heard the door closed. He glanced at the table and noticed it was bare.

Tony told Tanya, "Turn the damn radio off." Then he turned to Steve and said, "Billy tells me you're a very capable orchestrator. I can use you if you'll do things my way."

"I'll try," Steve replied.

"Good, that's what I wanted to hear. Now then, I don't want to make a big deal out of these appearances with symphony orchestras. Don't write anything for the woodwinds. We'll just make copies of what we have and let them double up on the parts. The only instruments I want you to write for are the French horns and strings. Keep the French horns in unison and pick up existing lines. I don't want my charts cluttered up with a lot of new lines. When you write the string parts, give them footballs and use them sparingly. I don't want to hear them sawing away throughout my arrangements. Now that you've heard what I want, do you have any suggestions?"

"Perhaps you'd like to use their percussionists?"

"I don't like a lot of rattling bang behind my vocals, and I hate timpani," Tony told him. Then he asked, "What did you have in mind?"

"It would depend on the actual arrangements you wanted scored up, but I was thinking of the bells, vibraphone and marimba, nothing loud or heavy. We could use some of their toys for color, like the bell tree, tambourine and triangle. Since these appearances are going to be televised, you might want the musicians to be busy if there is any camera panning of the orchestra."

"I suppose we can use them," Tony said, "but keep it light. What else?"

"I don't think it would clutter up your arrangements if I wrote a few new things for the French horns. I'm not talking about thickening up the chords, just a few counter lines during the ensembles."

"All right, but don't get carried away with a lot of fancy things. How many days will it take you to orchestrate three of my charts?"

"One or two days should be adequate."

"I'll give you more time than that," Tony told him. "When I decide on the songs, I'll tell Billy. Now you'll have to excuse me, I have another engagement."

A few days later, Billy found out what songs would be used and relayed the information to Steve. There was more than enough time to get the job done, and Steve enjoyed the assignment. Among other things, it took his mind off the problems with Faye. He tried to keep his writing simple, but ended up writing some rather ambitious things. Before copying the parts, he edited out a few instrumental passages that might be difficult for Tony to sing through.

When the Symphony Orchestra rehearsed the charts, Tony had the string players tacit out many of their lines. No revisions were made in the percussion parts, but some of the French horn lines were eliminated. Steve felt that Tony had removed some of his best writing, but he wasn't surprised or upset. Revisions and differences of opinion on musical ideas were part of the business.

When the performance was over, Steve turned in his bills. He wondered if there would be a problem getting paid. He charged for everything he wrote and a lot of his writing was not used. At the end of the week, Steve received his regular pay envelope. When he opened it he found two checks and a note. The second check was for his music preparation work, and he was paid in full. The note was from Tony and it stated: 'Thanks for the job well done. You gave me everything I asked for and more. The next time I need new music, you will be my first choice.'

Steve smiled as he finished reading the note. His feeling of self-worth bounced up a notch, and for the first time in months, he felt good.

The exhausting schedule of one and two night concert appearances continued until they reached New York. Tony had a series of engagements booked within the surrounding area, and for two weeks, they unpacked their luggage and stayed at the same hotel. The musicians had it made. Plenty of free time during the day, and most of them used it to see the sights of the city. The road crew and Tanya remained as busy as ever. When they finally had an evening without any performances, Billy asked Steve, "Would you care to go out and hear some jazz?"

"Why not, I've always found drinking to be more enjoyable when it's accompanied by good music."

As they reached the lobby, Billy asked, "Do you mind if I call Tanya and asked her to go along with us? I doubt if she'll be interested, but I'd like to invite her anyway." Billy found a house phone and asked the switchboard operator to ring her room. When she answered, Billy did his interpretation of Tony Sutherland's voice.

"Tanya, I didn't like the travel arrangements you made for the boys last night. The musicians were five minutes late arriving at the theater. Don't use that service again. If you have hired them for any of my other engagements in this area, cancel them out and find someone else."

"Yes, Mr. Sutherland," she replied.

"And another thing, I've been looking at last month's bills and I think you're paying too much money to the airlines. We should be able to get better rates than that. Have you been getting at least three quotations before you book us?"

"Well last month was rather hectic, so I had a travel agency book some of the flights."

"I thought so. It's your job to see that I'm not overcharged, and you're not doing your job. I should fire you, but I'll give you one more chance if you'll start doing what I tell you to do. I'm horny for a flat chested broad, get up to my suite right away."

There was a long pause before Tanya said, "Billy, I don't think that was very funny."

"I'm sorry Tanya, but I couldn't resist it. You know how much I enjoy impersonating Tony. What are your plans for the rest of the evening?"

"I bought a book and was going to read it. Now that I've finished a few pages, I realize it's the same damn book I read a few months ago. What did you have in mind?"

"I'm going out and do the town with Steve. We wondered if you'd care to join us and hear some music. How about it?"

"I must admit it sounds better than reading a book for the second time," Tanya told him. "When are you leaving?"

"We're ready to go now, but we will wait for you in the lobby if you're interested."

"I'm interested, but what should I wear."

"Clothes I suppose. Put on anything that's comfortable."

"What are you two wearing?"

"We're wearing sports coats and... For God's sake, Tanya, what difference does it make?"

"It makes a big difference to a girl, I don't want to look out of place."

"Well, I don't think we have to be color-coordinated," Billy told her. "You want me to come up to your room, pick something out and dress you?"

"That won't be necessary. I'll dress myself and be down in fifteen minutes."

They waited about thirty minutes for her and Steve said, "I'm going to the men's room." "I'll join you," Billy replied. "It looks like this is going to take longer than we thought."

As they were standing at the urinals, Billy said, "I'm glad you suggested this. I was so filled up, my teeth were about to float away. Man, this feels good. I think it's better than sex."

"If you're serious about that statement, I think you've been seeing the wrong women."

They returned to the lobby and continued to wait for Tanya. After about ten more minutes, she arrived and said, "I'm sorry to be late, but I had a call from Tony. He started raving at me, and I thought it was you. I screamed into the phone, just who do you think you are... Go shove it. When I heard the response, 'I'm sorry. They must've given me the wrong number,' I realized it wasn't you. I hung up the phone and started to laugh. Then I started shaking. When the phone rang again, I wet my pants and had to change my clothes. The phone started ringing again when I left the room. Let's get the hell out of here."

They took a taxi to a club where Billy once worked. After they were seated and a waitress arrived to take their order, Tanya asked, "What do you have that's one hundred proof?" Steve looked at her and said, "Don't drink that stuff. It will knock you on your can."

"What do you know about my capacity?" She asked. "Shit, I bet I could drink both of you under the table."

They gave their orders and Billy noticed an attractive girl sitting beside him. He started a conversation with her and ignored Tanya and Steve. As he continued promoting, his chair kept moving closer to her table until he was sitting next to her. In a few minutes, another man sat down beside her. She introduced him as her husband, and Billy rejoined Tanya and Steve.

Tanya said, "Welcome back stranger what's the matter, you afraid of a little competition?"

"You'd better believe it. That guy is her husband, and he acted like he wanted to lay one on me. I think married women should wear dog-tags or something."

The band took a break and Billy said, "I know two of the guys that are playing here. I'm going over to the bar and say hello to them."

Billy left their table and started talking with the musicians. After a short time, they moved from the bar and joined three girls at a table. When intermission was over, the regular bass man stayed at the table with the girls and Billy sat in for him.

Steve was impressed with Billy's playing. With the exception of one number he did with Tony Sutherland, this was the first time Steve heard him perform on his instrument. Billy was truly enjoying himself. He was playing the kind of music he liked and doing it with enthusiasm. He heard all of the chord changes and played some choice lines. By the end of the set, he was getting tired and his beat showed it.

When he rejoined them, his first words were, "That's the most fun I've had in a long time. But if they played just one more up-tempo number, I think I would've had a heart attack." The three of them talked for a few minutes before Billy said, "I'm going back to see the guys." Steve noticed that he went back and zeroed in on one of the girls.

Tanya was working on her fifth drink. She had been rather talkative, but now she was talking less and getting the words out mechanically. Her eyes looked glassy and Steve asked, "Are you all right?"

"If you're talking to me, you'll have to speak louder," she told him. "I can see your lips moving, but the only thing that comes out is mush."

"Tanya, I think we had better get some food and coffee. You're going to have an awful hangover in the morning if you don't get something on your stomach."

"What makes you think you're an authority on the subject?" She asked. "Do you have a degree in drinking? Show me your sheepskin or shut up, because I know I can hold my liquor better than you can. Ha, when you try to speak, you can hardly make a sound."

Just then, Billy appeared at Steve's side. He leaned close to him and said, "I think I'm going to score. She's got her car here, and we're going out for a ride. Can you get Tanya back to the hotel by yourself?"

Steve looked at Tanya and saw her slowly sliding off her seat. He grabbed her just before her head disappeared beneath the tablecloth. When he pulled her back into her seat, she burped and nodded her head. Steve said, "I don't think she'll give me any trouble. Go out and have a good time." Billy hurried away and Steve ordered food and coffee.

Tanya had a difficult time trying to eat solid food. After many abortive attempts to get something down, Steve called the waitress back and ordered soup. He spoon fed her and eventually she came around and could stand up. Tanya could not walk in her high heels, so Steve took them off. He strapped them together and hung the shoes around his neck. As they staggered out, everyone in the club was waving goodbye and wishing them well.

Steve found a taxi and they started back to their hotel. When they were about half way home, Tanya woke up and said, "Stop the cab and find me a restroom."

The driver pulled up to a hotel, and Steve helped her find what she wanted. He waited outside the door for what seemed an excessive amount of time. When another girl started to go into the room, Steve asked her to find out if Tanya was all right. In a few moments, the two girls appeared and Tanya said, "I fell asleep."

Steve finally got Tanya back in her room. She was face down on the bed as he removed her shoes from around his neck and tried to leave quietly. As he opened the door, Tanya spoke. "The next time you guys decide to go out on the town, don't do me any favors by asking... by ask... don't ask..." She fell asleep again as her voice trailed off.

Steve closed the door and started toward his room. As he approached the elevator, the door opened and out stepped Billy. They looked at each other and Steve said, "That must've been the *quickie* of all time. Was it that good or that bad?"

"It wasn't anything. After she got me all hot and bothered, she told me it was her time of the month and she couldn't do anything. What a tease. She gave me her phone number and said the curse would be over in a few days, but that doesn't help me out tonight. Oh well, I'll guess I'll lay it on the sill and slam the window on it a few times. See you tomorrow, buddy."

The following evening, it was business as usual. When Tony walked into his dressing room, Tanya was waiting for him. He looked at her and said, "I tried to call you several times last night. Where were you?"

"I was out with Billy and Steve."

"Apparently it didn't agree with you. My God, you look awful. Don't do that anymore."

"Don't worry, I won't," she replied.

After the engagements in the New York area, Steve returned to Los Angeles. He found his luggage and spent a few hours drinking in a bar at the airport. When he felt drunk enough, he found a taxi and headed home to see Faye. He unpacked his suitcase and they went for a walk. Faye hardly spoke and finally Steve asked, "Do you still want a divorce?"

"Yes! I think it's the only sensible thing for us to do."

"Do you want to keep the house?" He asked.

"No! It's too big for me and I don't want the frustration and expense of maintaining it. Why don't you keep it?"

"I don't think I'd be comfortable living alone in it," he told her. "We might as well just put it up for sale and split whatever it brings. I'll call a few realtors tomorrow and get it listed. What do you want to do with the furniture and the cars?"

I'd like to keep the new car. I know it's in good shape, and I'm comfortable with it. If it's all right with you, I'd like all the furniture except for your living room chair and the stuff in your study. We could have the furniture appraised. Whatever its value is you can subtract it from our savings."

"Keep the furniture, Faye. It doesn't mean anything to me, and take the new car. I'll keep the old one and we will divide up our savings. We have a lot of things to do before I rejoin Sutherland, so don't argue with me about it. This time, I won't be staying long."

"You never do," she said.

"Do you have to say bitchy things like that? No, don't bother to answer and don't interrupt me. I want this thing over with as much as you do, maybe more. I'm sick and tired of your pretentious attitude. All you ever think about is yourself. If things don't go your way, it's a living hell to be around you."

"Is that so?" Faye responded. "Well, you're consistent in one thing and that is constant criticism. I've taken enough criticism from you to last a lifetime. You're big on criticism and short on praise. You have never complemented anything I've done. You take me for granted all the time, unless you want to have sex. A girl needs reassurance about a lot of things, but you have never taken the time to make me feel like anything but your wife."

"Stop it Faye. We have been through this scene too many times to do it again. Let's stop going out of our way to make each other uncomfortable. Find yourself a lawyer and I'll get the house listed. Let's get the divorce over with - as easily as possible."

Steve rejoined Tony Sutherland and they left for Europe. He found himself drinking more and enjoying it less. They made a whirlwind tour, and their last overseas engagement was in London, England. It was a three-day engagement, and after the final show, Steve went to the hotel bar and started drinking. He was on his third cocktail when a voice beside him said, "What's your problem?"

He turned, looked at the girl and said, "I don't have any problems. I just enjoy a good drink."

"You're new around here, aren't you?"

"Yes, I'm new," he said.

"Do you work at the hotel or are you just passing through?"

"Just passing through," he replied. "I'm a musician on tour with Tony Sutherland's show."

"That sounds exciting. Is this your last night in London?"

"Yes, tomorrow we return to the States." He didn't know if she was on the make or a prostitute, not that it made any difference. Since the liquor wasn't calming his anxieties, he thought a romp with a woman might be the answer. He bought her a drink and found out she was a prostitute. They agreed on a price and went to his room. After undressing, she spread herself on the bed. Steve poured a drink. When he finished it and started to fix a second one, the girl said, "Well, if you didn't want it, why did you pay for?"

That made some sort of sense to him, so he joined her in the bed. After it was over and she had left the room, he didn't know if he felt better or worse.

The next day, they flew to San Francisco and arrived late. There was a snafu with the ground transportation, so Tanya made alternate arrangements to get the equipment and personnel to the theater. Then she stayed behind to make sure everyone's luggage was picked up and delivered to their hotel. The musicians cleaned up as best they could at the theater, and Tony was furious because of the foul-ups. As the customers came into the room, Tony's road crew was still running some sound checks and putting the staging in place.

Tanya arrived at the theater a few minutes before curtain time and was subjected to Tony's wrath. The show started late, and Tony was still chewing out Tanya as the orchestra started to play. After his first song, Tony apologized to the audience for the delay and proceeded to give his usual unpretentious performance.

The sound system worked beautifully, the staging didn't collapse, and the lighting was effective. No one seemed to notice that some of the musicians had not shaved. As the performance concluded, the audience gave Tony a standing ovation. He left the stage in a good mood and forgot about his time pressure tensions prior to the performance.

After he was settled in his hotel room, Steve called Faye and asked, "What's up?"

"We have a buyer for the house," she told him. "When can you come back here to sign the papers and move your things?"

"Our next day off is Tuesday. I'll check with the airlines and see what's available."

"Can't you make it sooner than that?"

"No I can't. When I've made reservations, I'll call you back. Hopefully, I can get an early morning flight out of Detroit. I'll be in touch in a day or two."

Steve went downstairs to the cocktail lounge and saw Tanya. She was alone in a booth, so he walked over and joined her. During their conversation, he mentioned that he planned on flying from Detroit to Los Angeles on Tuesday. He asked if she had any airline schedules.

"I have a briefcase full of them," she told him. "After I calm my nerves, you're welcome to come upstairs with me and look them over."

"Thanks. I'll take you up on that."

They finished their drinks and went to Tanya's room. While Steve was looking over the schedules, Tanya received a call from Tony Sutherland. After a few moments, she returned and said, "That's a coincidence, Tony wants to fly to LA on Tuesday. He has to go back to sign a new recording contract. You may have company on your flight."

"I doubt it, because I'm not going to fly first class. According to your brochures, there are two morning flights out of Detroit. The first one leaves at eight."

"Let me have their schedules. I'll call Tony back, give him the information, and then perhaps I can relax."

"Here they are," Steve said as he handed them to her. "I'll let myself out."

"Would you mind staying for a while? I'd like to have someone to talk with."

Tanya called Tony and gave him the information. He wasn't satisfied with the departure times and asked her to charter a jet. "See if you can get one that will leave around 2 AM," he told her. Tanya mentioned that Steve was going back to LA on the same day and wondered if he could catch a ride with him. Tony told her it would be alright.

She hung up the phone and told Steve, "Forget about the airline schedules. If I can find an available charter jet, and I'd better, you'll be flying with Tony."

Steve stayed with her for a couple of hours. They didn't talk about anything that mattered, but by the time he left, they had developed a genuine friendship.

The following day, Tanya found a charter service and booked a jet aircraft. Steve called Faye and told her he would be arriving early Tuesday morning.

She was delighted and said, "I'll arrange to get the day off. What time do you want to meet me at the airport?"

"With the time difference, we will probably arrive shortly after 3 AM, but don't show up at that time. Tony is very unpredictable, so we might be late getting off the ground. Why don't you plan on showing up at five? If we get in earlier, I'll have a leisurely breakfast at the airport to kill time. Don't bother to park. I'll meet you outside - in front of the main entrance."

After the last performance in Detroit, Tanya drove them to the airport. Tony gave her a few last-minute instructions before they boarded the Lear Jet. When they were airborne, Tony became talkative. Eventually, he asked Steve why he was going to Los Angeles.

"I guess you could call it a business trip. My wife is divorcing me. We found a buyer for our house, so I have a few papers to sign and some things to move."

"It sounds unpleasant. Here, take this," Tony said as he handed him a small pouch.

"What's inside?"

"Cocaine! When you're doing something you dislike, it will make things easier."

They slept the rest of the way to Los Angeles. Tanya had arranged to have a limousine pick Tony up at the airport. After he got in it, Tony lowered the window and shouted, "See you tomorrow afternoon. We fly at one and good luck with your business."

Steve waved his hand at him and watched the limo drive off. He found a coffee shop and had a light breakfast. Afterwards, he went to the men's room and took out the pouch of cocaine. It was the first time he had used it, but he had seen others use the stuff. After sniffing a small amount into each nostril, he made his way through the underground passageways. Then he went to the street and waited for Faye.

She arrived a few minutes early and told him, "Driving the freeways at this time of the morning is almost like having your own private road. What a pleasure. Did you get any sleep during the flight?"

"Yes! I feel well rested."

"The movers left extra boxes for your things. They're in your study. I found a darling apartment and hope to move in next week. Have you given any thought as to where you're going to live?"

"No, not yet. I think I'll have my things put in storage. When the job with Sutherland is over, I'll start looking for something. In the meantime, would you mind if my mail is forwarded to your place?"

"Of course not. I'll be glad to hold it for you. I have no idea when I'll be able to get the telephone company to install a phone. If you want to call me, you'll have to leave word at the apartment manager's office. Here's their phone number and my new address. I have two parking spaces assigned to me. Do you want me to take your car?"

"Yes. After I get settled someplace, I'll stop by and pick it up. Take it to work once in a while so it doesn't get out of the habit of running. The drive will be good for it."

They arrived at their house and started packing. When the title company opened, they drove over and signed the papers. Faye wanted to show him where her apartment was located, so they drove over to the complex and she pointed it out to him. They stopped for lunch and then went back to their house and continued packing. It was early evening when Steve had all of his things boxed up. He asked Faye, "Would you care to go out for dinner?"

"I'd love to. Where do you want to take me?"

"Let's go to the restaurant at Ports O' Call. You've always liked that place, and so do I."

They drove to the coast, looked at the sunset, and continued their drive to the restaurant. After their meal, they ordered after dinner drinks and watched the ships. By the time they returned home, they were exhausted and went directly to their beds.

Steve woke up and smelled coffee. When he arrived in the kitchen, Faye said, "Do you realize we spent an entire day together without one argument?"

"I guess there's a first time for everything," he replied. "What's for breakfast?"

"I'm fixing French toast for you. I had my breakfast an hour ago. When you finish, will you put your things in the dishwasher? You know how I hate to come home and see a dirty sink. Here it is and here I go. If I don't hurry and get dressed, I'll be late for work."

Steve ate breakfast, put everything away, and waited for Faye. When she came back, he walked her to the car. She got in and told him, "Yesterday was nice, and I really appreciated your thoughtfulness throughout the evening. After the divorce, I'd like to have us stay in touch with each other. Who knows, maybe we can develop a friendly relationship. The past few years have been awful for both of us, but I remember the good years. Promise you'll call me from time to time."

"Sure thing, Faye, you can count on it."

Steve went back to the house and called a few storage warehouses. When he found one that had a suitable space, he drove over and paid two months rental. He brought the keys back to the house and wrote a note to Faye asking her to have the movers deliver his things to the mini warehouse. After calling a taxi, he took a last look around his study. Everything was packed and labeled, so he locked up the house, went to the street and waited.

The tour continued, and Steve found himself spending more time with Tanya Allan. It provided a harmless relationship, and there were not a lot of other things to do during the off hours. It was good for both of them.

During the final week of the tour, Tony Sutherland was going to host a TV special. At the time, they were performing in Dallas, Texas. The TV producer wanted to tape Tony's entire nightclub act. The guest artists would be filmed during the afternoon in the empty showroom. When he had everything on film, the producer would take it to the studio for cutting, splicing and overdubbing. When he finished with it, the entire show would look like it was performed before a live audience.

One version of the show had been sold to network TV. It would be two hours long, less commercials. The producer was still negotiating with overseas buyers for a one-hour version. The night before the actual filming of Tony's live show, the producer's assistant arrived. Tanya found a seat for her in the showroom. After watching the show from out front, she came to the stage and started making notes. Tanya had run off copies of the show sequence, and Billy had obtained an extra copy of his piano conductor parts. That evening, Tanya and Billy stayed with the assistant producer until she had figured out camera placements and angles for all of Tony's songs and monologues.

The following afternoon, the TV crew arrived and installed the additional equipment in the showroom. Five hours before the performance, everyone was on stage for sound checks. The assistant to the producer was giving orders like a drill sergeant. When everything appeared to be in order, she notified her boss.

The producer went into the showroom and Tony Sutherland appeared on stage. They started running down the entire show. As it proceeded, the producer made numerous comments to his crew. He had a filthy tongue and didn't mind shouting obscenities over his mike. No one had any doubts about who was in control of the filming. When they finished the last song, the producer said "Let me hear the 60's Melody one more time and then we'll get the fuck out of here."

As Steve dressed for the show, Billy came into the musician's room and introduced him to Pat Anderson. Then he continued to tell them, "Steve, we have a problem. Tomorrow, one of Tony's guests will be Carl Kay. The producer just pulled a fast one on us. He wants them to sing together on this song."

"So what's the problem?" Steve asked.

"We have two problems. They both had hit records on this song a few years back, so the first problem is to use the background music from their respective records. The second problem is the bad one. They've been singing this song in different keys. Tony's chart is in the key of A and Carl's is in F. what we need is a new arrangement in the key of G. I've pencil marked my piano conductor part to show you where Tony sings and where Carl will be singing. The only time they sing together is during the final eight measures. Now here's the sticky part: when Tony sings, he wants to use the background from his chart. The same goes for Carl. When we get to the final eight measures, use your own discretion. Save as many lines as you can, but when things go out of the range of the instruments, write something new. We need it by noon tomorrow. Can you do it?"

"I'll need help copying the parts," Steve told him.

"No problem my man. Pat and I will help. We can work here tonight. Tanya is making the necessary arrangements for us to use the stage and Tony's dressing room."

"Billy, you can't work all night, do a TV taping during the day, and conduct a show tomorrow night."

"Sure I can. I've done it before."

"Go back to your room after tonight's show and get some rest," Steve said. "If we need help finishing the parts on time, you'll get a call from us around eight. At least you'll get a few hours sleep. Do you have Carl's parts with you?"

"No, they're in my hotel room. I'll dash back and pick them up."

"While you're there, you might just as well try to get a few hours sleep. After we finish tonight's show, it will probably take me an hour or two to check over Tony's parts and re-orchestrate the instruments that go out of range."

Billy and Steve left for the stage. Steve sat down behind his stand and tuned up his instruments. He noticed the assistant to the producer standing opposite him in the wings. She was wearing a headset and would probably be relaying directions to the stage cameras. She looked vaguely familiar, but he couldn't connect the face with a name.

The show and filming went by without a hitch. Tony was up for his performance and his supporting personnel gave their best. When it was over, Steve gathered the instrumental parts to be re-orchestrated and went to work.

After checking over the parts, he found three passages that had to be reworked. He identified three inserts and re-orchestrated the instruments. Then he wrote background music for the last eight measures of the arrangement. The whole thing took less than an hour. Steve took the music to Tony's dressing room and started titling parts. Before he finished, Pat walked in carrying his uniform, shaving kit and Carl's music.

He told Steve, "I checked over Carl's parts and only found one woodwind line that went off the instrument. The line occurs in two places and only runs for a few measures. It isn't very important, so I circled it on the parts and we can take it down an octave. How did you make out?"

"Like a bandit. There will only be three short inserts and new lines for the last eight measures. I'll show you where the inserts occur."

Steve explained them and they started transposing and copying parts. Around 4 AM Pat said, "I sure could use a cup of coffee."

"No problem," Steve replied. "Tanya made coffee before she left, and it's behind the counter. I should've mentioned it earlier. My back tells me it's time to get up and stretch, so I'll join you. How far along are you on your parts?"

"I'm in good shape," Pat said. "The woodwinds and trumpets are finished. I have two more trombones to do, and then I'll start the piano part."

"Aren't you going to make a piano conductor part?"

"Why bother. This is a one-shot chart. I'll be playing the piano, and all I need are the chord symbols and bass notes. Billy will be conducting and he doesn't need much information. I'll cue in the intro and ending and that should be enough for him. Hell, we're not going to make any mistakes in the copying, so who needs a complete piano conductor part. How are you doing?"

"The string parts, percussion and drums are finished. After I copy the bass and guitar, I'm through. This is a piece of cake. Why don't you give me one of your trombone parts, that way we should be able to finish about six? We'll be able to get a solid three or four hours sleep before the afternoon filming."

Everything went as planned, and they were back in the show room at noon. The first thing they rehearsed was the duet. After running it down twice, the producer started telling Tony and Carl where and how he wanted them to stand, move, and look during the filming. While this was going on, Billy came over and said, "Nice job, Steve."

The assistant to the producer said, "You are Steve Post. I knew you looked familiar. I'm Claudia Fleming, do you remember me?"

"Yes! You were the dance captain for the Erwin Booth Revue."

The producer yelled, "Cut the gabbing. We've got work to do. If you want to talk with each other, do it on your own time. If anyone interrupts me again, your god damn ass will be mine."

When the afternoon filming was over, Steve went over to Claudia and said, "It's good to see you again. I'd like to find out what you've been up to. When can we get together?"

"It will have to be tonight or never," she told him. "We pack up and fly back to Los Angeles after tomorrow's filming."

"Tonight's fine with me. I'm always wide-awake after the evening show. I'll plan on picking you up at your room when I get back to the hotel."

"Good! I'll look forward to it. By the way, just so you won't screw away your evening looking for me, my room number is 230."

In a few hours, Tony and the musicians were back on stage grinding out the same old show.

Claudia was through for the evening and returned to her room. Her back was stiff from standing throughout the day, so she did calisthenics for about 30 minutes and took a cold shower. Afterwards, she dressed and watched TV until Steve arrived.

When she let him in, Steve asked, "Where would you like to go?"

"Why don't we just stay here? The chairs are comfortable, and I'm tired of seeing people. We can have room service bring something up if you're hungry. If you want something to drink, that's already in the room. I can fix anything you'd like as long as you say martini or gimlet."

"Martini would be fine. Would you like to have me make it?"

"Sure, mix up a batch. But go easy on the vermouth, I like mine about 10 to 1."

"Ahh, you sound like a confirmed drinker who knows what she likes. Claudia, you look wonderful. How come I got older but you didn't?"

"I appreciate hearing that, because I've spent a few dollars trying to hold back time. The nose job was done years ago, and I had my second face lift last year. But look at this, the body is still the same old me."

"You sure keep it firm," he said. "You must work out all the time."

"I work out a lot, but I was always built like a brick shit house. It was my strongest asset. My body allowed me to dance for years, and I loved every minute of it. A few times, I thought I was going to make it big. Somehow, it never quite jelled. But I don't have any regrets about giving it a go; it was a satisfactory living for a long time. When I get uptight, dancing is still a therapy for me. There's nothing like going to a dance studio and working out. After I'm exhausted, I forget about the bull shit side of this business and feel good about me, what I've done, and what I'm going to do. Listen to me talk about myself. Of course it's my favorite subject, but I'd like to know what you've been doing."

"I haven't done anything that's very earthshaking," he said. "This is the first time I've been on the road since we worked together in the Revue. After the summer tour, I moved to Los Angeles and became a studio musician. Now you've heard the whole story of my life."

"You never used a lot of words, but that story is ridiculous. Don't you think it's oversimplified? Did you ever get married?"

"Yes," he said. "Shortly after I moved to the West Coast, I met a girl at one of the music preparation agencies and we were married."

"Well, do you have any children?"

"No, and in a few more weeks, I won't have a wife. She's divorcing me."

"When I saw you last night and earlier today, you seemed to be a little bit down. I guess that explains why. No matter how you go about it, getting a divorce is a painful experience."

"It sounds like you've been through one or two of them also."

"Just one, but that was enough for me. Shortly after I moved to New York, I thought I'd found my prince charming. He was a choreographer for a show I was dancing in. What a talent, no question about that. He really helped me with my dancing. Before Bobby came along, most of the men I met were the macho type. What a bunch of creeps, all they wanted to do was lay me."

"That's life," he told her. "Boys just naturally want to poke fun at the good-looking girls. That's what happens when you make it look so attractive."

"Flatterer! You sound like you're trying to soften me up. You're not going to try to hit on me, are you Steve?"

"Do you consider me one of the macho types you were talking about?"

"No, you are one of the rare exceptions. I always felt safe around you. If I didn't, you would not be in my room."

"I'm glad to hear that," he said. "Are you going to tell me what spoiled things for you and Bobby?"

"It's rather embarrassing, but I'd like to tell you about it anyway. Bobby was always so attentive and helpful. Perhaps you weren't always aware of it, but I was very insecure about my dancing talents. Bobby helped me build up my confidence. For the first time in my life, I got so I could perform up to my ability. When he proposed, I could hardly believe it, but I didn't give him a chance to change his mind. He was a gentle lover, and I gave myself to him completely. I felt like I was living in heaven, until I found out he worked both sides of the street."

"You mean he was bisexual?" Steve asked.

"You got it. When I discovered it, I was sick, really sick. I know I'm not carrying the Holy Grail between my legs, but I thought what I gave him was better than what a guy had to offer. I spent a year in psychoanalysis before I got my head together. That covers my divorce, now I'd like to hear your story."

"I don't know, Claudia; I guess I'm not very easy to live with."

"You're not very easy to talk with either, now give. I bared my soul to you, and you won't even give me a glimpse at your problems."

"When I said I'm not very easy to live with, it's true. I haven't enjoyed the music business for a long time, and it bothers me. I've been taking a lot of my frustrations out on Faye, and she got tired of being my whipping post. Besides not getting much satisfaction from my profession, the amount of work available to guys like me is drying up. If a lot of things were going on in the studios, I wouldn't be on the road with Tony Sutherland."

"If you don't like your work and there isn't much of it, why don't you do something else?"

"You sound like my wife," he replied. "I'm hanging in there, even though the current business climate stinks, because I don't want to do anything else."

"Oh I see, you enjoy being down. I don't blame Faye for leaving you. No one wants to be around a person who likes to feel sorry for himself."

"Doctor Fleming, I presume. If you are trying to save my marriage, forget it. It's over, and I'd like to forget about marriages."

"That's one thing we can agree on, Steve. I'll promise not to mention it again if you'll fix me another drink."

"You had two stiff ones already. What do you want to do, get tight?"

"What I want to do is my own business. Besides it's my booze. Are you going to make me another martini, or do I have to fix my own?"

"I'll fix it," he said, "but then I'm leaving. Our conversation is beginning to sound like we're married."

No, please don't go. I could use a good laugh, and you're funny. I promised you that I wouldn't mention the word *marriage*. So what do you do, you drag it back up and even associate that terrible word with us. I think you enjoy making yourself miserable, and I find that funny as hell."

"Among other things, you have a perverse sense of humor," he said. "Here is your drink, smart ass. I think you're full of crap all the way up over your eyebrows."

"I probably am, but not quite that high. Why don't you sit down, cool off, and join me. I haven't had anyone like you to talk with in a long time, maybe never. Steve, I like you even if you don't like yourself."

"I guess I'll have to stay, because you have to be the most screwed-up person I've met in my entire life. So tell me more: What are you doing for the rest of your life?"

"You can't fool me, that's a song title, isn't it? I don't know what I'll be doing the rest of my life, but I know what I've done so far. You do want to hear about it, don't you?"

"After hearing about your marriage, you have my undivided attention. I doubt if anything else you've done can top it, but I'm willing to listen and learn. Besides, I like your taste in liquor."

"Silly, I'm not in the liquor. I'm here beside you. My mother always told me that the way to a man's heart was through his sodden brain. 'Ply them with booze.' That's what she told me. Now then, are you ready to hear more about me?"

"I can hardly wait," he replied.

"Shall I start right after my divorce, or would you prefer to have me start with when you saw me last?"

"Why don't you start after your divorce. It's 2:00 AM and I will have to be back working at noon. That only gives us ten hours."

"That's hardly enough time," she said, "but here goes. After the divorce, I went into psychoanalysis. I didn't want to dance for a while, because I couldn't stand the thought of seeing anyone who knew me while I was married. There's that word again. Well, the analysis cost me big bucks, so I had to do something to bring in some bread."

"If you're going to tell me you became a hooker, don't bother," Steve said. "I've heard that story before."

"No, that's not my story. Besides, after my experience with Bobby, I'm sure I wouldn't have been any good at it. What I did was imitate children's voices on a daytime TV puppet show. I was a lousy girl vocalist, but I had a flair for imitating children's voices. I'd probably still be doing it if the show had been canceled. By the time the show went off the air, I had my head on straight again and went back to dancing. The Broadway shows that I got into 'kind of' came and went. You know how this business is, feast or famine. Well, I found myself in a period of famine. From what little you've told me, that's the way it is with your studio work right now, just lousy."

"No, Claudia, not lousy. Nonexistent."

"That's a good word. Well, after a lot of nonexistent work, I decided to take a secretarial course and brush up on my typing and cowering to men."

"How did that work out?" he asked.

"Pretty good. But I never completed the course, because I landed a job at a TV studio. Would you believe it -- as a secretary?"

"Yes! Since it was you, I believe that. How long did you work at it?"

"Oh, I guess it was about two months," she said. "I quit because another chance to dance came along. Unfortunately, the show closed within a month. When I tried to get my secretarial job back, they wouldn't have me. But that was when my luck made a change for the better, because I went to work for a music contractor. He didn't need a full-time secretary, just a part-time gal to make out payrolls and chase around. I picked up, delivered, and filed music. Sometimes I made out the contracts and delivered the paperwork to the TV studios and musicians union. It was perfect for me, because I could still take dancing jobs. Most of the work didn't have to be done at a specific time, but there were a few rare exceptions. If I was rehearsing for a show in the afternoon and couldn't deliver music or contracts when he needed them, I'd have one of my out-of-work dancer friends do it for me. Most of the things I did were just routine dummy work, but it helped pay the bills and still allowed me to do my thing."

"What kind of music did he contract?" Steve asked.

"He went after everything that came along in New York. But for the most part, he made his living from daytime TV soap operas. The job was a great experience for me. Among other things, I found out what it cost to get music and musicians for TV programs. As I became more knowledgeable of the business, he turned a lot of the detail items over to me. I even ended up doing most of the cost estimates. Those were fantastic years, but nothing good lasts forever."

"How well I know," Steve said. "Just about the time you think you've got it made, it's gone. What wiped out your fantastic years?"

"Age," she replied. "I noticed that I was the oldest girl dancing in the shows and realized my days were numbered. It was hard to let go, but I decided to walk away from it before there wasn't anything to walk away from."

"If you enjoy dancing that much, why didn't you try to get into choreography?"

"Hell, I never had an original idea in my life. Dreaming up dance routines wasn't my bag. There's a big difference between thinking up things and doing them, and I knew it. After quitting the dance profession, I needed something else that would provide additional income. Since I was spending most of my time in or around the TV studios, I decided to branch out from my music contracting work and do the same type of thing for TV production companies. At first, the work was spasmodic, but it kept growing as I became more familiar with the industry. Eventually, I started picking up odds and ends; assignments from independent TV producers. About the time I finally found myself making a damn good living, Jack had a heart attack and a lot of my work disappeared."

"Was Jack the music contractor?" Steve asked.

"Yes! He was a real sweetheart to work for, but after the heart attack, he threw in the towel and retired. His work fragmented to other people, and I could not pick up enough of it to keep busy. So I concentrated on TV work, but right now, I'm hustling more and getting less business than I had when Jack was still active. That's why I'm here in Dallas working for an independent TV producer. After tomorrow's filming, I'll go to Los Angeles with him. The editing and paperwork should give me about five more days of employment. After it's over, I'll return to New York and hope the phone will ring for something else. I don't like this kind of traveling, but there isn't enough work at home to keep me busy. I guess my life sounds a lot like yours. We're out here because we have to make a living."

"Traveling around the country is the only part of your life that sounds like mine," he said. "You've worked at many different things. The only thing I've work at is music. You may think you've never had an original idea, but I believe you've had quite a few of them. You are a very resourceful woman. Claudia, regardless of what you think, I know there aren't many around like you."

"When you finally start talking, you say all of the right things. I wish you would talk to the producer of this Special, and tell him I'm a' resourceful person. He seems to think I won't move my tail unless he yells and swears at me."

"That's just his method of showing leadership ability and getting things done," Steve told her. "Everyone has their own style. From what I've seen of him, he doesn't treat you any better or worse than the rest of his crew."

"Maybe not," she said, "but he sure is a bastard to work for. God, I hate him. Everyone around him has to take a lot of verbal abuse, everyone except his wife. She gives it right back to him when he gets carried away with his tongue. I like it when she's around, because he has to toe the mark. She's a jealous type and very possessive. If she caught him fooling around, and he does, I believe she'd castrate him and shove those things down his throat. If it ever happens, I'd like to be around to help her stuff him."

"Some people get their kicks in strange ways, but since you're a different kind of a woman, I believe it. At one time or another, he must've seduced you."

"Are you kidding?" She asked. "He tried, but I wouldn't buy it. The first time I worked for him, he said 'I could throw quite a bit of work your way for the right kind of consideration.' I told him straight out; if he mean sexual consideration, I wasn't that kind of a girl. After a few vulgar insults, he told me, 'Sinning with the right people could be good for you. If you want to get anywhere in this business, you'd better start believing that.' He made me so mad, I told him to go shove it. That remark didn't even faze him. He simply replied, 'That's what I had in mind, and you're going to be the recipient.' The guy has perseverance, I'll say that for him. He kept after me with filthy innuendos until I told him, bug off, you're the wrong sex. That statement really conned him, so now the clown actually thinks I'm a lesbian. He must've mentioned it to his wife, because she always seems to be pleased when I'm working for him. Perhaps she feels that I'm not a competitor. Who knows what goes on in her mind, but I'm sure she's been instrumental in my getting quite a few calls from him. Last year, he produced six TV specials. I worked on four of them, and it certainly wasn't because he was overjoyed with my work."

"You're not, are you?" Steve asked.

"I'm not what? A lesbian?"

"Well, you wear trim clothes without frills, and keep yourself in marvelous shape."

"So I fooled you too. Why didn't I think of that line years ago? It would've saved me from a bunch of hassles with men."

Steve yawned and said, "It's past my bedtime, and I'm spent after last night's long job. This man isn't going to hassle you anymore tonight. Claudia, your story was fascinating. I'll look forward to the next time you bring me up to date on what is going on in your life."

"Aren't you going to stick around until you've satisfied your curiosity?"

"My curiosity about what?" he asked.

"The answer to the question, is she or isn't she?"

Steve smiled and told her, "I think you're straight, but straight or not, I'm not going to try and bed you down. I'm sure it would be a pleasure to jump up and down on your bones, but I respect you too much to try that sort of thing."

As he started to leave the room, Claudia got up, put her arms around him, and said, "You are nice." They held each other for a few minutes before she spoke again. "Steve, if it wouldn't corrupt you, I wish you'd spend the night with me."

"It won't corrupt me. I'm a big boy."

"We'll see," she said. They turned out the lights and made love shyly.

The following evening, Claudia left for Los Angeles with the TV production company. Three days later, Tony Sutherland's tour ended.

Steve returned to Los Angeles and found a furnished apartment on the north side of the city. Then he stopped by Faye's apartment to let her know he was back and picked up his car. After his things were moved from the mini storage warehouse, he went to a doctor and asked for a complete physical checkup. During the examination, his doctor asked, "Are you having any specific problems?"

"Yes," Steve told him. "I'm always tired and my periods of depression seem to be more frequent."

Arrangements were made to admit him to a hospital, and they started running tests. At the end of the week, the doctor informed him that nothing in the tests pinpointed the cause of his chronic tiredness and depression. The doctor thought it might be wise for Steve to consider checking into a nearby sanitarium. "Do you think my problems are mental rather than physical?" Steve asked.

"I don't know, but I believe we should consider it. If you agree, I'll make an appointment for you and transfer your records."

Steve agreed to the transfer and called Faye. After he told her where he was going, she replied, "I've heard of that place, but I thought it was for people who had nervous breakdowns."

"I suppose it is," he said, "but that's not the reason I'm going there. I feel tired and depressed most of the time. Before it gets worse, I want to find out what's causing it and have it taken care of. The tests at the hospital did not disclose anything, so this is the next logical step. I didn't call to upset you, but I thought you should know my whereabouts in the event you wanted to contact me."

"You're right," Faye told him, "and I appreciate the call. Unless something comes up, I'll stop by and see you on Sunday."

Steve's psychologist was George Mickelson, and he asked all of the anticipated questions. After additional tests were run, they had another conference.

Dr. Mickelson told him, "I think you've been living on the edge for a long time. Your line of work creates a considerable amount of emotional stress, and you've been subjecting yourself to it throughout your adult life. I think you should get away from music for a few months. Of course, the divorce added more stress. Even though you have a stable personality, everyone has a breaking point. You've had too many disagreeable things happen at one time. You don't get a feeling of fulfillment from your work, and because of changes in your industry, you can't be choosy about what you do and still keep busy. Everything considered, I would be shocked if you weren't experiencing severe depression."

Steve asked, "What about all of the antidepressant pills, cocaine and alcohol? Did the tests disclose any physical deteriorations?"

"Not a thing, and I haven't noticed any signs that would indicate a harmful chemical dependency. Now that you've been away from controlled substances for a few weeks, do you feel a need for them?"

"No, not really," Steve told him.

"Are you experiencing any symptoms of withdrawal: nausea, tremors, anything at all?"

"No! I miss the booze, but that's about it."

"I think we run a tight ship here, but it's not a prison" Dr. Mickelson said. "I'll see to it that you can have wine with your dinner. We have many planned programs, and I believe it would do you a world of good, if you would participate in some of them. Pick out a few programs that sound interesting to you. It will put you in touch with people who are experiencing problems similar to your own. I strongly recommend our exercise programs. I'm sure they'll reduce your anxieties."

When Faye arrived on Sunday, Steve told her, "This place is run like a summer camp for children. They plan everything to fill your day. We even have planned free time. This is the first time since I was a kid that I've had my meals at regular intervals. Two days ago, I started an exercise program and was shocked at how little stamina I had."

"Steve, have the doctors found out what's the matter with you?"

"No, I'm afraid not. They've run tests like mad, but there doesn't seem to be any physical reason for the way I've been feeling. Just knowing that I'm okay physically makes me feel better. I guess it's a start."

"I don't think you belong in a place like this," she said.

"Faye, if it isn't my body, it must be in my head. I don't think I belong here either, but during the past few days I've seen numerous people who feel the same way. Some of them are really screwed up. I don't want the same thing to happen to me, so I'm going to stick it out for a while. It can't hurt anything, and it might help."

"Are they giving you any drugs?"

"No! I don't feel a need for them, so they don't give me drugs."

"Well, I suppose you're doing the right thing," she said. "I'll be tied up next weekend, but the following Sunday I'll stop by and see you. Can I bring you anything, magazines, newspapers or books?"

"Don't bother. This place has plenty of publications."

After four weeks, Steve was ready to be released. During his final conference, Dr. Mickelson told him, "When you checked in here, you were well into a complete nervous collapse. Fortunately, you had the good sense to submit yourself to our therapy while you could still function. You have been a most cooperative patient, and I believe you're ready to get out of this place."

"I still find it hard to believe. How could I have had a nervous breakdown and still play my musical instruments? Besides, I was able to do all the necessary things to get through the day."

"Steve, if you continued to try and function without outside help, in another month or two you would not have been able to do those things. That's when you hit rock bottom. You have seen all sorts of people in here at various stages of nervous collapse. You are one of the lucky ones. You responded to treatment, and for all practical purposes, you are well. In your case, it wasn't anything permanent and it should not happen again. You had the bad luck of having too many distasteful things hit you at one time."

"Doc, you're probably right. I certainly don't feel the way I did a few months ago. Right now, I'm anxious to leave this place and get on with my life."

"That's the right attitude. Now, just one more thing before we split. I want you to stop by my office once a week for a short conference. If it's okay with you, we will schedule our get-togethers for Tuesday afternoons at 2 o'clock. Unless something unexpected develops, our meetings will be over within five or six weeks."

Steve continued to exercise on a regular basis and he started practicing on his musical instruments. This was the first time throughout his professional career that he'd been away from them for over a month, and he was surprised at the deterioration of his finger dexterity and embouchure. It took four weeks of hard practice before he felt comfortable playing them. Then he started calling music contractors, and much to his surprise, he was hired to play background music for a new TV miniseries. He made his last visit to Dr. Mickelson's office and mentioned the job during the conference.

"Steve, how do you feel about going back to work?"

"I'm excited and looking forward to it. After the long layoff, I am even nervous. I believe this is the first time I've been uneasy about playing a job. It's a strange feeling, and I hope it doesn't get worse when I get on the soundstage. If it does I might go to pieces and not be able to cut it."

"Your uneasiness does not surprise me. It is a natural reaction, and I'm going to write you a prescription. This medication will calm your anxieties and get you through the day. How many days will you be working?"

"Probably three, maybe four," Steve said.

"This prescription should be adequate. There's enough medication for that length of time. Now then, if the periods of deep depression start again, contact me immediately. Good luck with your recording dates."

Steve had the prescription filled and took some of the medicine before the initial session. Shortly after it got underway, his anxieties disappeared. The following day, his confidence had returned and the medication was not necessary. He put the bottle in the cabinet with his antidepressants and other drugs. Recording work was like a tonic, and he was sorry to have it end after a few days. Nothing else in the way of work turned up for two weeks, and then he received a call from Billy Baker.

"Billy, where are you calling from?"

"I'm in the city and calling from my hotel room. Tony is finishing up a recording session for his new album."

"Are you conducting or playing on it?"

"No, I'm not doing much of anything. Everything is being handled through the recording company. They hired the conductor, arrangers, musicians and sound technicians. Since these people are new to Tony, I guess he wanted to see one familiar face. I've been hanging around the studio with them and trying to stay out of the way. Until a few minutes ago, I had it made. Do you remember Carl Kay?"

"Yes," Steve replied. "He was one of the guests on Tony's TV show."

"That's the guy. Well, he just had a heart attack. Carl was supposed to open tomorrow night in Reno, and Tony wants to fill in for him. I was asked to round up as many people as I can find from Tony's last tour. Are you available?"

"I'm very available and could use the work."

"Good. I'm relieved to hear that. We'll be in Reno for two weeks. As yet, I don't know how we'll get there, but I'll check back with you in one or two hours."

Steve tried to call Faye, but she wasn't at her apartment. Billy called back within the hour and told him, "Pack your suitcase and meet me at United Airlines. We fly out of the International Airport in three hours."

Steve called for a taxi and threw his things into the suitcases. He carried them outside and went back to get his musical instruments. After trying to call Faye, he wrote a note to her and put it in his coat. On the way to the airport, he had the driver stop by her apartment. He left the note in her mailbox and started back to his cab. Before he reached it, he saw Faye. She was coming up the walkway with someone he didn't know. Faye introduced him to Jim Decker and said that they had been out to dinner. Steve shook hands with Jim and explained why he stopped by Faye's apartment. Afterwards, he hurried to the taxi and continued on his way to the airport.

After they were airborne, Billy relaxed and started talking. "Tomorrow morning, Tanya will be flying in from Dallas with the music library. The last time I talked with her, she told me Tony's staging was on the road. The truck won't arrive until the day after we opened, so tomorrow night we will have to make do with whatever is available at the hotel. Do you know any musicians in Reno?"

"I know two guys who moved up there last year. They may have moved on by now, but I doubt it. Both of them had friends in that area, and they wanted to make Reno their permanent home."

"What did they play?" Billy asked.

"They were trumpet men."

"Were they any good at it?"

"One was outstanding, but the other guy could barely blow his nose," Steve told him.

"When we get on the ground, call the outstanding one. I need him, and see if he can find us another good trumpet man. I also need people for the guitar and second trombone chairs. If you can't get in touch with your friend, I'll call the Musician's Union and pick out a few names from their availability list. The rest of the musicians will be flying in tomorrow morning with Tanya. Tony won't arrive until tomorrow afternoon. He wanted to stay in Los Angeles and listen to the final tracks this evening. He's really enthused about this new record."

When the stewardess arrived, both of them ordered drinks. Before they had finished them, the Captain's voice came over the speakers and announced, "Ladies and gentlemen, the Reno airport has been closed because of a snowstorm. We will be flying to Salt Lake City and should be safely on the ground before the snow reaches that area. If anything else develops, I'll let you know."

After landing, Steve and Billy found their luggage. With all of Steve's musical instruments, they had more cases than they could move without a cart. While Steve guarded their things, Billy left to try and get reservations on the next flight to Reno. As Steve waited, he noted flight cancellation notices appearing on the TV screens. He hurried to the nearest phone and called the Holiday Inn. They still had one room left, so he gave them his credit card number and made guaranteed reservations for the room.

After an hour, Billy returned and said, "They've closed the airport. I bet there isn't a room in the whole god damn city. I can't get us confirmed on anything tonight. When the weather clears, our airplane is expected to return to Reno. However, it will probably be on a first-come first-served basis. I've got reservations on a flight out at 4:30 PM but that won't give us enough time for a full rehearsal."

"I can't solve all your problems," Steve said, "but I did find us a room."

"Are you kidding me?"

"No! We lucked in and got the last room at the Holiday Inn. Do you snore?"

"Only when I'm asleep," Billy said. "A room, I'll be damned. I've always liked having you around, but until tonight, I didn't know why. Man, I'm ready to crash for a few hours."

By the time they found a taxi, made the drive and registered, it was after 1:00 AM. The bellboy loaded the luggage on his dolly and they went to the room. As the bellboy started carrying everything into the room, he said, "You guys don't exactly travel light. What's in all these cases?"

"Musical instruments," was Steve's replied as he went to the phone.

The bellboy finished unloading and asked Billy, "Can I get you guys a couple of girls?"

"No thanks, we have to practice," Billy told him.

The bellboy shrugged and started to leave, but Billy called him back and asked, "Can you find us a bottle of good bourbon?"

"I can find most anything for a price."

Billy gave him some money and closed the door. Steve was still trying to locate his friend in Reno, so Billy unpacked his things and went into the bathroom. When he returned he heard Steve saying, "Have everyone in the showroom at three o'clock for a rehearsal. If we're late getting in, have the guys start looking over their books."

Steve hung up the phone and told Billy, "Red Potter is available and he'll round up the rest of the musicians."

"Red Potter... I wonder if it's the same Red Potter I used to know? With a name like that, how could it be anyone else? What age is he?"

"Red is about your age," Steve said. "Perhaps he's two or three years older, but that is still in your ballpark."

"It's the same guy, I know it. He's a real monster of a trumpet man, or at least he used to be. Steve, you made a good choice. I'm beginning to feel better about this gig."

The bellboy arrived with the bourbon and asked, "Are you sure you guys don't want me to get you a couple of girls?"

"Not tonight friend," Billy said. "If it doesn't last at least eight hours, it's no good. And tonight, we don't have that much time." The bellboy slammed the door when he left the room.

After they had a few drinks, Steve asked, "Don't you think we should let someone in this organization know where we're at?"

"Let them guess," Billy replied.

They joked about it for a while, but eventually Billy said "I suppose we should try to make contact with the outside world. It probably wouldn't be a good idea to call Tony at this hour, so I'll contact Tanya. With the time difference, she should be about ready to get her butt out of bed."

Tanya was still sleeping when her phone started ringing. Her first words were, "Who the hell is this?"

"This is your leader, and it's time to rise and shine."

"Billy, you are not my leader. You're just another hired hand like me, except most of the time you don't seem to realize it. What are you doing up at this hour?"

"I haven't been to bed yet. Because of a snowstorm, our airplane over flew Reno. We crashed at Salt Lake City. I'm calling from the hospital to let you know that you have to conduct the orchestra tonight."

"Billy, I can't... You stupid son of a bitch. This is another one of your jokes, isn't it?"

Billy dropped the phone. It fell on the floor and he started laughing. He couldn't stop. Steve watched him roll around for a while and laughed along with him. The tears were still streaming down Billy cheeks as Steve picked up the phone and heard Tanya saying, "Billy where are you? Answer me damn it! Are you all right? Billy, what's the matter? Say something! You bastard, don't do this to me!"

Steve interrupted her by saying, "Tanya, settle down. This is Steve and nothing is wrong with Billy. Nothing except his sides are sore from laughing."

"Put him back on the phone."

"I can't, Tanya. He still laughing so hard he can't get off the floor."

"You guys are drunk, aren't you?"

"We've had a few drinks, but were not drunk."

"I'm going to tell Tony about this, you'd better believe it. I'm a registered professional secretary, and I'm not going to take any more of this kind of treatment. I'm supposed to be working with professionals, not clowns and liars."

"Tanya, Billy didn't lie about everything. We couldn't land at Reno because of a snowstorm, so we flew to Salt Lake City and crashed at a Holiday Inn… Pardon my laughing."

"You prick, you are just like him. Is he still on the floor?"

"Yes, I'm afraid he's there for the night."

"I'll get him for this. He's going to pay and pay dearly. I'll put broken glass in his coffee and make him leak like a sieve. I'll…"

"Tanya, stop it or you'll miss your flight. Speaking of flights, I don't know when we will arrive in Reno. We're scheduled to fly out of Salt Lake City at 4:30 PM, but we will try to catch an earlier flight. I've arranged to get musicians out of the Reno local for the missing chairs. A trumpet man named Red Potter will have them in the showroom at three for rehearsal. Can you remember all that?"

"Yes! I've taken it down in shorthand."

"Oh, I forgot, you are a registered secretary, aren't you?"

"After I take care of Billy, I'm going to get you too." She hung up on him.

Steve poured two more drinks and placed one of them in front of Billy's nose. They finished the bottle, and when they turned in, Billy's last words were "God, I love this life."

They got up early and were at the airport by nine. Flights started departing around 10AM, but they were running about two hours late. Steve and Billy tried to fly standby on an earlier flight, but didn't have any luck. They finally were airborne at five and made it to the hotel in time for the first show. As the Tony Sutherland Show was being announced over the speaker system, Billy reached for his baton. It would not come loose from the podium. Tanya had glued it down a few hours earlier. Billy pulled hard with both hands, and the baton separated into three pieces. As one piece of the baton flew across the stage, the band broke up with laughter. After the musicians regained their composure, Billy gave the downbeat with his bare right hand. His left hand was holding his stomach to try and contain his laughter.

As the show progressed, Billy wondered if Tanya had done anything to his bass. She hadn't, and they continued the performance without additional incidents. Billy was surprised and relieved to hear how well the new musicians played the show. He hadn't arrived in time to rehearse them, so this was the first time they had seen him conduct. With his limited conducting ability, he had anticipated a few train wrecks. None occurred, and he was amazed at the overall musical performance. When the curtain came down and the mikes were turned off, Billy addressed the musicians.

"Obviously, there is a music teacher someplace in this city and you locals have been taking lessons. I must say, all the rumors about Reno musicians not being able to read a note of music were wrong. I was prepared to hear our usual shitty performance, so tonight's musical rendition was a pleasant surprise. If you guys can keep this up for two weeks, I'm going to see to it that you make scale wages just like the professionals do. Of course, I'll expect you to kick back 10% back to me."

He had more to say, but Tanya interrupted him. "Billy, stop that oral dribble. Mr. Sutherland wants to see you in his dressing room, and he wants to see you right now."

They went to the dressing room and Tanya closed the door. Tony was still in his stage clothes and looking stern. Tony pointed a finger at Billy and spoke. "Tanya told me about your early morning phone call, and I think she's entitled to an apology. What do you think?"

"I agree," Billy said. "Tanya, I'm sorry about that call, and I apologize for upsetting you."

For a few moments, no one spoke. Tony looked at both of them and broke the silence by saying, "Tanya is a good little trooper and I'm sure she accepts your apology."   Since there wasn't any response to that statement, Tony spoke again. "Tanya, will you leave the room for a few minutes?   I have a few more things to say to Billy about this incident, and I think it would be best if you didn't hear my comments."

Tanya left and when Tony believed she was out of earshot, he said, "When she told me about your phone call, I could hardly keep a straight face. It was the funniest thing I've heard in a long, long time… but don't mention my amusement to Tanya."

"I won't," Billy replied.

"For such short notice, I think we put on a good first show. I want to compliment you on your choice of musicians. Where did you find the new men?"

"I didn't. A friend of Steve's found them. The new men are all Reno residents."

"In that case, thank Steve and his friend for me. I want you to call a special rehearsal next week. I'm having club arrangements made for five of the songs from my new record album, and I want to start performing them during this engagement. The arrangements should arrive in three or four days. I guess that's all."

As Billy walked out of the room, Tony noticed Tanya standing about twenty feet from his door. In a loud voice, Tony said, "If this happens again, I'm going to fire you."

As Billy passed Tanya, he had a dejected look on his face. He went to the coffee shop, saw Steve and Red, and joined them at the counter. While Red was filling them in on what he had been up to the past year, Tanya come into the room and sat down beside Billy. When there was a pause in the conversation, she spoke. "I'm sorry, Billy. I didn't think he would be that hard on you."

"It's alright, Tanya, I deserved it."

"I hope he doesn't fire you. I'd miss you if you weren't around."

"Thanks, Tanya. I didn't know you cared that much. Last night, I missed you too. It was cold and lonely in Salt Lake City. I sure could have used you."

"What do you mean?"

"You know what I mean."

Steve and Red stopped talking and turned their attention to Tanya and Billy. Tanya's face was getting red and the anger showed in her eyes. Finally she spoke, "You are a real dummy, dumb, dumb, dumb. Haven't you heard?"

"Heard what?" Billy asked.

"You can do that by yourself."

"It's not the same, Tanya. It's just not the same."

"That talk with Tony didn't scare you or change you one damn bit. Nothing that anyone says ever sinks into that thick scull of yours. All you ever think about is fooling around." She got up and stomped out of the room.

As they watched her go, Red asked, "Do you have something going on with that broad?"

"No. With Tanya, I'm all blow and no go."

When the new arrangements arrived, they had a rehearsal. Two of the arrangements were used in the first show and the other three were performed during the second show. The audience had responded favorably to the new songs and Tony Sutherland was on a high. He stayed his dressing room and listened to the dubs from his new record album for a few hours. It would be at least another month before his record was released, but he felt it would be big, really big. And he needed a new big selling record to boost attendance during his next tour. As yet, only a few dates had been booked, and they were almost six months downstream. After this engagement, the only immediate bookings he had were on a few TV appearances.

Tanya was still in the room and had suffered through countless playings of the songs. When Tony finally turned off his tape deck, her nerves were shot. Tony unplugged his tape recorder, wrote a note, and handed everything to Tanya. He had indulged himself with some cocaine while he was listening to his tape and was still in his own little world. Tanya held onto the things Tony gave her and kept her mouth shut. Tony paced across the room a few times and suddenly realized she was still there.

"Tanya, get that stuff to Steve Post right away. I want him to do two charts for me. Never mind that, it's all in my note to him. Hurry. Find him." Tony was laughing as she rushed out of the room. Tanya didn't stop at the house phone to call or page him. She went directly to his room and kicked on the door.

When Steve opened his door, she rushed in saying, "Pour me a drink. I don't care what it is, just pour me a drink. God, I hate it when he uses that stuff. Here is a note from Tony and some things he asked me to deliver."

Steve poured straight gin into a glass and added a few ice cubes. He handed the drink to her and then read the note from Tony. It said: "I've run off two songs from my new record and they are on the cassette in the recorder. I want you to make arrangements of them for my nightclub act. Try and have them finished by tomorrow night."

Steve plugged in the tape recorder and depressed the play key. When the sound came out, Tanya screamed, "Not again." He listened to the first song and then the sound stopped. There wasn't anything else on the cassette. He turned it over to play the other side, but no sound came out.

Tanya was sitting in a chair, shivering. She had finished her drink but was still holding the glass. As the blank cassette continued to wind its silent tape through the recorder, Steve removed the empty glass from Tanya's hand and refilled it. He gave it back to her, and as she raised it to her mouth, the phone rang. Steve picked it up and heard Tony's voice.

"Did you get my note?"

"Yes, but I can only find one song on the cassette."

"Are you sure?" Tony asked.

"I am now. The tape just finished going through both sides, and the only song is on the A side."

"I must've forgotten to push the record key on the second song. That's all right, do one song. I'll get the other one to you tomorrow. Is Tanya still there?"

"Yes, I'll get her for you."

"Steve, wait, wait just a moment. I want to ask you something."

"What is it?"

"Are you screwin' her?"

"No," Steve replied.

"Good, then put her on the phone."

Steve looked at Tanya and said, "It's Tony and he wants to talk with you." Tanya put her drink down, got out her pad and pencil, picked up the phone and said, "Yes Mr. Sutherland, this is Tanya."

"Thank God you're there. Tanya, I forgot to tell you that tomorrow night, two very important people will be here. They are from a booking agency in England. I want you to roll out the red carpet for them. Get them the best seats in the showroom, because they can do a lot for my career. Take care of their every whim, and charge everything they want to me. I gave them your name and room number, so they will be contacting you as soon as they check-in. I'm counting on you my girl, so don't let me down."

Tony hung up as Tanya was shouting, "What are their names?"

Steve worked all night and most of the day. Before the first show, he delivered everything to Tony's dressing room.

Tony looked at the music and asked, "What's this?"

"It's the chart you asked me to do."

"OH! Yes, the chart. I remember now. Thanks Steve, but I don't think we'll use it tonight. We had better save this thing until we have time to rehearse it. There are some important people in the showroom tonight, and I don't want to try something new. Why take any unnecessary chances with our new chart, right? When you get a chance to make out your bill, give it to Billy. I'll see to it that you are paid right away. I'm really looking forward to hearing this arrangement."

Tony didn't bother to call another special rehearsal, and nothing more was said about the second chart. Tony had other things on his mind. He was concerned about future bookings for his nightclub act and the promotion of his new record.

After the final performance of the two-week engagement, Steve and Billy went to the bar for a goodbye drink or two. In between making passes at the young girls, Billy said, "I think it will be at least five months before we hit the road again. Tony will be busy with promotional tours for his new record. He has a few TV appearances lined up, but he'll just use the musicians available on the programs. When Tony gets ready for another tour, I'll give you a call and see if you are interested and available."

Steve returned to Los Angeles the following morning and started calling music contractors. A few weeks went by before a job turned up, and it only resulted in two days work at a recording studio. When he finished the session and returned to his apartment, the phone was ringing. He picked it up and heard Faye's voice.

"Steve, I have been out of the city for a few days and just returned. I want you to be the first to know, Jim Decker asked me to marry him and I have accepted. We'll be married next week."

"How long have you known him?" Steve asked.

"Almost a year. We work for the same advertising agency. A few weeks ago, Jim was transferred to our branch office in San Francisco. He invited me up there for the weekend and popped the question. Everything happened so fast, I don't know where to begin. We don't even have a place of our own. Jim has been living in a hotel suite. We'll start house-hunting after the wedding, but I don't know how long it will take to find something suitable for us. I still have two months to go on my apartment lease. I'd like to leave my furniture at the apartment until we find a house. Would you stop by the apartment from time to time just to make sure everything is okay?"

"Sure, I'll watch the place," Steve told her.

"Thanks! Aren't you going to congratulate me?"

"Congratulations, Faye. I hope it's a happy marriage."

Calls for studio work continued to be few and far between, so Steve started playing with the rehearsal band on Sunday afternoons. It gave him someplace to go and broke the monotony of practicing by himself. After one of the rehearsals, he returned to his apartment and received another call from Faye.

"We found a house," she told him. "It's vacant so we can take immediate possession. Would you do me another favor?"

"I'll try," Steve said. "What is it?"

"I want my furniture. Would you make arrangements with a mover to get everything up here to San Francisco?"

"I suppose I could do that. What would be a good day and time for you to meet them and accept delivery?"

"The sooner the better, and time doesn't make any difference. I'm now a lady of leisure. All I have to do is be Mrs. Jim Decker. Steve, if you're too busy to do this for me, I'll drive to Los Angeles and take care of it myself."

"I have more time than work," he told her. "It's not an imposition, and I'll be glad to do it. I'll give you a call after I find out the specifics from a mover."

"Good, now I can spend tomorrow looking for drapes. Steve, I owe you a few favors, and I hope to be able to repay them someday."

Steve contacted a mover the following morning. A few days later, he left them into the apartment and made sure they took everything. He left Faye's keys at the manager's office and went home. As he started to fix lunch, he received an emergency call from a music contractor. He took down the information, grabbed the required instruments, and hurried to the recording studio.

The months continued in the same pattern. Days would turn into weeks without a call for work. When a call came, it was always for a last-minute panic job. It was a pleasant surprise when Billy Baker called and asked, "Would you care to go on the road for about two months?"

"Why not," Steve replied. "I'm not stirring much dust in LA."

"Okay, here is the deal. We kick off the tour in Chicago next Friday. We have a rehearsal scheduled for the early afternoon, so you may want to fly in Thursday evening. After you've made your airline reservations, call back and I'll fill you in on a few more of the details."

Steve checked into the Hilton late Thursday evening. He called Billy's room but did not get an answer. After unpacking, he went in search of a cocktail lounge and found one. About the time he was finishing his second drink, Billy walked in and joined him. Billy looked tired, but he still had his perverse sense of humor. He looked around the room a few times and said, "What rotten luck, I've laid all the girls in this room before."

"Your style stays the same, but I think your memory is shot."

"So are my nerves," Billy said. "Tony's bizarre behavior is driving me up the wall. You'd better get yourself prepared for the worst, because I think this tour is going to be a real bummer."

"Would you care to elaborate a bit more on that statement?"

"Tony's new record album is dying on the vine. He put a lot of time and money into promotional tours, but the record didn't make it into the top 100. Right now, it's sinking into oblivion. Tony hasn't had many disappointments in his career, so he's taking this one very hard. His popularity is slipping and his ego can't accept it."

"Sooner or later, everyone's career seems to hit the skids," Steve said. "Did he think he was immune from the changing tastes of the public?"

"I don't know what he thought, but he's still trying to push that record. We'll be selling them at the door on this tour. Tony had stage arrangements made for the rest of the songs on his new album, and we'll be rehearsing them tomorrow. I think it's a mistake, but what do I know? If record sales don't exceed 300,000, his options won't be picked up. That means he'll have to look for another recording company or throw in the towel in regards to recording for the mass market. It's a vicious circle. If you don't have a hit record on the market, most people don't want to attend your concert appearances. If you're not drawing well at your concert appearances, the recording companies don't want to risk their money recording you."

"It sounds like this is going to be an interesting tour," Steve said.

"Only if you enjoy suffering. Once upon a time I thought I had the easiest job in the business, but now I'm not so sure. Either way, it doesn't make much difference. Hell, after this tour I may not even have a job. That will make a big difference. Here's to nervous tension."

The regular show was rehearsed in a relaxed manner. When they finished playing the final bow music, Tanya brought out the new music and helped Billy pass out the parts. They rehearsed them, corrected a few bad notes, and then Billy told her, "We are as ready for him as we're going to get."

Tanya found Tony Sutherland and he came on stage. Tanya looked for a place where she could be out of the way but not out of hearing distance. She found a chair in the wings and sat down.

The orchestra played the first chart and waited for Tony's comments. He looked puzzled, but after a brief pause he told them, "Let me hear the next one." After they played it, Tony said, "Pass it in. I don't like it. Steve, will you do an arrangement on that song for me?"

"I did one about six months ago," Steve replied.

"That's right. I remember asking you to do an arrangement on that song, but we never got around to hearing it. Tanya! Where the hell is she at? Tanya, get your ass out here."

Billy had gathered all of the parts and was handing them to Tony as Tanya rushed across the stage. Tony pointed to the parts and asked her, "Where is Steve's arrangement on this song?"

"I'm not sure, Mr. Sutherland, but it's probably in your Dallas music files."

"Why isn't it here?" Tony asked.

"You didn't ask me to bring it."

"Do I have to tell you everything? Can't you think and act on your own once in a while? This song is from my new album, and you know how important that album is to me. Get on the phone and have Steve's arrangement sent up here at once."

"I don't think we'll be able to have it delivered today," she told him. "Shall I have it sent to the Detroit Airport and held for pickup sometime tomorrow?"

"I don't give a damn how you do it. Just get that arrangement, and get it as soon as possible. Don't stand there, call Dallas and get my music." As Tanya left the stage, the tears were forming in her eyes.

After they played the next arrangement, Tony asked the wind instruments to tacit out a few measures. When they finished the last arrangement, Tony's only words were, "Pass it in."

As Billy gathered the parts, Tony was yelling for Tanya. She leaned around the curtain and said, "Just a moment, Mr. Sutherland, I have Dallas on the phone."

"Call them back. I want to see you right now."

Tanya hurried back to Tony side as Billy was dismissing the musicians. Tony held the two arrangements he disliked as he addressed Tanya. "Send these two charts back to that dumb bastard in New York who calls himself an arranger. When you make out his check, pay him 50% of what his invoice states. He only did half a job, so he's only going to get half pay." Tony threw the music on the stage and the parts scattered everywhere. As he stormed away, he said, "Billy, I want to see you in my dressing room."

Tanya was on her knees gathering the discarded music as the musicians left the stage. Steve came forward and helped her pick up the parts. They didn't say a word to each other.

Billy entered the dressing room and Tony told him, "I want you to audition a musician tomorrow afternoon. His name is Fred Akers. He plays the reed instruments and just graduated from college. If you think he can play my library, we'll hire him."

"Are you dissatisfied with one of our reed men?" Billy asked.

"No. I guess they're all right."

"Then why should we consider changing musicians?"

"Billy, knockoff the questions and do as you're told. Fred will be in the concert hall at 2:00 PM and I want you to give him a thorough audition."

The Chicago concert was not a roaring success. The room was only 50% filled, and the songs from Tony's new record didn't exactly set the audience on fire: they received polite applause and that was all.

Tony's disappointment was complete when he found out that only 20 albums were sold at the door.

It was an apprehensive group of performers who arrived at the Detroit Airport the following afternoon. While they were waiting for their luggage, Billy asked Steve, "Will you get me checked into the hotel? There's something I have to do for Tony before I can make it to the high-rise bedroom building."

"Yes sir, rank has its privileges. Does Tony want you to roundup an audience for tonight's performance?"

"If I could, I would," Billy said. "He was pretty testy after last night's performance, and I hope it's not more of the same tonight. My butt needs time to heal."

Billy hurried off to audition Fred Akers. When he arrived at the concert hall, the stage crew was still working. After the Chicago performance, they had disassembled everything, loaded the truck, and drove straight through to Detroit. They hadn't slept, and their mood reflected it. In the midst of the chaos stood a young man with a lot of musical instruments. Billy introduced himself and said, "Let's move away from here before they kill us."

Billy couldn't find anyone with a key to the musician's room, so they sat next to the back wall as Fred demonstrated his skill on an assortment of reed instruments. When the stands for the musicians were in place on the risers, Billy went to the music cases and found the woodwind books. They move from the wall to the stage, and Billy had Fred sight read lines from some of the actual charts. Throughout it all, the stage crew kept working. Billy and Fred ducked their heads numerous times as a boom swung across the stage. When the crew was placing the microphones, someone in the wings shouted, "Is there a Billy Baker in this place?"

Billy waved his hands and shouted, "Right here, friend. You can't be one of our crew, because you spoke an entire sentence without swearing. What's up?"

"You're wanted on the phone, clown."

Billy excused himself and went to the phone. Tanya was on the other end and she told him. "When you finish the audition, Tony wants you to come directly to his suite. The number is 1011."

"Got it, doll. It's almost finished here, so I'll show up within the hour. After tonight's performance, would you care to fool around for a few hours?"

The line went dead, so Billy returned to the stage and listened to Fred Akers play a few more lines from Tony's music library. "I think I've heard enough, Fred. Put your horns away. You're a very talented young man."

"Thanks! That's what I've been hearing for quite a few years, but it has not resulted in very much work. I have letters of recommendation from my teachers and a few letters of introductions to entertainment directors, but they haven't helped."

"Well, you know how it is; things are a little slow right now."

"Do you think I'll get a job with Tony Sutherland?"

"I don't know, Fred. Right now, I'm not sure if there's a job opening."

"I was afraid of that. My uncle told me he knew Mr. Sutherland. He said he would lean on him and get me a job, but I guess he was just giving me the same snow job my teachers gave me."

"Maybe not, Fred. Your uncle may know something you and I don't know."

"I hope so, because I'm getting nowhere fast. When I contact music contractors, their usual response is, 'Do I know you?' When I tell them we haven't met before, they cut me off with things like 'get lost' or 'don't bother me, kid.' I'm getting pretty discouraged."

"Don't get discouraged," Billy told him. "Hell, it wouldn't surprise me if you got a job working for Tony Sutherland. Either way, I'll be in touch with you within a few days."

Billy arrived at Suite 1011 and knocked on the door. Tanya let him in and said, "Tony is on the phone." Tony waved and motioned for Billy to come to the desk. In a few moments, Tony hung up the phone and asked, "All right, Billy, what's the verdict?"

"Fred is an outstanding musician, but he needs seasoning."

"Seasoning! What the hell are you talking about? I don't want to eat him. Can he play my book or can't he?"

"Fred can play all of the notes, but he has not had much experience. Some of his phrasing is stilted, and he isn't familiar with your type of music."

"Billy, you didn't answer my question."

"Let me put it this way, Tony. All of our guys do a good job. Fred cannot touch them; because of his lack of experience. So, why do you want him?"

"I want him because his uncle is one of the biggest cocaine dealers in the country. He's a high roller and knows all the right people in casinos around the world. That kid's uncle can help my career, if he wants to go out of his way to do it. I want to give him a reason to help me. This year, I don't have an overseas engagement. That's a disaster, but it's the least of my worries. I can't even get booked in Lake Tahoe, Las Vegas, or Atlantic City. Billy, I'm going to ask you just one more time, can we use Fred Akers?"

"If we don't put him on lead, he'll work out."

"That's what I wanted to hear," Tony said. "Get on the phone and higher that young man."

"After I hire Fred, I suppose you'll want me to fire one of our musicians."

"Of course. It has to be done."

"Which one of the guys do you want me to let go?"

"I don't care. That's up to you."

"Tony, you're putting me in one hell of a spot. You want me to fire a musician, but I cannot explain to him why he's being terminated. If I mentioned cocaine, he might spread the word and put us in a barrel of snakes. This situation stinks, and I resent it."

"Billy, why do you think I keep you around? It's not because I believe you're one of the world's greatest conductors. You've always carried out my orders and done it with discretion. That's why you're my conductor. If you ever refuse to carry out one of my directives, I'll replace you. It's as simple as that. Now call Fred Akers and find out when he wants to join us. Use my phone."

Billy placed the call and told Fred that he had a job with Tony Sutherland.

"That's great," Fred responded. "When you want me to start?"

"Could you join us in three days?"

"Sure! I could start playing tonight, if you need me."

"No, Fred. That won't be necessary, but I would like to have you hear the show tonight and tomorrow night. Come by my dressing room about 30 minutes before the show, and I'll find a seat for you. We have the day off on Monday, but we use that day to travel to New York.

That's where you'll start playing with us. I'm going to put you on the third woodwind chair. After you hear tonight's show, I'll let you take the book home with you so you'll be able to get familiar with it. See you in a couple of hours and congratulations. I know you'll do a good job for us."

When Billy hung up the phone, Tony asked, "Which one of the musicians are you going to fire?"

"I'll give the ax to Jim, because I don't think he needs the money. I know he'll be upset when he hears the news, so I'll tell him after tomorrow's performance. Since we won't be giving him the required notice, you'd better have Tanya make out a check for two weeks pay."

Tony called Tanya and told her what he wanted. As she made out the check, Tony said, "I like you, Billy. I always have, and I'm confident you'll keep your mouth shut when it comes to giving Jim his final check."

After the Sunday night performance, Billy told Jim he wanted to see him in his dressing room. Billy closed and locked the door before saying, "Jim, this is your last night with us on this tour. I'm sorry to put it that way, but I don't know of any other way to say it."

"What did I do wrong?" Jim asked.

"Nothing, it's just one of those things. Here's two weeks pay plus the partial week you've worked for us. If you ever need a recommendation for a job, give them my name. I think you're a great musician, and I'll be glad to say that to anyone in the business."

"Then, if it wasn't my playing, it must have been something I said or did. Tell me what it was so I won't make the same mistake twice."

"You didn't do anything wrong," Billy told him.

"Nobody gets fired without a reason. What was it?"

"Yes they do... all the time. Jim, I just don't care to discuss it."

Before they left for New York, Billy introduced Fred Akers to everyone in the show. Afterwards, one of the musicians asked, "What happened to Jim? Is he sick?"

"No. He's not sick," Billy replied. "I don't have any details, but Jim went back home and is doing something else."

Steve was not overjoyed with Jim's replacement, but he worked with Fred and whipped him into shape. The engagement in New York was better received than the ones in Chicago and Detroit, but not much. Steve tried to call Claudia Fleming, but all he got was her answering service. She was out of town on an assignment.

When the New York engagement ended, they traveled to Boston. Originally, they were scheduled to be in Boston for three days. Because of poor advanced ticket sales, the last day of their engagement had been canceled. Tony decided that they would spend their day off in Philadelphia. His next engagement was in that city, and he wanted to get away from Boston.

After they checked into their hotel, Steve placed a long-distance call to Claudia Fleming. He was pleasantly surprised when she answered the call.

"Claudia, this is Steve. What are you doing today?"

"I'm not doing a thing. I just finished working one week for Drew Daily Productions, but right now, all is quiet. My answering service told me you called a few days ago, but you didn't leave a number where I could reach you. Are you in New York?"

"No, I'm calling from Philadelphia. I'm back with Tony Sutherland for a few months, and we have a two day engagement here.

It doesn't start until tomorrow, so I have an open day. I'd like to see you again. If you are free for the day, I'll fly to New York and take you out to dinner."

"Steve, you surprise me. So you'd fly to New York just to see me? I'll be damned. Did you think I was that good? No, don't answer that question. It might hurt my ego."

"Claudia, you were very good, and I was very lucky. I enjoyed our evening together, but I'm not calling to find out if you'll put me up for the night. I'd just like to spend a few hours talking with you. What do you say?"

"I think you're trying to talk me into doing something foolish," she told him.

"No way, you have my word of honor as a former Boy Scout. See, I'm holding my fingers up."

"I suppose you are, but I wondered which ones... or one."

"Claudia, you're a real nut. Maybe that's why I enjoy being with you. Just say the word, and I'll catch the next flight to New York."

"The word is probably, 'sucker', and I don't mean you, I mean me."

"You're beginning to make me angry," he told her. "If you don't trust me, just say so and I'll forget about making the trip."

"Steve, don't forget about it. Of course I trust you. I'm not too sure about myself, but I trust you. Does that make any sense?"

"None at all," he replied, "but I'd still like to get together with you."

"I'd like to see you too. If you promise me one thing: I've got an idea that's simply delicious. Do you want to hear it?"

"Of course. I've never heard of a delicious idea. This may be my only chance."

"All right, here's what I have in mind. You stay where you are at, and I'll fly to Philadelphia. What you think of that idea?"

"Actually, I like it better than mine. It surprises me, but you're always full of surprises."

"Good. I'm glad you like it, but I won't come to Philadelphia unless you promise to pursue me."

"Have I been making the wrong kind of promises to you?" he asked. "Do you want to be seduced?"

"No! At least I don't think so, but I'd like to be pursued. From time to time, a girl needs to know that she's still attractive to the opposite sex. Will you promise to pursue me? Don't laugh, this is very important to me. Will you promise?"

"Claudia, I promise to chase after you until your legs give out."

"Don't make promises you can't keep," she told him. "I know darn well that my legs are in better shape than yours."

"They're prettier, too. When do you think you'll arrive at the airport?"

"I'll probably show up in about three or four hours. There are shuttle flights between the two cities, and they fly when the airplane fills up. Why don't you plan on meeting me in four hours. Jesus, I feel like I'm getting ready for my first date, and I like the feeling. This is going to be fun, I know it."

Claudia walked into the terminal carrying her luggage. Steve took her suitcases and told her, "You look radiant."

"I'm not surprised," she said. "I just had a hot flash. God, those things are awful. They started last month. When the first one hit, I thought I was having a heart attack. It really scared me. I even promised God that I'd stopped being bitchy, if He'd let me live. Let's find a cab before I have another one."

They found a taxi, and Steve asked the driver to take them to the Marriott. Shortly after they started the drive, Claudia unbuttoned her jacket and flapped it for a few seconds. When she removed it and threw it on the seat, Steve asked, "Are you all right?"

"No. I'm not all right. In a few minutes, I'll feel better, but I don't think I'll ever be completely all right again. This is going to be a bad one, so don't look at me until I say you can. I'll probably break out in perspiration and look like a whore in heat. Steve, this is a difficult experience for me. I don't know how to describe it, but I'm beginning to feel like a disaster area. I need to know that I'm still a desirable woman. Do you mind my using you this way?"

"I don't mind," Steve told her, "but it certainly wasn't what I expected."

"Are you sorry that I came to Philadelphia?"

"No, I'm not sorry. It's good to have you here, even if you aren't in your right mind."

Claudia started to unbuttoned her blouse, but the driver shouted, "Hey lady, you can't do that my cab. You'll have to cool it until you get to the Marriott."

"Shut up!" she told him. "Can't you see that I'm going through one of the most humiliating experiences of my life? I'm hot, but not that way."

The driver thought about the remark as Claudia finished unbuttoning her blouse. After a short pause, he spoke. "Oh, I see. You looked too young for that, but I guess I'm not an authority on the subject. Do me a favor, will you? Don't take off your blouse. I've been cited for so many violations in this cab, one more would probably cost me my license."

Claudia fanned herself for a few moments. Then she buttoned her blouse and wiped her face. The two men continued to look ahead as she touched up her makeup and put on her jacket. After a final look at her hair, she put her mirror way and said "Thanks boys! It's over and I'm fully dressed. Face and all."

Steve lit up a cigarette, looked at Claudia and said, "I can see that this calls for a completely different game plan. The one I had mind probably wouldn't do a thing for you. I know how we can spend the rest of the afternoon. There's a swimming pool at the hotel. We'll just sit beside it and talk. Whenever you warm up, I'll dunk you in and out until you cool down. How does that sound?"

"Steve, a pool sounds heavenly, but I'll dunk myself. As soon as I'm unpacked, can we go there and stay forever and ever?"

"Sure," he replied. "I'd rather stay there than go back on tour with Tony Sutherland. Being with you is enjoyable. Playing with the Tony Sutherland Show can be summed up in two words: *numbing boredom.*"

When they stopped in front of the hotel, the driver got Claudia's suitcases out of the trunk and placed them on the curb. As Steve paid the fare and offered a generous tip, the driver told him, "Keep the tip, buddy. I don't want you to think I make my living this way. I'm a part-time driver and a full-time author. You'd be surprised at the amount of material I get from my fares. Believe me, that little lady of yours is going to be in my next book. Take good care of her, because she's something else. Here's my card. When you get ready to check out, give me a call. I'm looking forward to driving you two again."

Steve took the card and picked up the luggage. On the way to the room, Claudia asked, "What were you two talking about?"

"You made quite an impression on our driver. He wants to include you in his next book. I guess nutty people are in fashion these days. They walked a few more paces and he said, "Whoa, girl. This is your room."

Claudia walked in, looked around and asked, "Where are your things?"

"They're in my room," he said. "I'm two doors down the hall, right next to the elevator."

"A room of my own...how about that! Chivalry isn't dead after all. If you want to impress me by throwing money around, I'm not going to complain. "Go back to your room and get into your swimming trunks. It will probably take me longer to get ready than it will you. When I'm dressed for splashing, I'll come down the hall and see where you live."

"You sound a little pushy. Do you like to give orders and act bossy?"

"Yes I do," she said. "It gives me the illusion that I'm doing something worthwhile and important. Now get out of here and let me get unpacked."

When Steve heard a knock on his door, he opened it and Claudia came charging and saying "I just used the last Kleenex in my room. Do you have any extras?"

"Yes. They're in the medicine cabinet. The manager of this place must be bucking for promotion. If he isn't, he probably controls the in-house coin concessions. I ran out of tissues shortly before I left for the airport. Those packages came from the machine in the hall."

Claudia took one of the packages, and they left for the pool. On the way she asked, "Are you sick?"

"I was sick in the head, but there isn't anything wrong with me now. This is as good as I get. Why do you ask?"

"When I took your tissues, I couldn't help but notice a lot of medication. You've got enough stuff in there to set up a small pharmaceutical service. What's in all those bottles and boxes?"

"They contain medicines prescribed by a couple of doctors. Since the last time I saw you, I spent a month in a sanitarium. It wasn't anything serious, and they couldn't find a thing wrong with me. They said I had the bad luck of having too many distasteful things hit me at one time. It was just a case of nerves brought on by the divorce, my work, and things in general."

"You take all of that junk?" She asked.

"No, not really. If you're wondering if I have a chemical dependency, I don't. The doctors confirmed it, and prescribed more medications. I guess you could call them my security blanket. I have something for every occasion: tension, depression, and anxieties."

They reached the pool and Claudia took off her outer garment. She dropped it on a chair, stood up straight and asked, "Does this do anything for your anxieties?"

"It sure as hell does, it sets them on fire."

"So am I." Splash... and she was in the pool.

When she climbed out of the pool and collapsed on a chair, Steve asked, "What kind of work do you do for Drew Daily Productions?"

"Wet-nurse. I think that's the best way to describe it. Drew Daily's secretary, Lois Martin, asked me to fill in for a week. I think she wanted to go out and look for another job, but she didn't say that that was what she had in mind. I first met Lois when Daily's career was really big. At that time, Drew was doing a lot of recording and TV work in New

York. He was a dynamic type of guy who seemingly couldn't do anything wrong. Now he's nothing but a basket case."

"So the super guy turned into a super slob. Do you know what caused the change?"

"Booze," she said. "He's stoned most of the time. Don't get me wrong, I don't have anything against drinking. God knows, I've help make the distilleries what they are today."

"You're making me thirsty," he told her. "Shall we get dressed and go to the cocktail lounge?"

"Not yet. The sun is still out. After being around Drew Daily, I promised myself that I wouldn't take a drink during the daylight hours. When I saw what drinking did to him, I couldn't help but think the same thing could happen to me. I don't know what caused him to increase his alcohol consumption, perhaps he started to lose his audience, and maybe it was the other way around. Either way, he is destroying himself with heavy drinking. Sometimes, he can't even hold his water."

"A superstar and his secretary must have a very intimate relationship. Did you have to change his clothes, wash him up, and powder him?"

"You don't know how close that comes to being the truth. What a job. Why Lois stayed with him all these years, I'll never know."

After a short pause in the conversation, Steve said, "That's it? Aren't you going to tell me more?"

"Since you insisted, I'll drone on. During the day, Drew was usually half-assed sober, so the routine secretarial work wasn't too bad. The living hell came when he had to perform. During my week with him, he only performed three times. That was enough, because he went to pieces before each performance. Each evening went like this: I'd put on his stage makeup; comb his hair; and start brushing off his clothes.

Before I would finish, Drew would ask me to check on the audience attendance figures. During all of this he would be drinking. When I'd bring back the disappointing news, it was always the same. He would say,' that's bad, that's bad.' Then he'd run his hands through his hair, put his face in his hands, and make a mess of himself. I'd start prettying him up again after he had another belt or two, but then he would ask me to re-check the latest attendance figures and the whole damn process would repeat itself."

"That's fascinating," Steve said. "I believe your big problem was being too slow with the brush. It sounds to me like Daily was trying to speed you up. What do you think?"

"I think it's too hot." Splash.

While Claudia was splashing, Billy Baker walked by and told Steve, "I've been watching you two from the second floor. That woman really enjoys swimming."

"Yes, you're right. She does like the cold water," Steve replied.

"When she decides to come out, will you introduce me?"

"No! It would be redundant. You met her last year in Dallas. That's Claudia Fleming."

"That's the girl who gave orders like a drill sergeant? She sure looks different when you get her out of those tomboy clothes. What is she doing here?"

"She's visiting with me. That's what she's doing. Claudia is an old friend of the family."

"I don't know what's going on down here, but I'm not buying that friend of the family routine. Hey, Claudia, this is Billy Baker talking at you. It's good to see you again. What are you doing in Philadelphia?"

"Hi, Billy. I'm visiting with an old friend of the family."

Billy threw his hands in the air and said, "Besides being all wet, you're also a flagrant eavesdropper."

Claudia came out of the pool and grabbed her towel. As she dried off, she asked Billy, "Why are you all dressed up in your Sunday best? Do you have a heavy date?"

"Yes, a very heavy one," Billy replied. "It's with Tony Sutherland. We're having dinner together. He invited me down to the waterfront to have some seafood. It always bothers me when he offers to do something nice. Based on experience, it usually means he's really going to give it to me. Well, it's almost time to be picked up. Since my date doesn't like to be kept waiting, I'd better get out front before he starts blowing his horn. Perhaps the three of us can have a drink later tonight. I think I'm going to need one."

As Billy departed, Steve said, "The daylight hours are over. Shall we get dressed and have the first drink of the day?"

"Why do you keep asking me to get dressed? Don't you like what you see? I thought it was supposed to be the other way around. Steve, are you confused or am I going to pot?"

"I must be confused," he said, "because I can't remember all the questions. I'm also hungry and thirsty."

"Why don't you have something sent out here. I like the pool, and I don't want to get dressed. I want to stay here..."

"I know, forever and ever. Claudia, can't you see that sign? It says 'no food or beverages allowed in the pool area.' We'll have to get dressed or die of hunger and thirst."

"You don't believe everything you read, do you? If you won't have something sent out here, I'll go get it. What do you want to eat?"

"Meat," he said, "Anything that has a lot of meat in it. Hey, you can't go in there in your swimsuit. Can't you read the signs? They won't let you in the restaurant if you're not fully clothed."

"Don't try and tell me what I can or can't do. Who the hell do you think you are, the manager? Read the signs. I'll be back in a few minutes."

Steve threw an ashtray at her as she went through the glass door. It hit the door as it was closing and fell to the walkway. A short time later, Claudia came back and sat down. Steve glared at her for a while before he asked, "Has anyone ever told you that you're an independent bossy bitch?"

"Many times," she said.

"Sometimes you make me so mad I could kick your butt."

"Did you say kiss or kick?" Splash.

In about 15 minutes, a waiter came into the pool area pushing a cart with food. He stopped beside Steve, looked at Claudia and asked, "Is this where you want it?"

"Yes," she replied. "That's the injured man."

As Steve signed the bill for the dinner, Claudia climbed out of the pool and dried off. When the waiter left, Steve asked, "What did you tell them?"

"I told them you were sick, and I was your nurse. I also mentioned that you were on a high-protein diet. How's the food?"

"Delicious."

"Are you still mad at me?" She asked.

"How could I be after this surprise. You've provided me with a great meal, a private dining room, moonlight and a mermaid for a dinner companion."

"Well, I'm still mad at you. This is for throwing an ashtray at me." Claudia picked up the pitcher of water, poured it over his head and stuck her tongue out at him. Steve continued to eat as if nothing had happened. After swallowing the last of his food, he spoke. "This is the first time I've had a shower with my meal. It was rather refreshing. Did you perform the same service for Drew Daily?"

"During my last night with him, I wish I would have thought of it. Dousing him with water would have expressed my anger in a womanly way. Oh well, it's too late now."

"Did you lose your cool?" He asked.

"Completely, but not without good justification. That hateful man provoked me into saying angry words."

"Don't stop your story now. Tell me how it happened. What did he do?"

"I don't know whether to tell it to you or not," she said. "I think he was awful, but you might laugh at the whole thing. If you do, I will be mad at you too."

"If I promise not to do anything more than smile, will you tell me about it?" He asked.

"I'll take your word, but you better not back down on it or you will be sorry. Midway through his show, Drew always makes a brief exit while the band plays bow music. In the wings is a tray with a pitcher of water, glasses, towels and extra stage makeup. When Drew exits, he always takes a drink of water or something stronger. While he is drinking, I would wipe off the perspiration and touch up his makeup. During my last night with him, he performed the most dreadful act while I was touching up his makeup. He unzipped his pants and urinated on the stage. It smelled just awful, and the stuff splattered on my legs. To make things even worse, the stage crew saw the entire incident. At the time, I was so embarrassed I couldn't say a word."

"He must have been blind drunk to pull a stunt like that," Steve said.

"Pretty close to it. When the show was over, he tried to apologize in his own egotistical way. I think his words were, 'I'm sorry about that. Let's kiss and makeup.' That was when I went into a rage. I can't remember all of the things I said, but I ended up calling him an imbecile and telling him that I wouldn't puke on the best part of his body let alone kiss him."

"Claudia, you have a knack when it comes to finding powerful expressions. You probably made a lasting impression on him with those remarks. If you ever need a reference, I don't believe you should count on getting a *zingy* one from Drew Daily."

"I'm not counting on anything from Daily. I don't even want to think about him. Steve, let's get in the water."

"You must be mad," he said. "Swimming at this time of night might be alright for mermaids, but it's too cold for me."

"If you get cold, I'll warm you up."

Later, Billy walked into the pool area and saw two figures standing in the water. He shouted, "This is the lifeguard and you're breaking the rules. Touch swimming is not allowed in this pool." The outburst didn't even generate a response, so he walked over to them and asked, "Aren't you two getting a bit waterlogged?"

Steve continued to look at Claudia as he said, "This lifeguard is a drag, but he may have a point."

"Of course I do," Billy replied. "Folks, I just want to do my job. Honest. It's true. No one freezes to death in my pool. If you'll untangle yourselves, put on some clothes and meet me in our cocktail lounge, I'll buy a round of antifreeze."

After they had dressed, Claudia and Steve went to the lounge. It was huge, and business was good. As they made their way through the lounge looking for Billy, Steve introduced Claudia to numerous people who worked for Tony Sutherland. When they reached the end of the room, Steve saw Tanya Allan. She was drinking alone, so they joined her. After the girls were introduced to each other, Claudia mentioned that she had just met a lot of the people on tour, and everyone had one thing in common: "They were all getting bombed."

Tanya looked at her and asked, "What else is there to do?"

When Steve asked if she had seen Billy, Tanya told him, "That clown just left with a broad. Do you know that tired old routine he keeps pulling on the young ladies? Sure you do. Well, he used it on a girl at that table." Tanya pointed to the table next to them, but she leaned too far out of her chair.

Steve helped her get up from the floor, and she told him, "Thanks, Steve. Tonight I'm not only unsteady, I seem to be spilling more than I'm drinking. Will you call that waitress? I hardly had a chance to touch that one before it was gone." She looked at Claudia and asked, "Did I get any on you?"

Claudia just shook her head in a 'no' manner and watched as Steve called a waitress to their table. After they gave their order, Steve asked, "How can that be? Are you telling me that someone actually took Billy up on his routine?"

Tanya tried to straighten her dress. Eventually, she gave up and said, "When Billy finished his childish come on, I couldn't believe my ears. The girl told him, 'I don't want to die stupid,' so he took her to his room. That was that. She must be a strange person or a third-class nymphomaniac, because nobody in their right mind goes to bed with Billy. I hope she gives him a good case of clap. He deserves it."

When the waitress delivered their drinks, Tanya put both of her hands on the glass and drank it straight down. After it was drained, she crashed the glass on the table and said, "I didn't give that one a chance to get away. Claudia, I want to let you in on a secret. Move closer so the others can't hear us. That's good. Claudia, this place has the best miracle drugs in town. Why don't you go to work on Steve and see if you can talk him into buying more of the same?"

"I heard that remark," Steve said, "and you'd better forget it. I'm not buying you a drink, and you're not buying another drink. You've had more than enough."

"Maybe so."

"Tanya, can you make it back to your room on your own?"

"Why not? If I can't drink, I'll sleep. Piss on you."

Tanya got up, but she could barely walk. Steve saw Fred Akers at a nearby table and motioned for his help. They supported Tanya and helped her move through the room. Claudia followed them. When they were outside in the fresh air, Tanya started to cry but stopped. They reached her room, and Claudia unlocked the door.

After they were inside the room, Tanya said, "Tony really laid into me last night. He told me I was doing a lousy job with his makeup, and that's one of the reasons attendance is off. Jesus, how do they know that? If they don't show up, how do they know?"

Claudia tried to get Tanya out of her clothes, but she wasn't making much progress with the limp body. Steve asked Fred to help her, but he replied, "I don't want to undress Tanya."

"Fred, she won't even remember you were in the room. Stop acting like you're sixteen years old and help Claudia. I'm going to order some food and coffee."

Room service arrived. Steve wrapped a towel around Tanya's neck and started feeding her. After awhile, Tanya said, "Steve, thanks for looking after me. Why do you treat me so nice?"

"Because I like you. You're my friend. Now keep eating or I'll spank your bottom."

"Think that might help? Have I been a naughty girl?"

"No. I don't think you've ever been a naughty girl. Adolescent and goofy, yes, but only when you drink too much."

When Steve finished the feeding, Claudia washed Tanya's face and placed a cool damp cloth across her forehead. The men gathered all of the pillows in the room and propped her up in the bed. Steve took the room key and told her they would be back to make a bed check in an hour or two. As they started to leave the room, Tanya said, "Not a naughty girl, too bad."

Fred told them he was going back to the lounge. As they watched him walk away, Steve asked, "Shall we join him?"

"I'd rather not," Claudia replied. "I've seen enough drunks for one night. Why don't we go to one of our many rooms and just talk?"

"That's fine with me, but I'm going to have a drink or two with the conversation. I do some of my best talking while I'm drinking. Let's go to my room. It contains a hidden stash of gin and vermouth."

As Steve mixed a shaker full of his magic ingredients, Claudia sat down and kicked off her shoes. He poured a drink for himself and asked, "Can I tempt you with a martini?"

"No! I don't want to take a drink. Almost everyone I know in this business is a heavy drinker, and I don't want to become a lush just because it's the 'in thing' to do."

"Suit yourself," he said.

"From what I saw tonight, this group you're working with is about the worst bunch of confirmed alcoholics ever gathered for a performance. How do they make it through the show?"

"With great difficulty. If you would care to have firsthand knowledge, tomorrow night you can witness our performance and judge for yourself. If it's anything like our previous engagements on this tour, there will be a surplus of empty seats. Unless something changes and changes fast, this cross-country jaunt is not going to go down in history as one of Sutherland's greatest triumphs. Shall we look in on Tanya and see if she's still among the living?"

"If she is, tomorrow she's going to wish she wasn't."

Steve opened the door, and they walked over to Tanya's bed. Steve bent over her to make sure she was breathing. When his face approached hers, Tanya opened her eyes and asked, "Are you going to kiss me goodnight?"

He kissed her on the cheek, straightened up and said, "I think she'll live."

They returned to Steve's room and sat down on the bed. "That girl likes you," Claudia said. "She trusts you. Did you or are you having an affair with her?"

"No, and no respectively," he replied.

"I don't believe you. Tanya idolizes you. Have you ever asked her to go to bed with you?"

"No!"

"Maybe I worded it wrong. Have you asked her to sleep with you?"

"No!"

Claudia's voice increased its intensity. "You're jiving me, aren't you, Steve? Who are you trying to kid? She wouldn't act that way if there wasn't a reason."

"There's a reason," Steve said, "but you probably wouldn't understand it."

"Try me."

"Okay! I'll skip the details and make it short. The other musicians ignore her. Billy teases her, and Tony abuses her. I treat her with respect and kindness. I know what it's like to feel down, and I don't like to see anyone else going through the same thing. When Tanya gets depressed, she knows I'll take time to listen to her troubles. It helps her get through those low periods. That's why she likes me."

There was a long pause before Claudia spoke. "I did it again. I exploded like a firecracker and ran off at the mouth. A few minutes ago, I was mad at you. Now, I'm mad at me. I feel foolish and tacky. Why do I carry on like that when I don't even know what I'm talking about?"

"I'd like to think it was because you were a little jealous," Steve said.

"I'm also a very weak person. Fix me a martini. I think I'm rapidly sinking into the second stage of alcoholism. Steve, this may come as a shock to you, but under this brazen exterior lurks the most insecure person on the face of the earth."

"Here you are, Miss Insecurity. You'd better drink fast, because the sun will be up in a few hours."

"Don't grin at me like that. I can't help the way I am. Stop grinning or I'll kick you in the crotch. You look and act like you're doing the devil's work, and I've met more than enough devils for one lifetime. Be nice to me, and I might be nice to you. Why can't you treat me the same way you treat Tanya?"

"I'll try, but I don't think it will work."

"Why not?" She asked.

"You are not like Tanya in any way, shape or form... And I feel differently toward you. Claudia, you are the most interesting person I've ever met, and you seem to be completely self-sufficient. Tanya is just a young, lonely, insecure girl without close friends."

"Close friends! Do you think I have a lot of close friends? Name one. My ex-husband certainly isn't a friend. I don't have a steady boyfriend, and all of the girls I know hate my guts. If you think I'm self-sufficient, you're nuts. I'm frightened every day of my life. I don't even have a regular job. If that damn phone doesn't start ringing for work, I will probably starve. I feel all alone and lonely, and I don't like that feeling. Steve, please lie down next to me and hold me."

The following morning, they went to Tanya's room and knocked on the door. She opened it and was fully dressed: peaked, but dressed. The three of them went to the coffee shop and saw of Billy. He was alone, so they joined him.

Billy look to Tanya and told her, "You should start taking better care of yourself. Have you seen a doctor recently?"

"Yes! Last night I had a consultation with Dr. Post. He said I was taking my job too seriously. Outside of that, he gave me a clean bill of health."

"He's a quack," Billy said. "You look like you could use some professional advice. I'd get a second opinion before it's too late."

"My hangover will be gone in a few hours," she said, "but you're problems will be with you for days. Did you look into the mirror this morning?"

"Yes, my princess, and I'm counting on you to hide those scratches on my face. You work wonders on Tony, so why not me? May I have a few moments of your time before we hit the stage?"

"No! You told me I looked bad, so why should I help you look good. Unless you change your tune, the only help you'll get from me is iodine on the open wounds."

"So that's how it's going to be," he said. "You're going to make me kiss your ass before you'll help me. All right, you win. Pull down your pants."

"Billy, I'm not interested in hearing any more of that kind of talk. As far as I'm concerned, you're on your own with your scratches."

"You're a hard woman, Tanya. How can I make you change your mind? Tell me the words."

"Find the words yourself, lover boy. You've still got eight hours before you have to show off your face to the audience."

Billy looked at Claudia and Steve for a few moments before saying, "At least you two look well rested. I didn't expect it, but life is full of surprises. Did you have a fight or something?"

Claudia developed a slight blush as Steve replied, "We ran out of things to say about the family, so we turned in early. How did your evening go, or shouldn't I ask?"

"The first part wasn't so hot, but the last part made up for it. The last part was fantastic. Offhand, I'd say it couldn't have been better, unless of course Tanya replaced what's her name. Tanya, are you listening to me? Love of my life, do you like those words?"

"You are not even coming close," she told him.

"Billy, you didn't have much to say about the first part of your evening," interjected Steve in an effort to change the subject. "Was it a wash out or just another super-secret-hush-hush conference?"

"I guess it was all of those things," Billy replied. "During the drive back to this place, Tony did enlighten me on one item. He has pinpointed the cause of declining attendance on this tour."

Tanya bit her lip and frowned.

"I can hardly wait to hear these words of wisdom," Steve said. "Come on, Billy, aren't you going to let us in on the big secret?"

"Why not! The rooms aren't filling up, because I'm not setting the right tempos. I offered to buy a metronome, but Tony said it wasn't necessary. I believe his words were, 'I know when the tempos are right and when they are wrong. I can feel it, so from now on, I want you to keep your eyes on the palm of my left hand. When my palm and fingers wave upward, increased the tempo. When they wave downward, slow it down. Just watch me at all times, and I'll correct this problem.' So look out buddy, we may have five or six little tempo changes during every song."

Tanya laughed and told Billy, "You finally said the right words."

"I did, when?"

"Never mind. I'll take care of those scratches. Who knows, I may even make you look more handsome."

"I'm not asking for miracles, Tanya, just make me look presentable. This tour is going from bad to worse. Trying to keep my eyes on Tony is going to be nothing but a riot. My head will be swiveling from front to back like a marionette. I'll be his quick-to-react puppet, and the musicians won't know who or what to follow. What fun."

When they finished breakfast and were having a third cup of coffee, Claudia called her answering service. Someone had tried to reach her a few minutes earlier, so she returned the call. After hanging up the phone, she hurried to Steve and told him "I've got a job with a TV production company, and I'm going back to New York. One of the people on the set got sick, and I told them I'd be on deck within a couple of hours. Find a cab and hold it. I'll pack and be out front in a few minutes."

They made it to the airport in record-breaking time, and Claudia was lucky. She walked onto a flight that was ready to leave for New York. Steve stayed in the airport and watched the plane take off. When it was airborne, he returned to his room and got a few hours sleep.

That evening, when Steve was walking to the stage, Billy came out of Tony's dressing room. Steve looked at him and said, "It's not handsome, but it's not bad."

"Yeah, this is the new me. Tony laughed his head off while Tanya worked her wonders. At least he's in a good mood. I made his day, and now I hope the audience will make his night. I must remember not to sweat. If I sweat, Tanya won't guarantee her work."

As Steve took his place on the stand, Fred Akers turned toward him and asked, "May I shake your hand?"

"Sure, here it is. What brought this on? Did you finally come to the realization that someone else might know more about music than you do?"

"Music doesn't have anything to do with it," Fred said. "Your room is next to mine, and I hardly slept last night. The moans and groans from your roommate kept waking me up. I think you do good work, and I wanted to congratulate you."

Billy blotted his face with a handkerchief before giving the downbeat. The tempos gradually went up and down throughout the evening. It was amusing to everyone on stage except for Billy and Tony. They were dead serious.

When the concert ended, Billy made an announcement. "Alright children, except for the rhythm section and Fred Akers, everyone is dismissed."

"What's up?" Fred asked.

"How should I know? I'm just the leader of this outfit, but don't put your instruments away. As soon as the theater clears, Tony wants us to work out some new things with him."

After the audience left, the musicians returned to the stage. A short time later, Tony Sutherland joined them. Tony went directly to Fred and told him, "Tomorrow, your uncle will be here. I want to show him that we're proud of you. Therefore, I decided to feature you on one or two numbers. Billy, have the boys get up *It Doesn't Matter.* Fred, this is what I have in mind. After we are sixteen measures into the second chorus, the other wind instruments will stop playing. That's where I want you to start your featured performance. You'll be out front with me, and I want you to play some licks behind my vocal. When we reach the third and final chorus, the rest of the band will join us. You'll continue playing throughout the third chorus. Billy, take it from the top. That will give Fred plenty of time to get ready for his featured solo."

Billy kicked off the tempo. When Fred started playing, he filled all of the cracks and more. After they had concluded the song, Tony told him, "You're covering me, Fred. Let me hear my voice. After all, everyone wants to hear the words. All I want you to do is play a few fills at the end of my vocal phrases. Billy, let's try it again."

"From the top?"

"No. I don't think that's necessary. Start it right on the second chorus."

They charged through the song again, and when it was over, Tony told Fred, "That's better, but it's not quite what I had in mind. Billy, have everyone get out *Love Me Forever.* Now then, Fred, what I have in mind for this song is more straightforward. After I sing the first chorus, we will feature you on a solo. You play a full chorus with only the rhythm section backing you up. After your solo, we'll go back to my chart and pick up where we left off. Let me hear how you intend to play your solo. Billy!"

"Give Fred a vamp to get him started," Billy told the musicians. "Here we go again with a one, two, three, four…"

Fred wasn't completely familiar with the chord changes on the song, but that did not keep him from playing the hell out of his sax. Notes cascaded like sheets of sound. His technique was absolutely amazing. They finished the chorus and waited for Tony's comments.

Tony looked at Fred Akers and asked, "Was that jazz? Were you playing jazz?"

"Yes," Fred replied.

"That's what I thought. Now I don't want you to think I have anything against jazz, but it's out of context with my music. Let me hear you play that solo again, but this time, make it sound more country."

They went at it again, and when they finished, Tony told them to take a break. He called Billy to his side, and they had a brief consultation. Billy went to the phone, called the Marriott, and asked to be connected with the cocktail lounge. When someone answered, Billy told the voice, "I want to speak with one of your customers. His name is Steve Post. You can't miss him, because he's usually drunk by this time of night."

When Steve answered the phone, Billy told him, "Hey, Steve baby, this is Billy. We've got a little problem down here. I know you're dying to help us out, so here's what I want you to do. Grab some manuscript paper and a pencil or two. Call a cab, and on the way down here, write a few lines for Fred Akers. The songs are, *'It Doesn't Matter'* and *'Love Me Forever.'* Write out a couple of choruses of background figures on *'It Doesn't Matter'*, and do one solo chorus on *'Love Me Forever'*. Hell, you'll probably have them finished by the time you get here. Oh yes, one more thing, write them for tenor sax."

When Steve arrived at the theater, Billy met him at the door. They went directly to the stage, and Steve talked over the parts with Fred. After Fred played them a few times with the rhythm section, Tony asked, "Can you have those lines memorized by tomorrow night?"

"No sweat," Fred said. "These things are simple."

"That's what I like to hear. That's my kind of man. I'm sick and tired of people who make excuses and tell me something can't be done. Fred, I like your attitude. What was that phrase you said? I know,' No sweat.' That's good. I may include it in my monologue tomorrow night when I introduce you. Well boys, everything seems to be under control, so we might just as well call it a night and get in some sack time."

Fred had his solos memorized the following evening, and Tony was delighted with his performance. After the show, Fred and his uncle spent over an hour with Tony Sutherland.

The next day, they started a series of one night stands that took them down the East Coast. Throughout this segment of the tour, tempos changed, music was rewritten, and the lineup was revised continuously. As the musicians became more disenchanted with each passing day, alcohol consumption and drug intake increased. By the time they reached Miami, most of Tony Sutherland's entourage were exhausted and disgusted. Tanya was the only person who didn't appear to be down. During the two-day engagement in Miami, she spent her leisure time with a male visitor from Dallas.

After the Miami engagement, they caught an early morning flight for San Francisco. During most of the trip, Tanya and Steve sat together. As Steve raised his first drink of the day, Tanya noticed the tremor in his hand and asked, "How long have you had the shakes?"

"They started about a week ago. It isn't anything serious, just a slight case of morning nerves. After my first drink, they ease off and disappear."

"Steve, I think you've been overdoing a good thing. If I were you, I get to a doctor - fast."

"Yes, mother."

"Don't yes mother me. Promise me you'll see a doctor."

"Tanya, you worry too much. When this tour is over, I'll see a doctor if I can't kick the habit. Does that satisfy you?"

"Not really, but I guess it will have to do."

Enough of this heavy talk about me," Steve said. "Tell me about your friend. From what I've seen, he is really giving you the rush."

"You're right. Jim Jackson may just rush me to the altar. Most of the guys I know just want to fool around. Jim is different. He wants to marry me. Does that shock you?"

"No, not at all. I think any man would be lucky to get you. If anything, I'm surprised that it didn't happen a long time ago. Are you going to take him up on it?"

"I don't know. We've been seeing each other off and on for about two years. Jim is nice enough, but I'm not sure I want to spend the rest of my life with him."

"You'll never know unless you try it," Steve said. "Marriage doesn't have to be forever. If it starts to go sour, you can always get out of it. I think everyone should take a shot at it from time to time."

"I suppose you're right. Right now, marriage sounds better than roaming around the country with Tony Sutherland. This kind of traveling gets to be *old stuff* in a hurry, and the demands on your time never let up. I'm not building anything on the road except more of the same, and I'm tired of this way of life. It's probably time to pack-it-in and settle down with some guy. If Jim wasn't such a good-old-boy, I jump at the chance to be his wife."

"What do you mean by that?" Steve asked. "What is a good-old-boy?"

"Maybe I used the phrase wrong," she said. "But to me, it describes a macho man who likes to let everybody be aware of his presence. That's my Jim. He's got a loud boisterous voice and can't keep his mouth shut. My God, he can't even sit still in a restaurant and enjoy a meal. Whenever he sees someone he knows, he has to rush over to them and shake their hand or slap their back. Sometimes, I get the feeling that Jim thinks he's a show business personality. He's always telling jokes, and I've never seen him without a smile on his face. He even smiles when he's mad. Force of habit I guess, and his idea of a real good time is to bull-shit all night long with the boys. Another thing I don't like about Jim is his drinking. He's beginning to put on weight and developing a potbelly. With the exception of those few annoyances, I like him, really like him. What you think?"

"Nobody's perfect. In comparison with what most wives say about their husbands, your complaints are nothing. Jim sounds like a winner to me."

"I think so too. After we're married, I'll change some of his bad habits, and he'll be just fine."

"Yes, I'm sure you'll try," Steve replied. "Apparently, you've decided to take him up on his proposal."

"I think so. It's the best and only offer I've had so far. Besides, I want to get married, settle down, and live a normal life."

Shortly after they started the evening performance, one of Steve's hands started to tremble. He couldn't get it under control and missed a few notes. About 10 minutes later, it happened again during a flute passage. Steve threw his flute on the floor, folded his arms and just stared into space.

When it became obvious that he wasn't going to play again, Fred Akers picked up Steve's book and placed it on top of the third woodwind book. Fred played the lead as the show continued. Near the end of the performance, Steve kicked the flute off the back side of the riser. It was his only movement in almost an hour. He continued his blank stare for the remainder of the show. When the curtain came down, Fred tried to talk to him, but he would not respond.

Billy saw Tanya standing in the wings and shouted, "Call an ambulance. Steve has freaked out."

Fred and Billy stayed with him until the ambulance arrived. A paramedic tried to talk Steve into getting up from his chair, but he didn't hear him. When they carried Steve from the stage and started to strap him on a stretcher, Fred turned away from the site and started vomiting. Billy went with the ambulance to the nearest hospital and filled out the paperwork as best he could.......

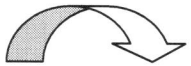

Steve stopped reminiscing, looked at his watch, and realized it was time for Faye to pick him up. He had been in the sanitarium for three months and was anxious to get out. This time he had a chemical dependency, so it resulted in a longer confinement.

Faye met him in the lobby, and they went to her car. As they drove off she asked, "How does it feel to be a free man again?"

"Words can't describe it," he told her.

"I didn't see your medication. Did you remember to bring it?"

"It's in the suitcase, but I don't intend to use it. After going through withdrawal, I'm through with medications. From here on in, the strongest drug I'll take is coffee."

"How are you set financially?" Faye asked.

"I'm in good shape. Besides what's left in the bank, I'll have money coming in from the musicians' pension fund. I put in for early retirement a few weeks ago. During the many good years, a lot of money was paid into that fund. I'll have an adequate income, not fabulous, but more than enough to take care of my needs. How are things going with you and Jim?"

"Pretty good. Jim enjoys his work, and I've managed to adjust my life around it. We had a rough period for a while, but I think we've resolved our differences. Jim has many of the same faults you had."

"I find that interesting," Steve said.

"I thought you would," she replied. "His work usually comes first, and I get what's left over. Jim has to attend frequent evening meetings, and I resented them. For a while, I felt hurt and angry about being second in line for his time, but Jim convinced me that I was being rather selfish and self-centered. You used to tell me the same thing, but I didn't believe you. I guess I've always wanted everything to go my way, and I still do. I doubt if I'll ever change, but this time around, I'm trying to be less demanding."

"Faye, I believe you matured."

"Thanks! I appreciate hearing those words. If you would have substituted grown-up for matured, I would have appreciated them even more. Matured sounds rather old. Either way, I must be getting better at something, because Jim has become much more attentive. He doesn't take me for granted anymore, and that means a lot to me. Jim also understands my need for a separate identity, so he didn't kick-up much of a fuss when I decided to take a part-time job. We're both working at the marriage, and I think the worst part is behind us."

"Good! I'm glad to hear you talk that way."

"If you're not doing anything on Sunday, we would like to have you over for dinner."

"Thanks, Faye, but if you don't mind, I'd like to take a rain check on it."

"You've got it, but don't drop out of sight."

"I won't," Steve told her.

"You're not going to sit in your apartment and hibernate, are you?"

"No, I'm not going to hibernate. I'll keep busy, but it won't be with music. I'm planning on taking a few short trips up and down the coast. After I get tired of that, I'll probably enroll in some of the night courses at one of the colleges. I don't have any hobbies, so I'm considering cultivating one or two."

Faye pulled off the road and parked beneath the carport. When she took the keys out of the ignition, she told him, "This is your new home. Your apartment is right behind us. I'll go with you and explain where Jim and I put everything."

They started walking toward the apartment, but Steve stopped and turned around. "That's strange," he said. "You parked next to a car that looks just like mine."

"It is your car, and after driving it back from Los Angeles, I agree with you. It is strange. If it were mine, I'd buy a gun and put it to sleep."

"Faye, you don't understand my car. It behaves like a demanding mistress. It won't put out for you unless you give it constant attention."

"I'll bet you even offer it a drink before you ask it to perform." She said. "When you get back to the sanitarium for your checkup, I strongly advise that you avoid discussing your car."

Steve laughed and said, "Everything considered, I think you're right. Did you make a special trip just to get the car?"

"Not really. Jim had to be in LA two weeks ago, so we drove down and loaded everything you had into and onto the two cars. During the drive back home, we looked like a couple of gypsies."

Faye opened the apartment door, dropped two sets of keys in his hand, and gave him a quick tour of the place. When they completed the walk-through, she told him, "I bought enough food for a few days, and it's in the pantry and refrigerator. They looked so bare, I simply had to put something in them. All of your musical instruments are in the spare bedroom closet. When Billy Baker found out where I was living, he shipped everything back to me. We stored them at our place until this morning. Well, what do you think of your apartment?"

"I like it. You two went to a lot of trouble getting me resettled, and I won't forget it."

"Steve, you're not going to completely forget about music, are you?"

"Probably not, but I don't intend to play anymore. For many years, playing was enjoyable and financially rewarding. I feel very fortunate to have had those years, but the music business has changed. Since most of the work I found satisfying has disappeared, I'm not going to beat my head against the walls looking for something that is almost nonexistent."

As they left the apartment and started to walk back to Faye's car, she asked, "Are you going to take Dan Daily up on his offer and play with the kicks band?"

"I doubt it. I can't see any point in practicing all the time just to go out with the boys on Sunday night and make music. I think it would be a poor anti-climax, and it's not the way I want to spend my time."

"Dan thought it would be good therapy for you, and I feel the same way. "Won't you even consider it?"

"Faye, I'm planning on going to some of the rehearsals with Dan. Hearing and seeing what they are doing should be most enjoyable, and I'm looking forward to it. But I don't intend to play with the group. I doubt if I'll ever play again."

As Faye drove away, Steve waved goodbye and started his new life.

Chapter 7

The Trip

Stan and Doris were wide awake at 6 AM, so they decided to get up and get going. By 8 o'clock, Stan had everything in the car except for Doris and her makeup kit.

Doris had been trying to call their daughter. After numerous attempts she said, "I'm worried about Allyn. We haven't heard from her in almost a month, and she does not answer her phone. I've been trying to call her for days, but she's not at home. I think we should delay our trip until we find out where she's at and if she is all right."

"She hasn't been right since she was 16 years old," Stan replied. "Put your makeup on and let's get rolling."

"I don't want to leave until I've had a chance to tell Allyn about our trip. If she wants to contact us, she won't know where we're at."

"We don't know where she's at, so why should she know where we're at? Sometimes, Allyn drops out of sight and sound for months at a time. If we do the same thing for two weeks, I'm sure she will survive. I'll even make book on it. Doris, are you going to put on your makeup, or do I have to do it for you?"

"Don't be so pushy. If you'll try to call Allyn, I'll fix my face."

Stan picked up the phone and dialed. After a moment he shouted "Hey, Doris, guess what?"

"What is it honey?"

"Allyn isn't at home."

Stan headed the car for the Golden State Freeway. After they were on it, he said, "You forgot to fasten your seatbelt. Buckle up, girl."

"What good would it do? If you hit anything at this speed, a passenger couldn't survive. Why do you have to be in such a hurry?"

"I want to get out of the traffic as fast as possible so we can relax."

"Stan, I'm only going to tell you this once. If you don't slow down, I'll cut you off until the trip is over and I'm safe at home."

"Don't do that. See, I'm slowing down."

They poked along at 50, and when they reached Route 101, Doris said, "Pull off at the next place that has a phone. I want to call Allyn."

"Can't it wait until tonight?" he asked.

"No, it can't. If you drive past a telephone, I'm going to roll down the window and scream rape. And I'll keep on screaming until you find a phone or someone comes to my rescue."

"I'm sure you would. I see a station up ahead. Doris, it's the first place I've seen that looks like it might have a phone. I'm pulling over, so roll up the window and keep your mouth shut."

Doris went to the public phone. After what seemed like an eternity, she returned to the car and said, "Allyn's home and she's just fine."

"Where was the little saint off to this time?"

"Lots of places. She took a trip with some friends, and they just roamed around. She told me all about it."

"I can believe that. Tell me, how can you talk on a pay phone for almost an hour?"

"With the right credit cards, anything is possible," she said. "I know you'll be glad to hear this bit of news. Allyn has a new love life. Her boyfriend sounds simply wonderful, and I'm so happy for her. After we return from our trip, she's going to bring him home to meet us. I can hardly wait."

"I can," he replied. "That girl goes through boys like they're candy. I hope the new one has been spending some of his time on this planet. The last one talked in a language that was completely foreign to me. Where does she find them? Is there a place called idiotville?"

"I wish you wouldn't talk that way about our only child. Allyn is all we have."

"Heaven forbid that we should be so destitute. Why don't we change the subject and talk about something or someone we both like."

They drove on in silence until they reach San Luis Obispo. "Is this where we change highways?" Stan asked.

"Yes! We want to get onto Route 1."

By the time they reached Morrow Bay, they were talking to each other on a regular basis. After wandering through a few of the shops and driving up and down the ocean front property, Stan asked, "What do you think of this place?"

"I think it's beautiful. Why haven't we taken this trip before?"

"We've been too busy to go much of any place. But in a few more months, things will be different. We will have all the time in the world, and thanks to Jerry Ross, we can travel any place at any time. The Ross account turned out to be a real winner. Before Jerry came along, we were the only poor Jews I knew. Now we've got it made."

"I'm not Jewish, and you don't owe all of your success to Jerry Ross," she told him. "We were doing all right before he came along."

"Just barely getting by, my dear. Prior to Ross, I spent most of my time looking at floors hoping to find money. Sometimes, what I found made the difference between paying the rent and being thrown out on the street."

"Things were never that bad," she said. "You've always kept your eyes on the floor and you still do. Sometimes it's very embarrassing, like last week when you walked into the mirrored wall at the Hilton. When it comes to finding money, you're just like a kid. Why are you stopping the car?"

"I saw a screwdriver on the road."

Stan brought back his find and they drove on. After they entered a park, he made a left turn and stopped at a golf course. "Care to get in nine holes before the sun goes down?" he asked.

"Shouldn't we look for a place to stay?"

"If we do, we won't have time to play golf."

"Stan, it is still a busy season in this area. I think we should look for a room."

"I think we should play golf. There are motels all over the city. We won't have any trouble finding a place to stay. Let's get some fresh air and exercise."

They rented a cart and Stan teed off. After hitting his ball 200 yards right down the middle of the fairway, he turned to Doris and said, "Five dollars says you can't beat that one."

"You know I can't out drive you, and so do I. I'm not throwing my money away on a sure loser. But I can win the hole, five dollars says I'll win the hole."

"You're on, woman. Show me what you can do."

Doris smacked her ball slightly over one hundred yards, and they were off. When they finished the hole, each of them had taken six strokes. They continued the match with determination and poor golf. By the time they reached the eighth hole, the sun was down and the mosquitoes were out. They picked up their balls and headed toward the clubhouse. As Doris swatted her hands at the mosquitoes, she asked, "Can't you go any faster?"

"Ten hours ago, you were complaining that I was driving too fast. Now you're telling me I'm going to slow. What do you want from me? I'm driving the same way now as I was then. My foot's to the floor."

They started looking for a place to stay, but every motel they went to was filled. After they were turned down by four places, Stan went into a Best Western and was turned down again. He returned to the car and said, "We are in luck."

"Do they have a room?"

"No, but they found one for us in Paso Robles."

"Isn't that out of our way? I thought we were going to see the Hearst Castle tomorrow?"

"Doris, get off my back. Paso Robles and Morro Bay are the same distance from the Hearst Castle. We'll just be taking a scenic inland route instead of driving along the coast."

They drove the winding highway in the black of night and eventually found their motel. Stan checked in and got the room key. He drove around the pool area and parked. When they got out of the car, Stan said, "We're upstairs, and if you'll help with the luggage, I believe we can make it in three trips. Of course, that doesn't include the golf clubs, tennis rackets, and ten pairs of shoes."

They loaded up with all they could carry and reached the stairway at the same time. With luggage in each hand, there was only enough room for one person at a time. "Ladies first," Stan said, "Besides, I want to look at your legs."

Doris giggled and swung her hips as she went up the stairs. They unpacked, showered, went to bed, showered and got dressed. When they arrived at the restaurant across from the motel office, it was closed. Stan looked at his watch and asked, "What kind of a restaurant is this? Look at the sign. They close at 9 PM and don't open up again until it's time for breakfast."

"Honey, you're not in Los Angeles. Folks do things differently when you get away from the big city. That looks like a restaurant to the north of us. Let's walk over and check it out."

"Let's walk over and eat. I'm hungry."

After they ordered their meals, Stan told Doris, "I want you to take a good look at all of the places we pass through on this vacation. When I close my office, I think we should move away from Los Angeles. I'm tired of dirty air, busy freeways and wall-to-wall people. It's time for a change, and I think we should find a nice quiet place with two or three golf courses."

"I'd rather stay in LA, keep off the freeways and only breathe the air when we're inside. I like my home and friends. If we move away, nobody will know where to find me. Besides, I don't want to live in a place where they close the restaurants and lounges before midnight."

"We could live with it. For a saner way of life, it would be a small sacrifice."

"If you're serious, I think I'm going to file for divorce. Stan, you've never lived in a small community. You don't know what it's like. I do, because I grew up in a tiny town before moving to Chicago. It was not for me."

"The night you set me up, you said the same thing about Chicago."

"At that time, I meant it. I'd been going through a very bad period. I didn't like Chicago, my job or my life. Dancing in that club on Rush Street had been a frightening experience. It was a scary neighborhood, and seeing all of those creeps in the audience every night had almost wiped me out. I was a nervous wreck. That's why I took up ice-skating and latched onto the job at The Stevens. I wasn't a bad dancer, but I sure was a lousy skater. When I was on skates, each performance was nervous city. Every time I made a sharp turn or sudden stop, I was afraid of falling down and breaking the caps on my teeth. Fortunately, the girls on each side of me knew what they were doing. When I'd lose my balance, they were willing to hold me up. I only fell down four times during that engagement, and each time it was backwards. Since I had a well endowed rear end, nothing was hurt."

"I always liked your big butt," he said. "As a matter of fact..."

"Shut up. Here comes our waitress."

They ate the food, but it was not anything to rave about. During the walk back to their motel, Doris asked, "Why didn't you call me?"

"When?"

"During our early years in Chicago. When we worked together with the Erwin Booth Revue, I thought you liked me. You had my telephone number, but years went by and you didn't call, not once."

"I was busy trying to get through college. I did not have time for anything except studying, playing my horn, and booking jobs. I thought about you, but not much. Those weren't the best years of my life. Even with intense concentration, I flunked out of law school. Very few people were calling me for playing jobs, so out of desperation, I started contracting musical entertainment. When a job required a big band, I would hire myself as one of the sax men. Why not? I wasn't very good, but I wasn't bad. When I got that temporary job at The Stevens, it turned my life around."

"Of course it did, you discovered that I was still alive."

"That too, Doris. Still alive and skating. I enjoyed seeing you again, but that wasn't what I was talking about. I found that it was possible to make a good living in this business without much talent. All you had to do was find someone or some place that had a need for entertainment. That's the key. You can always find talented people willing to do the job. There has always been more talent around than places for them to work. When I was doing music contracting work, I never hired a musician who didn't play better than I did. Why should I when it wasn't necessary. The big problem was, and still is, finding a place that wants to present entertainment and is willing to pay the price. I've been lucky enough to play on both sides of the street and make a living at it. I find out who's buying entertainment, and then I take a nice commission from entertainers for finding them work."

"You don't have to explain to me how you make your living," she said. "You may think I'm pretty dumb, but I know what's going on." They got ready for bed and Doris asked, "Have you ever resented me, because I seduced you?"

"Never, not for a moment. I always thought it was supposed to be the other way around, but I never resented the way it worked out. When you kept asking me for a ride home after the last show, I wondered what was going on. But I must admit, I never suspected you were setting a trap for me."

"You didn't give me any choice. When you took me home, you were always the perfect gentleman. Besides, I was running out of reasons as to why I needed a ride. Not once did you ask if you could come up to my apartment."

"I knew you had a roommate, and I did not want to impose on her sleep. Sometimes, we jabbered until the sun was high in the sky. Those talks were the most agreeable therapy I have ever known."

"I can't imagine why," she said. "You certainly didn't make any indecent proposals. After you started kissing me good night, I thought we might develop some sort of a relationship. But nothing happened. That was it. Just a good night kiss. Afterwards, I'd lie in bed and worry that I would lose you. I had to do something, so I told my roommate to stay out all night. I even told her she couldn't come into the apartment until the transom over the door was closed. That was my signal to make sure we weren't disturbed. I was prepared to keep you alone with me indefinitely. I'd made up my mind that I wouldn't let you go until you proposed. If it became necessary, I even had a gun. I'm not sure which one of us I was going to use it on, but I had a gun."

"Doris, you were a lewd woman, wicked, wicked."

"Maybe so, but it worked."

"It certainly did. You gave me three surprises that night. The first one was going to bed with me. The second one was a shocker. You were still a virgin. But the third one really puzzled me. When we finished, you started to laugh. I had heard of a lot of strange things that went on afterward, but never laughing."

"I couldn't help it, Stan. It didn't feel like I thought it would."

"Well, a laugh wasn't what I expected. A shrug perhaps, but not a laugh. Doris, you didn't build up my confidence by behaving that way, and I needed all the confidence I could find. When my assignment was over at The Stevens, I didn't have a single job in sight. There wasn't anything in my future but insecurity. If I continued working, or trying to work as a performing musician, I probably would've starved. My future looked so insecure, it even frightened me. Why you wanted to get involved with Stan Bernstein, I'll never know."

"When you married me, it was the first time in my life that I felt secure. Someway, somehow, I knew you would take care of us, and I wanted to be taken care of. Being a performer wasn't as much fun as I thought it would be, so I was relieved when it was over."

"You didn't exactly walk away from it right after the marriage. You hung in there for a few years until I got my feet on the ground. Without the income from your dancing, we would've been in big trouble."

"After the marriage, I didn't mind dancing from time to time. I knew it was temporary work and not something that would go on indefinitely. That made a big difference. Enough of this talk about the past, I'm looking forward to tomorrow."

"I'm looking forward to tonight."

"Again? Stan, if this is the way retirement is going to be, I think you should keep working."

The following morning, they had breakfast on the premises. When they finished, Doris asked, "What did you think of it?"

"I'm glad they were closed last night."

The drive back to the coast took less than an hour. When they reached the ocean, Stan made a right turn, and they drove to San Simeon. As they were passing through, he saw a Holiday Inn and said, "Look at that. We're back to civilization. That's where we'll have our next meal."

They continued their drive to the Hearst Castle and found the parking lot. Stan got in line and was lucky enough to purchase tickets for a tour that started in two hours. To kill time, they drove back to the ocean and watch the waves. After the return trip to the parking lot, Doris asked, "How's your heart treating you these days?"

"I haven't taken a nitroglycerin tablet in two days. Getting away from the office is making a new man out of me."

They boarded the tour bus and rattled up the hill. When the bus dropped them off, Stan said, "With all of the money this place makes from tours, I think they should provide better transportation. That road was rougher than the worst freeway in Los Angeles, and the bus was something else. I'm sure I rode on a similar model when I was in high school. Do you suppose that bus was left over from the days when the old boy lived here?"

"Stop being picky," she told him. "Our guide is trying to talk with us. Be still."

"Be still yourself. You are doing all the talking."

Doris jabbed him in the ribs as the tour started with the gardens and then the outdoor swimming pool. By the time they were shown the motion picture theater, both of them were fascinated with the details and massive wealth spent throughout the mansion. The tour concluded at the indoor swimming pool, and they returned to their bus. As they started to go aboard for the return ride, Stan asked, "What do you think of it?"

"If they'd replace the plumbing fixtures in the bathroom, it would do wonders for the place."

"Geez woman. At the time, I bet they were the best that money could buy."

"I doubt it. I think they cut corners in the bathrooms. Their fixtures look just like the ones we had in the girls' dressing rooms at The Stevens."

"Now who's being picky. Doris, I've never seen so much wealth under one roof in my life. The entire mansion was spectacular."

"Everything except the yucky bathroom fixtures," she replied.

The ride down the hill was just as bumpy as the ride up. However, one thing was added to the return trip, the constant squealing of the brakes. Halfway down the slope, Stan told Doris, "I think this bus needs a complete overhaul. It does not sound safe."

"I think it's a thrilling ride. Relax and enjoy the view. Look at the trees and the riding paths."

"I'll look but I won't enjoy the ride. What this place needs is an overhead tram."

They drove back to San Simeon and stopped at the Holiday Inn. As they walked toward the restaurant, Stan said, "I worked up a ferocious appetite from all that walking. I'm so hungry, I may eat a table for an appetizer."

When they walked into the restaurant, it was empty. One of the employees told them the restaurant closed at two and would not reopen until five. Stan shook his head as they walked out and exclaimed, "I'll bet this is the only Holiday Inn in the world that closes its restaurant for three hours during the afternoon."

"Should we cross San Simeon off of our list as a possible retirement area?" Doris asked.

"Definitely. This place may have been good enough for Hearst, but it's too 'backwoodish' for me."

They worked their way back down the line of motels and finally found one that was serving snacks in the bar area adjacent to the dining room. A girl came to their table in an abbreviated cocktail waitress costume and took their orders. When she left, Stan said, "That certainly is an attractive girl we have for waitress."

"Stan, what the hell is the matter with you? Are you overdue for an eye exam? That girl has pimples all over her face."

"She has? I was so fascinated by her legs, I didn't get around to noticing her face." He immediately dropped both hands to his right side to block the jab at his ribs.

After the snack, Doris went to the ladies room, and Stan went to a phone to call his office. When Doris return, Stan was still talking on the phone. After he hung up and made a pit stop, they returned to their car and started driving back to Paso Robles. On the way, Doris asked, "Is everything okay at the office?"

"Sure thing. Helen knows what she's doing."

"Then what took you so long?"

"Helen was giving me the high points from a preliminary promotional proposal. I'm afraid Vic Bailey has his head in the clouds on this one. If he doesn't, he's getting greedy. I asked Helen to contact another agency for a second proposal and cost quotation."

When they reached the city limits of Paso Robles, the sun was still out. "I believe there's a decent public golf course in this area," Stan said. "If you're interested, I'll give you a chance to win back your five dollars."

"I won't play unless you give me strokes."

"How many do you want?"

"Nine."

If we have time to play nine holes, that's one per hole. No! It's too many. I'll give you two, because I think we only have time for seven or eight holes."

"Stan, that's all we played last night, and you beat me by six strokes. I want nine."

"I won't give you nine. Maybe three, but that's all."

"Honey, your religious background is showing up in your words. I know you'll settle for more than three, so let's stop this dickering. I'll compromise with you and take eight strokes."

"No you won't. I'll give you four, and that's my final offer."

"Does the game end when the sun goes down?" she asked.

"That's right. But if it takes us more than thirty minutes to find the golf course, we'll have to renegotiate our deal."

"Okay sucker, you're on for five big ones."

Stan stopped to ask directions and then sped to the course. When they arrived at the clubhouse, Doris said, "You sign us in while I go to the restroom."

"You just did that, didn't you?"

"So I'm doing it again. Don't worry, I'll be ready by the time you sign in and get us a cart."

As Stan finished loading their clubs on the cart, Doris walked out of the clubhouse. She was carrying her slacks and wearing her short shorts.

Stan shouted at her, "What are you doing in those things. Doris, you're going to catch cold."

"How come you recognized my face?" She asked.

"Don't try to start an argument with me. Get in and stop wasting time."

She threw her bare legs over the front end of the cart as they drove to the first tee. It took Stan five strokes to hole out and Doris had six. When they started the next hole, Stan's drive sliced out of bounds, so he had to hit a second shot. Doris got on the tee and lined up her club with the ball. Then she broke her knees, squatted a bit and wiggled her behind. It didn't feel right, so she decided to take a few practice swings. Doris stepped away from her ball and started swishing the air with her club. Stan became impatient and told her, "Stop shaking your butt and waving your club. The way you're carrying on, we won't have time to play three holes. Enough is enough. If you don't hit that ball pretty soon, I'm going to hit you."

"You don't scare me you changeable bastard. You've always told me the big trouble with my golf game is that I hurry it. Tonight, I'm concentrating on my game, and nobody is going to make me hurry."

It was dark after four holes, so Stan forked over five dollars. They returned to their motel room, put on their swimming suits and soaked in the pool. When the evening air started to get cold, they returned to their room and showered.

After putting on fresh clothes, Doris asked, "Where shall we eat tonight? Would you like to get in the car and drive someplace else?"

"That might not be a bad idea. We haven't had a really good meal since we left home. On second thought, let's not. I'm too pooped and hungry to spend what's left of the evening driving around the city. I saw a sign for one of the chain restaurants when we returned from the golf course. The sign looked like it was only a couple of blocks away, so let's push our tired bones one more time. If we walk slow, I think we can make it."

They walked toward the sign and found the restaurant. When they stepped inside the door, it was 'people everywhere'. Doris looked at Stan and asked, "Do you want to wait?"

"Yes! If all of these people like this place, I think we should stick around."

When they finished their meal and started the return walk to the motel, Stan said, "That was the best meal we've had so far."

"Does that mean you want to consider Paso Robles as a possible retirement city?"

"No. Cross it off the list. We can find a Denny's almost anywhere. Besides, I didn't like the way my golf game turned out on their one and only course. Next time, I'm not giving strokes unless we start earlier in the day. If you're going to carry on the way you did this evening, sunup would be none too soon."

The following morning, they had a leisurely breakfast and started packing. When Stan returned from his first trip to the car, Doris asked, "Did you notice the sign that stated the road was closed north of the Hearst Mansion?"

"Yes. I'm disappointed, because I wanted to see the Big Sur area. Perhaps we can do it some other time. I guess we'll have to take 101 to Monterey."

Stan left the room with another load of luggage. Doris had kept her makeup case and decided to visit the bathroom one more time. When she walked out, Stan was on the phone saying "It will only take us a few hours to make the drive. I'll call you after we're settled."

As they got in the car, Doris asked, "Was that another business call?"

"You might call it that. I wanted to find out if Carl Kay was home. He was and we're having dinner with him tonight. Tomorrow, he's appearing at a fund raiser in Las Vegas. I thought he might have left a day early, but Carl said he was flying out this evening."

The drive to Monterey wasn't very enjoyable. It was a busy highway with nothing of interest on either side of the road. After they registered and were in their room, Stan called Carl to let him know they had arrived. When he asked for directions to Carl's house, Carl told him, "Just wait at the motel and I'll pick you up. With all of the short winding streets in Carmel, giving directions would probably take longer than driving over and picking you up. Besides you'd probably get lost trying to find me. If I stop by in an hour, will that give Doris adequate time to rest up from the drive?"

"That should be more than enough time. We'll be waiting for you out front by the pool."

"Carl will pick us up in thirty minutes," Stan said.

"That doesn't give me enough time."

As Doris hurried undressing, Stan asked, "How much time do you need?"

"At least an hour."

"That's what I figured. Okay, you've got an hour."

As Doris went to the shower, she asked, "Aren't you going to call Carl back so he won't have to wait around for us?"

"No need, dear. Carl won't be here until you've had an hour to rest up. I told you thirty minutes just to see how fast you could move. After all of that stalling during last evening's golf game, I wanted to see you hustle."

In a moment, Doris returned around the partition with two bath towels tied together. A large knot was on the loose end. As she swung the towels, Stan ran through the doorway. After he was outside and a good ten yards away from her, he took a defiant stance and told her, "Come and get me if you dare."

Doris slammed the door and fastened the chain lock. She went to the window, opened it a few inches and said, "You're locked out, and I'm not letting you back in for thirty minutes. Then we'll see how fast you can move."

Stan opened the door with his room key, but the chain lock wouldn't let him enter the room. He smiled and went to the office to look for some literature on the area. He knew that thirty minutes would give him more than enough time to shower, shave and dress.

Carl Kay picked them up and they exchanged greetings. During the short drive to Carmel, he said to Doris, "I understand you used to be a dancer. Do you ever miss it?"

"I miss some of the people but not the work. The constant practicing and rehearsals became boring. Besides, I was never at ease on the stage."

"Neither am I, but I get such a tremendous high from the experience, I tolerate the uneasiness. Stan also mentioned that you two are considering moving away from Los Angeles. During the trip up here, did you run across anything that looked good?"

"We were considering the Hearst Mansion," Stan said, "but Doris didn't like the bathroom fixtures. Outside of that place, nothing else has turned us on. Are you still planning on selling your house and moving back to Nashville?"

"I think so. When I had my heart attack and had to take it easy for a while, Carmel was a good place for me to change lifestyles. But now that I've been here for a few years, I'm beginning to develop a sinus condition. I guess it's time for another change, and I miss Nashville. As long as I'm thinking of moving and you're looking for a new place, would you be interested in my house in Carmel?"

"How much are you asking for the place?"

"I think it should bring about $400,000."

"We're not interested," Stan replied.

After they arrived at Carl's house, he gave them a quick tour that ended in the dining room. He offered them wine... and a short time later, his housekeeper served the meal. When they finished, Doris said, "That's the most delicious meal we have had since we left home. Maybe ever. Do you think Laura would mind if I asked her for the recipe?"

"I doubt it very much. I believe she'd be flattered, but you'll have to hurry if you want to get it. As soon as she cleans up the kitchen, she will be going home."

As Doris went to the kitchen, she said, "I think all men have one thing in common. They like to see women hurry."

While she was out of the room, the men discussed some of Carl's upcoming engagements and possible future bookings. Eventually Carl asked, "How is the promotional plan for my new album shaping up?"

"I have a preliminary proposal from Vic Bailey in my office. Yesterday, Helen read the high points to me, and quite frankly, I'm disappointed. As soon as I return from this vacation, I'll have a conference with Vic and his people. In the meantime, I've asked Helen to request a proposal from another agency. If Vic is not willing to back off quite a bit on the costs, I think we should consider other sources. Carl, how would you feel about having a whole new image?"

"If it's necessary, I suppose I could live with it. But why change? The old image has served me pretty well. Do you think I need a new image?"

"No, but Vic Bailey does. Since you're hoping for a crossover with the new album, Vic wants to project a new Carl Kay. His publicity plan includes large as life posters of you placed in all major record stores. They will go on display as soon as the album is released. However, he wants to get you out of your Western attire. If you are dressed in a tuxedo, Vic believes you will have better luck with the easy listening customers."

"I think that idea is a bummer," Carl said. "I don't want to offend my regular fans in an effort to obtain new ones. Stan, I don't even own a tuxedo. On the few occasions when they were compulsory, for an award show or something like that, I have always rented a tux. If my regular fans saw me dressed that way, they would think I was going to a masquerade. If the posters don't cost too much, I'll go along with them. But the tuxedo is out, no way."

"I thought you would say that, but I wanted to sound you out on it before the meeting. Vic has something else in his proposal that I think we should throw out, but maybe I'm wrong. Since this is your first recording in over two years, Vic believes you should make this release special. He contacted two of the better known commercial artists for price quotes for an original painting on the record cover. Both of the artists get top dollar, so your cover will cost big bucks if you want to run with the idea. You can write it off as a business expense, but do you want another new painting to hang on your walls?"

"Stan, I don't even know where I will be living in a few months, let alone how much wall space I'll have. Let's cut corners and go with a photograph of something. Perhaps me in country attire. If we decide to use posters, the same shot could be used on both items. I don't mean to sound cheap, but why throw money away?"

Their conversation was interrupted as Doris came into the room saying, "I got the dinner recipe plus two more from Laura. She's sweet. Carl, why didn't you tell us that Laura used to do walk-on parts in the movies?"

"I didn't think it was necessary. Sooner or later, Laura always finds a way to tell everyone about that segment of her past. She enjoys talking about it, so why should I spoil her fun. Doris, does the word 'hurry' bother you?"

"Normally, I can live with it, but today it's somewhat abrasive. It has to do with something my husband, *smart-ass Bernstein*, pulled earlier. I'd rather not talk about it, but since you know the source, I know you'll understand that I'm not uptight without justification."

"Since you find the word offensive, I hate to use it again. But if I don't hurry, I'll miss my flight to Las Vegas. I put my luggage in the trunk of the car before picking you two up, so let's get going before I run out of time."

Shortly after they started the drive back to Monterey, Doris said, "Why not drop us off someplace where we can catch a taxi? Then you won't have to drive back to Carmel."

"Doris, I'm not driving back to Carmel, because we don't have a commercial airport. Our nearest airport is in Monterey, and it's only a few blocks behind your motel. Being from Los Angeles, you probably won't believe the limited airline service we have in this area. I could drive to Las Vegas almost as fast as I can fly commercially, but the drive through the desert is just too boring. My best and almost only way to get there is to fly to Los Angeles, change planes, and then fly to Las Vegas. The layover in Los Angeles is longer than the entire flight time, but that's the way it goes when you live away from the big cities."

Carl dropped them off at their motel, and they decided to walk the streets for a while. It was one motel after another broken by an occasional restaurant or retail store. When their legs got tired, they returned to their room and noticed the light on the telephone was glowing.

"There can't be a message for us," Doris said, "because nobody knows we're here."

"Nobody except Helen," he replied. "We had so much trouble finding a place to stay that first night, I made advanced reservations for this place. I told Helen where we would be staying when I talked with her yesterday."

Stan called the front desk, and they confirmed that Helen Hall had tried to contact him. He called Helen's home phone and found out that Norma Anderson wanted to talk with him. Next, he placed a call to Lake Tahoe and asked for Norma. The hotel rang her room without getting a response and then paged her. Norma answered the page in the hotel restaurant.

"Norma, what can the Bernstein's do for you this evening?"

"I need your advice, Stan. I want this job, but the money stinks. If I go to work for the pitiful amount Benny Fisher offered me, I'm afraid the word will spread throughout the industry. You know how this business is; that kind of news travels fast. When this engagement ends, I probably could not demand a decent wage anyplace else. Do you have any words of wisdom?"

"Did Benny offer any concessions during your talks?"

"Just one. If the business picks up while I'm with the show, he said he would offer me a better contract midway through my engagement."

"That's a good sign, Norma. I think Benny will dicker if we approach him in the right way."

"I won't sleep with him if that's what you have in mind. I've never slept with anyone just to make a few more bucks, and I'm not starting now."

"Norma, cool that kind of talk. I think you know me better than that. Besides, Benny has not been able to get it up for at least two years. When it became a permanent thing, he told me it was the biggest drag of his life. Tell me, have you seen the show?"

"Yes," she said. "I saw it last night as Benny's guest."

"What did you think of it?"

"I thought it was a good show, but apparently I'm in the minority. There were only about 100 people in the audience for the cocktail performance. With such a poor turnout, I felt sorry for the cast. He introduced me to some of the performers after the show, and they seemed like nice people. I'm sure I would enjoy working with them. Damn, I wish Fisher wasn't such a hard nose. He wants me to give him a yes or no answer tomorrow."

"Don't do it. But if you do, don't sign anything until I've had a chance to talk with him. Based on what you've told me, I believe we can do business with Benny. Yes, I'm encouraged. Sit tight until I call you back."

Stan placed another call to the Lake Tahoe Hotel and asked for Benny Fisher. He was informed that Mr. Fisher wasn't in the hotel and they did not expect him to return until the following day. Stan left the telephone number where he could be reached in the event that Benny changed his mind and returned to the hotel. He tried to call Benny Fisher's home but did not get any response.

By this time, Doris was ready for bed. "What were all the phone calls about," she asked.

"Just something I'm trying to do for Norma Anderson."

"I haven't heard that name in a long, long time. I thought you weren't taking on any more clients?"

"I'm not. Norma is not a client, but I consider her an old friend. She wants to start working again, and I heard of a possible job that she might be interested in."

"If that's the case, why are you making all of the phone calls? She's a big girl. Let her make her own calls. Did you see her recently?"

"Yes. She stopped by my office the day before we left on this trip. Things have not been going very well for her during the past year or two. Norma told me she was broke and had to go back to work. I guess her last husband did a lousy job managing her money. What he didn't lose on poor investments, he threw down at the gambling tables."

"Maybe she deserved it. Norma has always asked men to help her with her problems. I think she expects it. After all, she was the big beautiful Norma Anderson. If you turn your unpleasant tasks and business affairs over to others, eventually someone will take advantage of you."

"Dear, I think you're being a little hard on her. You don't achieve that kind of success without a dedicated effort. Norma concentrated most of her energy on doing what she does best, and she tried to make it better and better. In my limited dealings with her, she always behaved like a professional in every sense of the word. Perhaps Norma did depend on others to help her achieve her goals, but what's wrong with that? It usually works out to everyone's advantage. However, in Norma's case, she had a run of bad luck with husbands, and the last one was a real loser."

"Nuts! Norma has always had her head in the clouds. She likes her dream world and doesn't bother to take a hard look at what's going on around her. If the last husband took her for all she had, I say it was her fault for being so damned trusting and blind to what was going on."

"Perhaps you're right. Who knows?

Doris, I guess now is as good a time as any to tell you something that might upset you. When I saw Norma a few days ago, I loaned her $5,000.00"

"You what? You're not serious are you?"

"I was afraid it would upset you."

"Stan, sometimes the impulse to strangle you is almost irresistible and this is one of those times. How could you do it? That

258

woman has made more money in one year than we've made in a lifetime, and she had numerous years of doing it."

"It's not how much money you've made the counts, it's how much you have left over. Apparently, Norma doesn't have anything left over. During the short time I was her agent, I made some easy money booking her. After she gets back to work, I know she will pay back my loan."

Their argument was interrupted by the ringing of the phone. When Stan answered it, he heard Benny Fisher's voice.

"Stan, I thought you were going on vacation. Did you change your mind?"

"No, Benny, we didn't change our minds. We are on vacation and having the time of our lives. Right now, we're relaxing at a motel in Monterey and enjoying each other's company."

"That's good. I'm glad to hear it. Did you want me to call you back so you could tell me about your trip, or did you have something else in mind, like perhaps, Norma Anderson?"

"All right then, let's get right to the point. Norma just told me that you are trying to rush her into making a decision in regards to your production show."

"That's correct. Our show is not doing good business, so we must make a change and do it quickly. If Norma doesn't want to join us, we'll find someone else. As a matter of fact, I have found someone else who is willing to do business with us. I haven't signed the other girl yet, because I want to give Norma one more day to make up her mind."

"Apparently, you would prefer Norma to the other person?"

"Who wouldn't" Benny said, "but only if she agrees to our terms. I made her an offer that I believe is fair. Since Norma will have a significant amount of work with us, we expect her to come way down on her usual weekly price. If she agrees, we'll do business. If she doesn't, losing her is not going to close us down. There's always someone else who can do the job."

"Norma said you were a hard-nose, and I'm beginning to think she's right. Benny, I've always known you to be a good businessman, not a stubborn pain in the ass. You are acting like some of the superstars you've dealt with over the years. Now this possible deal between you and Norma doesn't mean a thing to me one way or the other, but I want to ask you two questions before you hang up on me. First, if Norma fills up the show room, isn't she worth more money than you're offering her?"

"Yes, but I don't know if she can do it."

"Second, if your drop at the tables goes up while she's appearing at your hotel, isn't that worth a lot to you? Isn't that the bottom line?"

"Yes it is, but I don't know if that will happen. If we start making more money in the casino, I've told Norma that I'll offer her a better financial deal midway through her engagement."

"That's interesting, but it's not a good business arrangement for anyone but you. Benny, I think you're making a big mistake in your dealings with Norma, and you are going to live to regret it. If you give her a chance, the woman can make money for you. I think you should modify your offer. I'm not suggesting you raise her basic weekly salary, but I feel your offer should include an immediate incentive clause."

"Do you have something specific in mind?" Benny asked.

"Yes! Whenever the showroom count exceeds 400 people, I think Norma should be paid something for the additional people she brings into the showroom. I also believe you should include some type of incentive in regards to the actual drop in your casino. I think Norma will maximize showroom counts and do it by pulling in the right kind of people. By the right kind of people, I mean the ones who stick around and gamble. If I'm wrong, it won't cost you one additional cent over your current offer. You have everything to gain by this type of agreement and nothing to lose. If Norma makes money for you, she's worth more. Fair is fair. If you would do what I suggest, I think Norma Anderson will accept your offer. If you don't, you're going to kick yourself in the butt for the rest of your life. She can make a bundle for you, but if you stick to your *take it or leave it offer*, you'll blow a chance to find out if what I'm saying is true."

After a long pause, Benny Fisher said, "I'll think about it."

"You do that. And one more thing, Benny, thanks for returning my call so promptly."

When Stan hung up the phone, Doris said to him, "For a guy who isn't representing anyone, you made quite a pitch."

"I was thinking of my $5,000.00."

"Stan, forget about the $5,000.00. I know Norma will be good for it. She's that kind of girl. Deep down, I think I've been jealous of her success. While I was dancing for peanuts, Norma turned herself into a multi-talent and set the world on fire. I didn't think it was fair, and I have resented the fact that she made it big while I didn't even cause a ripple. When you started talking about Norma, I let my feelings hang out and overreacted. I'm sorry. Will you forgive me for acting like a jerk?"

"There's nothing to forgive," he said. "Everyone feels the same way from time to time, and more often than not, it's completely justified. Take Carl Kay for example: he's a nice guy and a friend, but I'll bet there are at least a thousand other guys with more talent. Carl was lucky enough to be at the right place at the right time. Everything opened up for him. Even though most of his contemporaries have disappeared from the scene, Carl has been able to sustain his career. God knows why! By itself, I don't think talent means very much in this business. Perhaps it's the breaks and what you do with them that counts the most. But who knows, nothing about this business makes much sense. I'm glad to be getting out of it."

"My, my, you're profound tonight. Is this the other side of Stan Bernstein?"

"I have opinions just like everyone else. This is the side nobody sees or hears when I'm doing business as an arbitrator. Sure, that's what I do when I'm making deals, but I keep my opinions to myself while I'm conducting business. Do you know why? Well, I'll tell you why."

"Stan, you didn't give me a chance to answer your question."

"It doesn't matter. I'm going to tell you anyway. When you're dealing with a bunch of overgrown kids, being overly frank doesn't pay off. It usually ends up costing you an account. That's what I think I'm dealing with most of the time, just a bunch of children who want more. Most of them go through life just trying to see how much they can get away with."

"Honey, don't get so upset. If you don't settle down, your heart may start acting up."

"If I blew off my mouth more frequently, maybe I wouldn't have a heart condition. Do you mind if I make one more phone call before we turn in?"

"Go ahead," she told him. "I rather enjoy hearing you do your thing when you're angry."

Stan placed the call to Norma Anderson. When she answered the call, he told her, "I believe Benny Fisher is going to make you a better offer."

"Good. I am ready to go to work."

"Now don't get too excited, because nothing is definite. The new offer, if it comes, will be in the form of an incentive agreement. What Benny offered you previously will be your base salary, but you'll also receive a weekly bonus. The amount of the bonus will vary in accordance with the number of people you pull into the showroom and the increased drop in the casino. If you do good business, the bonus should double your take-home pay. If you do spectacular business, you'll make out like a thief."

"That sounds wonderful. How did you do it?"

"It's not done yet, and from here on in, you'll be the one who has to pull it off. Here is what I think will happen: when you see Benny tomorrow, he will ask for your answer on his initial offer. You tell him 'no'. If he doesn't suggest an incentive agreement as a counter offer, pack your bags and go home. Benny has been in this business long enough to recognize a good thing when he sees it. If he doesn't offer you an incentive clause in your contract right way, it's because he's trying to get the best deal for himself. Don't worry about it, because he'll call you after you get home and make you an offer you can live with. Take my advice, Norma. Do this thing my way. I don't have your talent, but you don't have my head for business."

"Okay, Stan. I'll stick to my guns. If he doesn't make me a better offer, I'll turn him down cold."

"Good girl. It's the right game plan for this situation. In the event that I'm wrong about Benny, don't sweat it. I'll find something else for you to do that's worthy of your talents."

"Thanks, Stan. Either way, I will let you know how this deal turns out. Be sure to say goodnight to Doris for me."

"She's asleep," Stan replied. I'll say good morning for you when she wakes up. One more thing, Norma: When the haggling over the bucks is out of the way, you will find Benny to be a princely guy to work for."

The following morning, the first words Doris said were, "Where shall we have breakfast?"

"The girl at the registration desk said the wooden shack just to the west of us serves the best breakfast in town. The place looks like a moderate wind would blow it down, but let's give it a try. If we don't like it, we'll leave our food and find another place that looks more sturdy."

They walked through the open doorway and took a quick look at the inside. There wasn't anyone waiting to seat them or a sign asking them to wait or seat themselves. As they looked around the room, they saw one empty booth and took it before someone else walked in. The help was busy, and the atmosphere was relaxed. They ordered and when their breakfast was placed before them, the portions were huge.

As Stan finished his second cup of coffee, he told Doris, "This is the best place so far. Since we've come to Monterey, we've had two good meals out of two, and I've only had to pay for one. While we're in the area, would you like to take the Seventeen Mile Drive?"

"Yes. We may not get the chance again, and after being so close, I'd hate to think I missed it."

They drove down Highway 1 until they reached the gate. After paying the fee, they started their drive through the wooded area. Most of the houses and grounds were magnificent. They stopped a few times in front of some of the more impressive ones so Doris could take a longer look. Shortly after they reached the Pacific Ocean and started driving down the shoreline, she asked him to stop the car. Doris wanted to take some pictures of the seals perched on a large rock a short distance off the beach. While she was taking pictures, Stan tried to wave away the birds. They pretty much ignored him and continued to leave droppings on the top of his car.

After Doris got her pictures, they drove on until they reached the lodge on the Pebble Beach Golf Course. She wanted to go through all the shops, but after a short time, Stan became bored. He walked to the golf course and looked it over until Doris finished buying a few more things. As they started going back to their car, she asked, "What did you think of the course?"

"It's nice."

"Do you want to play a round while we're here?"

"No, not at the prices they're asking." While you were sleeping, I looked over the literature on this place. Besides the $80 a person it costs to get on the course, I'd probably lose about $20 worth of balls. At those prices, I wouldn't enjoy the game. Besides, this isn't a course for weekend duffers like us. I can see why it was nicknamed 'the monster'." When they reached the car, he said, "It looks like you found a few items in the shops."

"Yes, they had some darling things. Everything I bought I liked."

"I should hope so," he said.

"Here, hold these bags. I want to show you the shorty nightgown I bought for Allyn. Let me hold it up so you can get a good look at it. What do you think?"

"Perfect. That's perfect for Saint Allyn of the bed. It doesn't even have a crotch in it."

"Stan, I'm sick and tired of hearing you talk that way about our daughter. As a matter of fact, I'm getting damned angry. I wish you'd stop it."

"So I'll stop it, but I'm more than a little angry about the way she keeps carrying-on. Do you blame me, or do you feel I should sanction it?"

They drove back to their motel in silence. Finally, Stan asked, "Would you like to stay here one more night or shall we push on?"

"I don't care. You are the big boss, so you make the decision. You seem to think you know what's best for everyone. You even pass judgment on your daughter without hearing her side of the story."

"I'm not interested in listening to any side of that story. If she wants to screw her life away, that's her business, not mine. Well, since I'm the boss, I say let's hit the road."

"You go on without me. I'm going home."

"Suit yourself," he said. I'll leave your things in the room." Stan packed his bags and started toward the door.

"Aren't you even going to offer me a ride to the airport?" Doris yelled at him.

"If it's a ride you want, I'll offer you a ride. But Doris, this isn't LA, so the next flight doesn't leave until tonight. Instead of sitting in the airport for the next five or six hours, I think you'd be more comfortable relaxing in this room."

"You think you know everything, don't you?"

"No. I'm well aware of the fact that I know very little. But I do know a few things, and one of them is this: With or without you, I'm continuing this trip. If you want to go home and sulk, do it, that's up to you. As for me, I'm going to see some of the world. You are not going to see anything until you're willing to pull your head out of your ass and stop acting like a child. What's your pleasure? Do you want to fly south, or would you rather ride north with me?"

"I haven't made up my mind yet, but I'll keep thinking about it while I pack."

A short time later, they were back on Highway 1 and headed for San Francisco. The tension between them had eased by the time they reached the Bay Area. When they stopped for lunch, Stan made a few phone calls. After returning to their table, he told Doris, "I tried to call Steve Post, but his phone has been disconnected."

"I've always liked Steve," she said.

"So have I, and I'd like to find out where he's at and what he's doing. I owe him for many favors, and I've never had the chance to repay them. Steve was always willing to help me when I needed it the most. When I was going to college and needed a summer job, he talked Freddie Hayes into hiring me. That's how I got that playing job with the Revue. When the season ended, he went out of his way to introduce me to a lot of people in the trade. My music contracting business would have turned out to be a miserable failure if I hadn't known those people. When the entertainment business started to dry up in Chicago, and we moved to the West Coast, he even got me some studio work. Steve knew my limitations and never recommended me for a job I couldn't handle. Those playing jobs helped pay the bills and kept my confidence up while I was trying to establish my booking agency."

"In a way, I guess he was responsible for the two of us getting together," she said. "We didn't meet until we were both working in the Revue."

"Yes, that's right. I owe him for that also, but I don't know whether to thank him or curse him for that. Doris, put down that pot of coffee. I was only kidding."

"You spoke just in time," she said.

"I know, I know. I wish you'd learn to control your temper. If you don't, one of these days you're going to hurt someone."

"I had someone in mind. Stan, I was devastated when you started to walk out on me this morning, and now this. Why can't you be nice to me instead of being such a smart aleck?"

"I guess it was a rude thing to say, and I'm sorry I said it. I apologize for being a smart aleck. Now then, shall we kiss and forget that it happened?"

Doris nodded her head. As he leaned over to kiss her, she pressed his hand against her breast. After the kiss, he whispered in her ear, "I'm not complaining, here, but I think you should let go of my hand. Everyone in this place is looking at us."

After paying the check, Stan made a few more phone calls. While they were returning to their car, he told her, "I struck out, but let's find a place to stay and perhaps we'll think of something."

They found a room at a large motel a short ways north of the Oakland airport. As they were unpacking, Doris asked, "Did you try to contact Faye?"

"No. I don't know her new last name, so that's out."

"Good. I'd just as soon not see her again."

"Why? What's the matter with Faye?"

"I was never comfortable around her. When we first moved to Los Angeles, she treated me like a poor relative. At the time, Steve was doing so well in the Studios and I think she felt I was beneath her. After we had been out West for about ten years, your business started to take off and Steve's work started to disappear. Then she changed her tune and started acting like she resented me."

"Doris, may I ask you a question without making you mad?"

"You can ask me any question you want, but whether or not I get mad is up to me. I won't promise a thing, but go ahead, try me."

"Are there any women you like?"

"Sure! I like Allyn."

As they finished unpacking, Stan said, "After Steve had his second nervous breakdown, I wrote to him on numerous occasions. He answered my letters for about three years, but the last two didn't generate a response."

"Did he mention any names in his letters?" She asked.

"Yes. I tried to call some of those people from the restaurant, but they must have moved on. Hey, I just remembered another name that Steve mentioned in his letters, Dan Daily. He is a bandmaster at one of the high schools, or at least he was. Let's see if he's listed in the telephone directory."

There were quite a few Dan Dailys listed, and he started calling them. Eventually, he contacted a Mrs. Daily and was told, "You reached the wrong number, but I know the person you're trying to get in touch with." She gave him the correct phone number plus the name and street address of the high school where Dan worked.

Stan tried the telephone number, but nobody answered. He got out a city map, located the high school and asked, "Care to get back in the car and take a short ride?"

"Why not," Doris said. "It beats watching TV."

They found the high school and saw the band. Apparently they had just finished marching practice, and the members were walking back to the band room. Stan approached the only adult in the area and asked, "Are you Dan Daily?"

"The last I knew I was. What can I do for you, whoever you are?"

"My name is Stan Bernstein and this is my wife, Doris. We would like to locate Steve Post. Do you know where he's at?"

"Yes, but it's a pretty long drive if you want to find him tonight. He moved to Reno."

"Do you have his phone number and address?" Stan asked.

"Sure. I'll write them down for you before I lock up the band room. Damn, look at that. One of the little monsters from the trumpet section is kissing a majorette. She looks like she is 18 years old, but I know it just ain't so. I'd better break it up before it gets out of hand. I don't care if they make out, but they're not going to get it on in my band room. Excuse me for a moment."

When Dan returned, he handed Stan a piece of paper with a telephone number and address. Stan thanked him and asked if he had any plans for dinner.

Dan told him, "Only that I'm going to eat it sooner or later."

"Would you care to have dinner with us and fill us in on what Steve has been up to these past four or five years?"

"On my salary, how can I refuse a dinner. Are you familiar with this area?"

"No. This is our first visit this far up the coast."

"I remember your name now. Steve mentioned it a few times. Since you don't know the area, let me recommend a restaurant just a short distance from here. It looks awful, but the food is great."

"During this vacation, we've been finding our best meals in places like that. Lead on and we will follow you."

When they walked into the small restaurant, the smell of fried food was everywhere. Doris was not overly happy about the place, but Stan was excited by the aroma. Dan told them, "This place has been open for 20 years, and they've never turned off their grill."

Doris believed him and wondered if they had cleaned it during that time. When the waitress took their orders, Doris asked for a salad and a piece of apple pie. The men ordered steak, French fries, onion rings, and fried mushrooms.

Dan told them, "Our mutual friend had a very long low period after his last breakdown. I tried to talk him into playing with a kicks band, but he refused. He'd go with me and listen to the boys work out, but he wouldn't join in. I thought it would give him something to do besides taking short trips and watching the boob tube, but he didn't want to participate in making music. Hell, he wouldn't even substitute in the front line when one of the regulars was sick or out of town."

"That doesn't sound like Steve," Doris said.

"Maybe not, but I know it to be a fact. About a year after he was released from the sanitarium, I caught a bug that my knowledgeable doctor called the flu. The damn thing really wiped me out, and I could hardly get out of bed. My kids had a winter concert coming up, and I didn't want them to skip it. If they don't have a performance staring them in the face, they forget about practicing and the band goes to pot. Out of desperation, I asked Steve to pinch-hit for me."

Stan asked, "Did he help you out?"

"Yes. He rehearsed the band and got them through their concert. The kids liked and respected him. After I got over the flu, or whatever it was, I tried to get Steve interested in music education. That turned out to be another dead-end, because he wouldn't hear of it. He was starting to slip back into a rather despondent mood and didn't seem to be interested in much of anything. At the time, I felt rather helpless and was beginning to worry about him, and then a surprising thing happened. Afterwards, he snapped out of his 'I don't give a damn' mood. He even started practicing and playing with the kicks band."

Stan put down his knife and fork just long enough to ask, "What was the surprising thing that happened?"

"How can I best explain it? Tell it like it was, I guess. It had been more than a week since I'd seen Steve. The kids and I just returned from a regular band contest, and I decided to drop by to see if he wanted to join me for dinner. I probably had this place in mind. By the way, how do you like the food?"

Stan said, "Fabulous." Doris poked at her salad and told him, "Not bad."

"Good, good. Anyway, I knocked on Steve's door, but nobody answered. I started to get back into my car, and then I saw him jogging down the street with some broad. What a shock! Steve usually doesn't even walk fast, let alone jog. I'm sure you two know how stingy he is with words. With the exception of Faye, I can't recall ever hearing him mention a woman's name. When he does get around to talking, it's usually not about himself. So when I saw him jogging with someone of the opposite sex, I was completely surprised."

"Do you remember her name?" Stan asked.

"He introduced me, but I don't remember her name. At the time, I was probably still in a state of shock. It was obvious that they didn't want me around, so I took off."

Stan had finished his steak and called the waitress back for more coffee. After his cup was filled, he asked, "I wonder if Steve's friend is anyone we know? What did she look like?"

"Solid as a rock but much more shapely. She was a fairly tall girl, but most of her height was in her legs. Good legs, really good legs. I stopped by a few days later, and she was still there. They had just come back from jogging, and Steve was tired out. The broad looked like she thrived on it. She must be a physical education teacher or something like that. I only saw her for a moment. She told Steve to go out and get some groceries and then disappeared into the shower. I remember that distinctively. She didn't ask him, she told him. Does that sound like anyone you know?"

Stan shook his head from side to side and said, "I don't think so. Do you remember anything else about the girl?"

"No. That was the last time I saw her. She hung around for a few more days before going back to New York. I believe Steve flew out to the East Coast a few times to see her, but I'm just guessing. I know he went back East on at least three occasions to see a friend, but he didn't mention any names. I'd hate to try and guess the age of that woman. But if I were pressed, I'd say she was about six or seven years younger than Doris."

Doris prodded her piety and said, "She is not. If it's who I think it is, she is the same age I am. As a matter of fact, she's three months older. It sounds like Claudia Fleming, and I bet she's still having facelifts."

The man looked at her as she went back to eating her pie, and then said, "That's the name."

"Dear, how did you figure that one out?" Stan asked.

"It wasn't hard. I know a lot more than you give me credit for; and I know Claudia. I roomed with her for three months. During that time, she never asked anyone for anything. She told them what she wanted."

After a short pause, Dan said, "Whatever she told Steve certainly did wonders for him. After her visit, he got enthused again with music and with life. He started playing jobs around San Francisco. Before long, he was going up to Reno and Lake Tahoe. When the house bands would need an add-on man in the reed section, more often than not, Steve would get the call. He has always been one hell of a sight reader. I don't believe anyone has ever put music on paper that he can't read the first time through. Last year, a guy called Red Potter asked if he would be interested in playing with the house band in Reno. Steve didn't even think twice about it. The following day he made the move. I heard from him last week, and he still likes it in Reno. The house band only works about thirty weeks out of the year, but that's all the work Steve wants. I guess a lot of the headliners and acts are coming in self-contained. Anyway, he sounded happy and very up. One of these days, I hope to drive up there and see him."

Stan thanked Dan for the information, and they went their separate ways. During the drive back to their motel, Doris said, "I wonder how Steve and Claudia got together?"

"That might be an interesting story. Would you care to take a side trip over to Reno and asked him?"

"Could we?" she asked.

"I don't see why not. We've got the time, and I'm rather curious myself. Let's do it."

The following morning, they decided to have breakfast at their motel. After they walked into the restaurant and were seated, Doris said, "This is more like it. Besides having a large room, they have a huge breakfast menu. I see a lot of things that aren't fried, and I just might order all of them. I'm starved. That meal last night left a lot to be desired."

"I enjoyed it," Stan replied. Dan used good judgment when he picked that place."

"Your taste buds must be all screwed up. I don't think Dan is a good judge of anything, and when it comes to guessing the age of people, he's a total loss. The nerve of that guy, telling me that I looked years older than Claudia Fleming! He probably isn't even a good bandmaster."

Stan made no comment. After they had their breakfast and returned to their room, he called his office. Among other things, he found out that Norma Anderson had reached an agreement with Benny

Fisher. He told Doris about it and suggested they stop by Lake Tahoe on their way to Reno. She agreed.

They headed for Sacramento. After locating Route 50, they were on their way to Lake Tahoe. When the lake came into view, the snow started falling from the sky. It had been over 20 years since Stan had driven on the white stuff and it showed. He slipped back and forth down the road until they reached the hotel. When they were safe and sound in their room, he said, "I'll bet this is the only area in the country that gets snow in late September. Until a few minutes ago, I had forgotten why I hated snow. Let's cross this place off our list of possible retirement areas."

He tried to call Norma, but she was not in her suite. Then he tried to get in touch with Benny Fisher and he was put on hold. After about five minutes, Benny came on the line with, "So you decided to take me up on my offer. I'm glad. When shall we get together?"

"Can we make it in an hour or so? Doris just jumped in the bath, and you know how that goes."

"One hour would be perfect. That will give me time to clean up a few things. I'll meet you at the ground floor cocktail lounge around four."

When they got together, Benny was in a cordial mood. After they ordered their second round of drinks, Stan asked, "Do you know where Norma Anderson is hiding? She's not in her suite, and I didn't even have any luck when I had her paged."

"She's rehearsing in the main showroom," Benny told him. "They've been in there since noon. Yesterday, Norma had some of her music sent to us. I called in the producer of our show, and the two of them got together last evening. They watched the second show and went into a huddle. When I left them at 3:00 AM they were still going at it. Norma is being very cooperative, and I think she's just what our show needs."

"When does she open?" Doris asked.

"I'd like to have her open in two days, but she told me, 'No way. I can't learn the new songs and dance routines in that length of time.' She asked for a week, but I believe that's an excessive length of time. We'll probably have to reach some kind of compromise and have her open in three or four days. I don't like to rush her, but I need a name over our marquee. I've spent the last two days going over our publicity campaign, and we're all set to roll. All I need is a firm opening date, and I hope to get that in a few minutes. Regardless of the actual opening date, our first releases start going out tomorrow. Let's go to the show room and catch the tail end of the rehearsal."

The security guards stationed outside the show room recognized Benny Fisher and opened the door for them. As they sat down in the back of the room, Norma was concluding one of her new dance routines. The producer told her, "That's wonderful, Norma. Now then, this is the way I see your last appearance before the finale. I want you to start your routine back with the chorus and..."

Norma interrupted him with, "I don't see it that way, and I'm not going to start my final segment buried in the middle of the chorus. We did that earlier in the show and once is enough. I'm the star of this show, and I'm going to be down front where the audience expects the headliner to be."

"Alright, Norma. Settle down. Since you feel so strongly about it, we will do it your way, but I'll have to modify what's going on behind you."

Norma stood her ground and didn't say a word while the producer made some notes on his clipboard. When he finished, he nodded to the piano man, and the musicians started playing the last routine. Norma started singing the words from a sheet of music she held in her hand. As she continued her song, the producer indicated how he wanted her to gesture and move. After they went through the routine two more times, the producer told them, "Let's knock it off for today. We'll go at it again tomorrow. Same time. Same place."

The people on stage started to leave, but Benny Fisher rushed forward and hollered, "Stay where you are. I want to know when the new edition of this show will be ready. When do we open?"

"I'll work out the changes for the chorus tonight and start rehearsing with them tomorrow. The revisions will be minor, so the cast should be ready in two days," the producer told him.

Benny looked at Norma and waited for her response. "I think I'll be able to memorize the new songs and have the dance routines set in three days, but that's the best I can do. What about my new costumes and the music revisions?"

Then he told her, "The costume designer and one of the wardrobe girls will be at your suite tonight. You can plan on having your preliminary fitting right after our first show. They should arrive around 10 o'clock. What has to be done to the music?"

"We are planning on using two songs from our current show that are in the wrong keys for Norma," the conductor, Bob Albert, told him. "The music has to be transposed down a third, and Norma has requested some re-orchestration on both arrangements. Besides that, we have some hookup problems between segments, so we will need some new interlude material."

"Who's going to do the work?" Benny asked.

"Norma tried to get her former arranger," Bob told him, "but he's tied up on a TV series in Los Angeles. During our last break, I got a hold of a guy who did most of the rewrites for our current show. He lives in Reno, and he'll drive up here tonight. He has two shows to play this evening, so I expect him to arrive around 3 AM - maybe sooner. It depends on the roads. He will need prints of our music. Will you make arrangements to have someone in the office around 2 AM who can run off the copies?"

"I'm not bringing in anyone at that hour," Benny told him. "You'll have to run them yourself. If you don't have time to handle it, ask a couple of your musicians to help out. I'll notify security, and they'll let you in. Be sure to let them know when you're finished so they can lock up. Alright folks, unless there are any objections, the new edition opens in four days."

No one objected, so Benny went back to his office to finalize the releases. Norma saw Stan and Doris at the back of the room and waved to them. After a short consultation with the conductor, she came back and greeted them. Stan asked if she would care to have dinner with them, and Norma replied, "I would like that, but I don't have time. I only had five hours of sleep last night, and I'm exhausted. I'm going to rest for a few hours before the costume designer gets here. Perhaps I'll eat something during the fitting. If you two don't have anything better to do, come up to my suite around ten. We can visit while they are costuming me."

"I don't think we'll take you up on that," Stan said.

"Why not?" Norma and Doris asked simultaneously.

"With all of that dressing and undressing, having me around might prove embarrassing."

"Not to me," Norma said. "Except for my face and hands, you won't see my skin. I'll be wearing a body stocking. That's the easiest way, and it provides some protection from the pins. Both of you have seen me wearing a lot less, and so has almost everyone else who has watched me perform."

When they arrived at Norma's door, room service was leaving: they left a second pot of coffee and extra cups. As Norma started to eat her dinner, two women arrived to fit the costumes. Norma took off her robe and continued to eat whenever the clothing was removed from her body. When the fitting was over, she looked at her watch and suggested they go downstairs to see the last show.

While Stan and Doris were enjoying the production show, Norma was busy jotting notes. After the finale, Norma asked if they would care to go backstage.

"Yes. I want to see it all," Doris said. "With the exception of The Strip, Stan never takes me anywhere."

As they started walking toward the stage entrance, Norma asked, "Doesn't this awful man even take you out to dinner?"

"Only after I've cooked two or three bad meals in a row."

When they reached the stage, it was deserted except for three men gathering music. After everyone was introduced, Bob Albert decided to blow off a little steam.

As the two musicians continued to gather music, Bob said, "The support services provided by this hotel sure leave a lot to be desired. Whenever you want something done at odd hours, you have to do it yourself. Besides conducting two shows a night and rehearsing five hours in the afternoon, now I have to run copies of the music. If the duplicating machine does its usual good job of acting up, I'll probably be the one who has to repair it. If I didn't need the money, I wouldn't put up with this crap. Norma, are you planning on staying up for another hour or two?"

"Yes I am. When the arranger gets here, I want to talk with him about my music."

"Suit yourself," Bob replied, "but I've written down all of your comments, my comments, and the producers requests. They are in my dressing room, and that's where I asked our man to meet me. After you finish showing Doris and Stan around, would you mind keeping an eye out for him? I may run a little late getting copies of the damned music, and I don't want him looking all over hell for me. He might get pissed off and decide to go back home."

"Sure thing, Bob. I'll see to it that he doesn't disappear. What's his name?"

"Steve Post. Here are the keys to my dressing room. It isn't much, but after your tour, you will at least have a place to sit down. When do they expect to have your dressing room finished?"

"If everything goes as planned, the last coat of paint goes on tomorrow, "Norma told him.

"Nothing goes as planned around here, so don't count on it. Aha, it looks like the troops have the music. Follow me men, and we'll see how many asses we have to kiss to get the prints of this shit."

As Norma started showing them around the area, Doris said, "That Bob Albert sounds a bit crusty. I didn't like his choice of words one damn bit. That kind of language isn't necessary, particularly around women. Stan, why didn't you make him stop talking like that?"

"Bob is bigger and stronger than I am, so the thought of it never entered my mind. Besides, I didn't hear him say anything that offended me. When you're all worked up, I've heard you use the same words on numerous occasions."

"Don't mind Bob," Norma told him. "He's just a typical insecure musician trying to act tough. I've heard much cruder language in the past, and I'll probably hear more of the same in the future. At least I can understand all of Bob's words. That's more than I can say for some of the creative expressions I've heard."

As the overhead lights started to go out, Norma told them, "Let's get over to Bob's dressing room while we can still see where we are going."

They didn't make it. By the time they were halfway across the stage, most of the lights had been turned out. Their only illumination came from the exit hallway lights. They felt their way and stumbled over shielded cables, wires and tracks as they crossed the stage. Just before they reach safety, Doris brushed her leg against one of the rough pieces of staging and snagged her hose.

When Stan heard the word "shit," he asked, "Did you or do you want to?"

"Shut up," Doris replied. "Stop trying to be funny, and help me get out of this maze."

They reached the hallway and found Bob's room. After Norma unlocked the door and turned on the lights, she went to the desk and looked at Bob's notes. When she finished reading the comments, she asked, "Have either of you seen Steve Post recently these past years?"

"With the exception of this past year, we've always stayed in touch with him," Stan told her. "About six years ago, Steve started into a bad period. We've all had them, but his lasted a long time.   I don't know it to be a fact, but I think that phase is behind him. At least that's the impression I got yesterday when we talked with one of his friends. I'm looking forward to seeing him again and being filled in on what he's been up to this past year. Besides my curiosity, Doris has a question or two she'd like to ask him."

Doris started to talk about their conversation with Dan Daily, but she was interrupted by a knock on the door. When Norma opened it she said, "Hi Steve."

He gave her a quick hug and told her, "When Bob told me this job was for you, I could hardly wait to get up here. Norma, you look wonderful. I've followed your career with more than a casual interest, but I haven't heard very much about you for a year or so. Did you decide to take a rest?"

"No. I decided to get a divorce. It wiped me out in more ways than one, but it was the right thing to do. I'm glad it's over, and I think getting back to work will do wonders for me. Come in and meet a couple of old friends."

Steve walked inside and saw Stan and Doris. His first words were, "I've been meaning to write, but something always seems to pop up before I get anything on paper. What brought you to this place? Stan, are you Norma's agent?"

Before he could answer, Norma said, "Yes he is, but he doesn't realize it yet."

Bob Albert charged through the doorway and dropped a stack of music on the desk. He reviewed what had to be done with Steve. When he finished, Norma told Steve what she didn't like about the existing arrangements. After she explained the texture she wanted in some of the background phrases, Bob said, "Let's lock up and get away from this place for a few hours."

As they walked to the parking lot, Steve asked, "How long are you and Doris going to stay in this corner of the world?"

"Probably another day or two. Our plans are indefinite, but we had hoped to see the entire West Coast during this trip."

"I'm sorry to hear you're not staying longer," Steve told him. "After this job for Norma is completed, I was looking forward to spending some time with you and Doris. I guess that's out, because Bob said he needed this music for a mid-afternoon rehearsal the day after tomorrow. I'll pretty much have to work straight through the next day and a half to get it done on time. Fortunately, I won't be playing during the next seven days. The hotel I work at has a self-contained unit in for a week, so the house band is off. I should be able to complete this job with a minimum amount of outside help, but it will be a tight schedule. Are you sure you can't stick around here for three or four more days?"

Stan looked at Doris and asked, "What do you think? Shall we do it?"

"I'd like to stay and visit," she told him. "I think we've seen the best part of the West Coast, and I'm not interested in just riding down the highway. Besides, I'd like to see Norma on the stage in her new costumes. Let's stay here and watch her opening night performance."

"The big honcho has spoken," Stan said, "so I guess we'll stay put for a few days. Steve, when shall we plan on seeing you?"

"I'll be back in about thirty-four hours. After the new music has been rehearsed, the three of us can spend the entire evening together. Norma, I'd include you, but I know you have other things on your mind."

After Steve drove away, they walked back to the hotel. When Norma reached her suite, she told them, "I'm glad you're staying for my opening. Now I can count on at least two friendly faces in the audience."

The sun was out the following morning, and the snow had disappeared. When they finished breakfast, Stan asked, "What would you like to do today?"

"I'd like to drive around the lake and see what this place has to offer."

As they left the parking lot, they noticed Norma's name and opening date on the sign in front of the hotel. During their drive around the lake, they saw workmen making the same addition on billboards. When they returned to the hotel, Stan asked, "What are your feelings about this area?"

"If I lived in San Francisco, I'd enjoy coming up here a few times each year. The entire area has a resort atmosphere, but I'm disappointed in most of the buildings. They look like they were put up in a hurry and were only meant to be temporary structures. The lake was the only thing that looked like it would be around for any length of time."

"I feel the same way. It's a nice place to spend a few days relaxing, but I wouldn't want to live here year-round. Let's go to the showroom and see if they're still rehearsing."

The security guard knew that they were guests of Benny Fisher, so he let them in. Except for Norma Anderson, the entire cast was on stage. They continued to work out for about fifteen minutes. When the producer dismissed everyone, Stan went forward and asked Bob Albert, "Do you know where we can find Norma?"

"Not really," he replied. "About an hour ago, she got a cramp in one of her legs. She couldn't walk let alone dance, so Benny Fisher had a masseuse come down here to relieve the pain. After she could move about, they took her to the health club. As far as I know, they're still massaging her."

They returned to their room, and Doris decided to shower after the day of sightseeing. While she was cleaning up, Stan called Norma. She had just returned from the health club and said she was feeling better. When he asked if she felt good enough to have dinner with them, she told him, "Yes."

One hour later, they met and went to the ground floor. By this time, Benny Fisher had seen to it that pictures of Norma were in the elevators and on display throughout the hotel. When they walked into the restaurant, she was recognized by some of the people in the room. Besides the constant stares, their meal was interrupted numerous times by people coming over to introduce themselves, asking for autographs, or just wishing her well. Norma looked radiant and acted vigorous throughout the meal, but when they were returning to her suite, she walked with a slight limp.

Stan noticed and asked, "Can I help you?"

"No thanks. I'm a little sore, but it will go away. My legs always let me know when I've overused them, so I'm calling it a night. Will I see you at tomorrow's rehearsal?"

"Yes. We'll be there," he replied.

Stan and Doris returned to their room and watched TV for a few hours. When they were ready for bed, Doris said, "This may surprise you, but I don't envy Norma anymore."

The following day, no serious mishaps occurred during the rehearsal. Steve fixed a few music copying errors, but no rewrite was required. Norma had walked through her dance routines rather than abuse her sore legs. After Norma thanked Steve for giving her what she desired in the revised music, he asked, "Are you free for the evening?"

"I won't be free for at least two days. I'm having my final costume fitting tonight. Tomorrow morning, the press will be here for pictures and interviews. We have a rehearsal in the afternoon, and the new edition of the show opens that evening. Fortunately we only have one show tomorrow night. Benny Fisher made an exception on opening night, because he wanted to throw a party for the press and invited guests of the hotel. When the show is over, we will probably be on our feet for another three hours. I can't say I'm looking forward to a few hours of shaking hands, smiling, and trying to eat, drink and be merry. But I'll do it, because Benny told me that the backstage party is a very important part of his promotional strategy."

"I thought your schedule would be something like that," Steve replied. "When you have some free time and want to get out of the hotel, give me a ring. Unless we have a new show to rehearse, I'm usually free during the day."

"I may take you up on that offer sooner than you think. I had a call this morning from my realtor, and he thinks he has a buyer for my house. If I can dispose of it, I'll want to lease something here and get out of my hotel suite. If I get lucky, will you show me around the area so I can get a feel of what's available?"

"I'll look forward to it," he told her. "We have some rather strange places around the lake, but I'm sure we can find something you'd like."

"Almost anything would be preferable to living in a hotel month after month," she said.

After Norma left, Steve asked, "Would you mind driving to Reno?"

"We haven't been out of the hotel all day," Stan replied. "Driving to Reno sounds good to me. What do you have in mind?"

"My own safety," Steve told him. "Sometimes, I fade fast after these all-night sessions. If it happens this evening, I don't want it to happen while I'm on the highway. Why not bring your toothbrushes and plan on staying overnight. I have an extra bedroom, and it even has a bed. Nothing more, but it does have a decent bed. Tomorrow, if we get up in time, I'll give you a tour of Reno."

They took him up on his offer and went to their room. Doris decided to take more than a toothbrush. She packed two changes of clothes and nightgown, robe, extra shoes, slippers, and of course, her makeup kit. As they put the baggage in their car, Steve told him, "Just follow me. I'll make one stop at the drive-in window of a fast food restaurant, and then we can stay put for the rest of the evening. What do you want on your hamburgers?"

"I want to cook," Doris replied. "If you want hamburgers and a salad, that's okay, but I would like to fix the meal."

"Doris, I've always enjoyed the way you prepare a meal, but I'm not inviting you to my place to have you slave away in the kitchen.

If you don't like fast food restaurants, we will eat out before going to my apartment."

"If I have a choice, I don't want to eat out. Take me to a grocery store and let me find some real food. Steve, I'm serious. We've been eating out for a week, and I'm tired of it. I miss my own kind of food. Be nice and let me play house for a few hours."

They stopped at a supermarket a short distance from Steve's apartment. After Doris bought what looked like a week's supply of groceries, they drove a few blocks to the apartment. Steve showed her around the kitchen and asked if they would care for a drink.

"Yes," Doris told him. "Can you make a vodka martini? I cook some of the best meals when I'm half smashed."

"I have all of the ingredients, and I'm a master at the art. Stan, do you want the same, or would you prefer something else?"

"A vodka martini sounds good," Stan replied.

Steve mixed two large drinks and handed them to his guests. Doris took a sip and said, "Delicious."

"Aren't you drinking with us?" Stan asked.

"Yes, I'm drinking. I have a cola in the refrigerator."

"A what?"

"A cola. I don't drink the hard stuff anymore."

Doris asked, "Does it bother you to watch other people indulge themselves?"

"Not at all. Most of my friends enjoy a good drink, and I don't see anything wrong with it. But for now, I choose not to join them. Maybe I am just 'on hold'. You know, just waiting until my friends' consumption catches up to mine, but I doubt it. I think I've had my fill of liquor."

"Since you have such strong feelings about this stuff, I'll try not to spill too much of it on the food," Doris told him. "Why don't you guys go to the living room and leave me alone to do my thing."

They agreed with her desire, and left her alone with the pots and pans. "How is the artist management business treating you these days?" Steve asked.

"I think I've had it with managing artists. When it comes to business, too many of them have vacant heads. All they think about is performing, hearing applause and seeing their name in lights. That's not good. Sooner or later, their career disappears. I've always felt that they should have something to show for their time in the business besides memories. I worry about their relationships with entertainment buyers, and I try to keep them from being ripped off in their financial dealings. But most of the time, I feel like I'm talking to the wind."

"If some of your clients don't think about tomorrow, that's their problem. You're paid a commission to find them work. Since you don't make a dime from their investments, why concern yourself with the way they spend their money?"

"I can't give you a logical reason for my involvement and concern in their financial affairs, but that's the way I am. I worry about their future."

"For a guy who worries a lot, you sure look good."

"I may look fine, fat and happy, but my heart has been telling me a different story. I think it's time for retirement."

"Retirement isn't for everybody," Steve told him. "I tried it for a few years, so I know what I'm talking about. Before you throw in the towel, I believe you should give it a lot of thought."

"I have given it a lot of thought. Perhaps I'm wrong, but it seems like the right thing to do. Since you've actually experienced it, would you care to tell me about your years in retirement?"

"There isn't much to tell," Steve said. "I can summarize it in two words, *inactivity* and *boredom*. I guess that's why retirement wasn't for me."

"That's the shortest summary I've ever heard. Unless it's painful, I wish you'd elaborate on your years in retirement. Maybe you could build it up to three or four sentences. Look at it this way, it might help me avoid some of the pitfalls."

"If you want to hear more, I guess I can stretch it. The first six months weren't all that bad. I took a lot of short trips, but traveling doesn't thrill me. There isn't any feeling of accomplishment. Next, I tried some adult studies at the colleges, but that didn't do it either. I didn't complete most of the courses, because I couldn't see any purpose in it."

"How about hobbies?" Stan asked. "Did you try to get involved with hobbies?"

"Sure. I tried most of them. The only one that did anything for me was golf, and I still get out and play the game one or two days a week. I just couldn't get into the other hobbies. It was probably out of desperation, but I turned again to music for relaxation. At first I just listened, but eventually I started playing with the rehearsal band. I've never been overly excited about rehearsal bands, but it was something to do. I don't think my lack of enthusiasm with kicks bands has anything to do with the fact that there isn't a monetary reward, it's something else. Perhaps it's the laid-back attitude of some of the musicians that turns me off. I don't like to hear first-class musicians give a second rate performance. When money isn't involved in a performance, some musicians don't put forth their best effort. If they aren't getting paid for it, I guess they feel what they are doing doesn't count. That kind of playing doesn't grab me. I'd rather not be involved if everyone isn't giving 100% all the time."

"I've always known you to be that way," Stan said. "In that respect, retirement didn't change you at all. After the long layoff, did you find it hard to get back into the discipline and frustrations of the music business?"

"It was easier than I thought it would be, but I had the right attitude. When I got back into the business, I knew the type of music I enjoyed playing was passé. It's just a memory and so are the working conditions. Everything changes and sometimes those changes trap you. I've accepted the music business as it exists today and found a place in it where I can function. Now don't get me wrong, I'm not thrilled with everything I play or write. But almost without exception, I prefer it to retirement."

"You're a lucky man," Stan told him. "You have something to do that keeps you busy, and it isn't giving you heart trouble."

"I suppose I am, but the sticky part is that I had to work this all out for myself. I used to have very intense feelings about music, and that was one of the things that helped screw me up. Now, I do the best job I can with whatever has to be played, and when it's over, I forget about it. If you run your business with a similar attitude, Stan, I believe you could live with it. Do what has to be done, but walk away when the bickering becomes absurd. And most important of all, don't always be available. Take periodic breathers and escape from the constant hassles."

"What you're saying makes sense, but I don't know if I could pull it off. I've never tried to function that way."

"Stan, I think you should give it a try. If you close up your business and then change your mind, what are you going to do? You and Doris worked long and hard to get your agency established. If you close it down, for all practical purposes, you are through. When I decided to come out of retirement, it wasn't a big deal. After six months practicing, I was ready to go back to work. You won't enjoy the same luxury, because it would probably take years to rebuild your business. I'm not trying to talk you into working until you have a heart attack, but I think you should look for a middle ground, something between being too busy and complete retirement. If you try it and still have heart problems, then go all the way and retire."

Doris interrupted their discussion by announcing, "Dinner is ready." Steve looked at the food and said, "This is the nicest looking meal my table has ever seen."

As they started helping themselves to the food, Stan mentioned that Steve told him retirement wasn't for everyone.

"You don't have to repeat the conversation," Doris said. "I've been listening to every word, and I agree with Steve. Rather than quit cold, I'd like to see you taper off. You could start by dropping the clients who cause you the most problems."

"But Doris, those people usually make the most money for me."

"Get rid of them anyway," was her reply. "You keep telling me that we don't need the money, so I believe you should only work with the clients you enjoy dealing with."

Stan thought about it for a moment and replied, "I don't think my commission from the nice people would pay the office overhead."

"So why not make up the difference yourself and have someplace to go. That way, we can both ease into your retirement. If you stop leaving the house all at once, having you around twenty-four hours a day, seven days a week, may give me a heart attack."

"My dear, your words are food for thought. Sudden retirement may not be the best thing to do. I don't mind admitting that I'm having second thoughts on the subject. When Steve told me about his years in retirement, I didn't like what I heard."

"Steve didn't tell you everything about his years in retirement," Doris said. "Not once did I hear him mention Claudia Fleming."

Stan looked shocked and told her, "Doris, that's not nice. If Steve doesn't want to talk about Claudia, that's his business. I wish you'd learn to keep your mouth shut when it comes to personal matters."

Steve smiled and said, "On your way here, you must've come in contact with Dan Daily."

"You're right," Stan replied. "We talked with Dan, and Claudia's name came up during the conversation."

After a long silence, Doris said, "I guess this busybody did it again. Steve, don't be mad at me. I'm sorry."

"I'm not mad at you or anyone else. Doris, you're a marvelous cook. After that meal, I'm at peace with the world."

"That's a lovely compliment," Doris said. "Since you're not mad at me, I'd still like to hear about Claudia."

Stan kicked her leg, but she kicked him back and asked, "How did you happen to run across her? To my knowledge, Claudia never kept in touch with anyone unless it had to do with business."

"I think your last statement is pretty close to right," Steve said. "As far as I know, Claudia doesn't have any close ties with anyone. It was a complete surprise when our paths crossed about six years ago. At the time, I was on my first tour with Tony Sutherland. Tony was hosting a TV program, and Claudia was the assistant to the producer. During my second tour with Sutherland, I contacted her while we were on the East Coast. She has had a very interesting life, and it's a delight to hear her talk about it. About a year after I went into retirement, Claudia showed up at my apartment."

"How did she know where to find you?" Doris asked. "Did you correspond with her?"

"No. I probably should have, but I'm not big on writing. Besides, there wasn't anything going on in my life that was worth writing about. She found out about me through Billy Baker. Billy was Tony Sutherland's conductor during my stints with him. When Sutherland's career went down the toilet, Billy returned to New York and went back to being a bass player in the clubs. I more or less stayed in touch with Billy, so he knew where I was living. Claudia ran into Billy at a club where he was working. When she found out what happened to me, she flew to San Francisco and looked me up. It was somewhat of a shock when I saw her standing outside my door, but it was a good shock."

"Did she try to call you before she traveled across country?" Stan asked.

"Claudia is rather impulsive, so I doubt it. If she tried to call me, I wasn't aware of it. But she couldn't have shown up at a better time. I was getting rather complacent about my do nothing life, and Claudia jarred me back into activity. She's quite forceful and restless. If I had to describe her in a few words, I think I'd call her a powerhouse of raw energy."

"I've never known Claudia to go out of her way to help anyone," Doris said. "You must be a very special person in her life."

"Perhaps, but I think you've misjudged Claudia. She's very intent on her work, but that doesn't mean she won't take the time to help a friend. In my case, I can't say enough nice things about her."

Doris thought about his last statement for a moment before saying, "You sound like you really like the girl. From what I've heard tonight, it wouldn't surprise me if you end up marrying her."

"I suppose that's a possibility, but I don't think it will happen. Claudia is a free spirit. If the phone rings for a meaningful job, she's off on a moment's notice to any place in the country. She's a very independent person. Both of us have been divorced, and that's an experience neither of us wants to go through again. Marriage might sound good someday, but I don't believe she's ready to try it again and I know I'm not. I enjoy Claudia's company more than anyone I know, but I don't think we could live under the same roof year after year. Most of us aren't willing to do what it takes to develop a lasting relationship. You two are a rare exception."

"If you think we get along perfectly, you're wrong," Doris told him. "We fight all the time. Just a few days ago, Stan started to walk out on me for the umpteenth time."

They continue discussing their lives until fatigue hit Steve. The following day, Doris was the first one to get up.   It was noon by the time she showered and dressed. As the men joined her in greeting the new day, she played house one more time and fixed breakfast. Midway through the meal, Steve's telephone rang.

It was a brief conversation, and when it was over Steve told him, "I won't be able to show you around Reno today. That phone call was from the music contractor at the hotel down the street from where I work. One of his reed men just got a hernia during rehearsal, and they rushed him to the hospital. Before I got my steady job, that contractor gave me a lot of substitute work, so I owe him."

As Steve carried his musical instruments to the car, he told them, "Stay as long as you like, but lock up the place if you decide to leave. I probably won't be back until five or six. Do you think you'll still be here when I return?"

"No," Stan replied. "We promised Norma that we would be at her opening this evening."

"Will you be back tomorrow?"

"I don't think so, Steve. We would like to get an early start and see some more of the country."

They shook hands, and Steve told them he would write more frequently. After he drove away, Doris cleaned up the kitchen. Stan wanted to take a look at Reno, so they spent a few hours seeing the city. During the drive back to the lake, Stan asked, "What did you think of it?"

"Reno is too Western for my taste."

"I feel the same way," Stan replied.

When they got back to their hotel, they rested before dressing for the show. Benny Fisher had seen to it that his showroom was filled with the right kind of invited guests. Audience response to the performance was good. When Norma made her appearances, the response was usually enthusiastic. As the show ended and everyone in the audience was making their way backstage, Stan asked, "What did you think of our girl?"

"Norma adds a lot to the show," Doris replied. "I don't consider her the best singer, dancer or actress I've ever seen; but everything she does - looks and sounds professional. I don't know what it is, but she projects something out of the ordinary."

"It's called *Presence!* When Norma's on the stage, she stands out from the other people."

Even though the backstage area was large, it was crowded with people. Stan and Doris went to a portable bar and asked for their usual martinis. With drinks in hand, they mingled with about 700 people. One hour and two drinks later, they decided to try the buffet.

As they started to eat, Benny Fisher stopped by and told Stan, "Everyone I've talked with is favorably impressed with the show. I think we're going to make big bucks from this edition."

Before Stan could respond, Benny was back mixing with the people. By this time, Doris had lost her enthusiasm for the party. They migrated over to Norma and started to congratulate her, but Benny Fisher interrupted them and told Norma, "There are some people from the San Francisco Press who want to meet you. They'd also like to take a few pictures."

Norma whispered to Doris, "My legs and feet are killing me. If this room doesn't clear out pretty soon, would you turn on the speaker system and start screaming fire?"

"Sure, and if that doesn't do the trick I may even start one," Doris replied.

When it became obvious that Norma would be on her feet until the wee hours of the morning, Stan and Doris returned to their room and got a good night's sleep.

They woke up early and had breakfast in their room. Afterwards, Stan wrote a thank you note to Benny Fisher and a congratulatory note to Norma Anderson. As they were packing. Stan received a call from his secretary. Helen told him, "Sonny Cross just called, and he wants you to get in touch with him as soon as you have a free moment."

"Did he mention what he wants to talk about?"

"No, he didn't," Helen told him. "Mr. Cross said he would be at his home for another hour. After that, you can reach him at the hotel."

"Thanks, Helen. I'll try his home phone right away."

Stan placed the call to Las Vegas, and Sonny Cross answered his phone. "We have decided to extend our superstar policy for an additional six months," Sonny told him. "I could give Jerry Ross a considerable amount of work, but I won't do it until quite a few things are worked out. I would like to have the three of us discuss this possibility in the immediate future. When will you and your client be available for a meeting?"

"I'm on vacation, Sonny. Could we get together in two or three weeks?"

"I'd prefer to get it out of the way in two or three days."

"Hang on a moment, and let me discuss it with Doris. Dear, would you care to see Las Vegas?"

"Why not," she replied.

"She's agreeable," Stan told him. "I'll drive into your city sometime tomorrow, and perhaps we can get together the following day."

Sonny asked if they would care to stay at his hotel, but Stan declined saying, "Thanks, but no thanks. From the tone of your voice, I think it would be best if Doris and I stayed someplace else. That way we can start our meeting without any obligations on either side."

Before they left the room, Doris looked at her map and said, "Since we have a day or two before you have to be in Las Vegas, let's drive into the desert and see the wide open spaces."

That sounded good to Stan, so they took route 50 and escaped from civilization. Within an hour, the traffic had all but disappeared. As they took some of the side roads and wondered about, it wasn't uncommon to travel ten to twenty minutes at a stretch without seeing another vehicle. Eventually, their solitude was broken. Ahead of them was a cattle drive. It looked like about two hundred animals and ten cowboys on horseback. Unlike the drives they had watched on films, this one was coming right down the highway. The breadth of cattle filled the area between the fence lines, and Stan did not want to press his luck by trying to drive through them. He stopped the car, and they watched the cattle gradually make their way around them.

"I'll bet you've never seen anything like this on the Los Angeles freeways," Doris said.

"I've never seen anything like this anywhere. Let's not frighten them, because they seem to urinate a lot. Remind me to have the car washed as soon as possible."

As Doris waved to some of the cowboys and cowgirls, she said, "If they start to stampede, I'll probably urinate along with them. Look calm. Make them think we're used to this sort of thing."

After the cattle passed, Doris suggested they drive to Tonopah and stay overnight. He headed their car south, and they arrived as the sun was going down. They drove through the city and saw a few abandoned mines. The mines appeared to be the high point of the local color. After checking into a motel, they walked up and down Main Street until they were hungry. A bellboy was standing outside the one and only hotel in the city, and it really impressed Doris. She told Stan, "This is where I want to have dinner."

They walked through the street door and found themselves in a small casino. It was crowded, and the noise was unbelievably loud. As they made their way through the people, Stan said, "I believe we've found where the action is in Tonopah."

They located the dining room and were seated. Although this area was not crowded, they felt cramped and closed in. The dining room did not have any windows, and the tables were so close to each other there was barely room to get into the chairs. Due to the noise seeping in from the casino, it wasn't their most enjoyable meal during the trip, but it wasn't the worst. During their return walk to the motel, Stan summarized his feelings about Tonopah by saying, "I thought Reno had a western flair, but by comparison, this place makes Reno look like a modern metropolis."

"Apparently, you prefer Los Angeles to Tonopah."

"Doris, that's a fact. If nothing else, this trip has convinced me that LA has a lot of redeeming features that I've been taking for granted. Perhaps we should plan on staying put for a while."

"Does that mean you're not going to close your agency right away?" Doris asked

"I'm still undecided about the agency. What Steve suggested made a lot of sense. If I can avoid getting too involved in my clients' personal and financial affairs, I might be able to lick my intermittent heart problem and keep the business open for another year. Then I'll reevaluate my feelings and perhaps continue on a year-to-year basis."

"If you drop the Jerry Ross account, I think your heart problem would vanish," she told him.

"Maybe you're right, but Jerry is largely responsible for our financial well-being. I'll have to think about it. Speaking of Jerry, let's get an early start tomorrow and plan on seeing his first show."

They left Tonopah around nine and found the drive monotonous. After about 70 miles, they turned off the highway at a junction and took the tour of Scotty's Castle. It wasn't as impressive as the Hearst Mansion, but it gave them an excuse to stretch and walk around. After the tour, they drove straight through to Las Vegas. When they reached the outskirts of the city, Stan stopped at a gas station. As the car was being filled, he went to the public phone and tried to make room reservations. There was a large convention in the city, so it took a few calls before he could find a place with a vacancy.

When Stan returned to the car, Doris asked, "Where are we staying?"

"I made reservations at the El Morocco for two days."

"Good. I like that place. The rooms are spacious and it's quiet."

As they continued into the city, the traffic congestion increased and Stan had to pay attention to his driving. When they reached Sahara Avenue, he drove east for a short distance and made a right turn onto The Strip. At the Stardust Hotel, he made a left turn, crossed the street, and stopped in front of their motel.

After unpacking, they went to the pool area and sat in the sun for a couple of hours. When they returned to their room, Stan called Jerry's secretary to let her know he had arrived. Two hours later, they were seated for the dinner show. Shortly after they finished their meal, the orchestra started playing the Jerry Ross overture. Before the instrumental medley concluded, Stan noted that all of the dinner dishes had been cleared from the tables.

Jerry Ross was greeted with warm applause when he appeared. As he made his way across the stage singing his opening song, he noticed a vivacious young lady in the audience. She was nodding her head to the music and snapping her fingers on the second and fourth beat of each measure - just the way a swinger should. Jerry continued across the stage, but when he returned to where she was sitting, he stepped onto her table. Without missing a word of the lyrics, he extended his hand and asked, "Care to dance?" She was more than agreeable, so he helped her stand on the chair, then the table, and finally the stage. Jerry concluded singing the first chorus of the song and motioned for his conductor to go instrumental. The conductor pointed his finger at the tenor sax man as Jerry laid his mike on the floor. The sax man played ad lib with the rhythm section as Jerry and the girl started to dance.

She turned out to be a spectacular dancer, so Jerry gave her room to move and mimicked her when he could. The entire incident was impromptu, but it was vintage Ross, a veteran showman working at his trade. Tonight, he was enlivening his show with a member of the audience. Tomorrow, it might be a sight gag and the following evening who knows what, but it always worked. When Jerry helped the girl back to her seat the same way he had helped her onto the stage, the audience broke into delightful applause.

Jerry walked backwards from the table and pointed a finger at the girl so the spotlight would remain on her. Besides being a courteous gesture, it also accomplished three other things. First, it milked the audience for more applause. Second, it distracted from his appearance if he happened to stub his foot or lose his balance. Third, and most important of all, it gave the band time to finish their instrumental chorus without any dead space on the stage. When it was time for him to start singing again, he dropped his finger. The spotlight disappeared from the girl and centered on him when he resumed his song.

Stan turned to Doris and told her, "That sort of thing can only be pulled off when everybody's on their toes. They sure did an outstanding job tonight. The orchestra, sound, lighting, and most importantly, Jerry Ross... taking chances. It was showbiz at its best, and the audience loved every minute of it."

"Shut up, Stan. I want to watch the show."

When the performance ended, they stayed in their seats until the showroom started to empty. They walked to the stage entrance and introduced themselves to the security guard. He escorted them backstage and turned them over to another guard stationed outside Jerry's dressing room door. After Jerry's secretary identified them, they were admitted to the room.

Since the show had been well received by the audience, Jerry was in a good mood. They carried on a cordial conversation for a few minutes and then Stan asked, "Would you be available for a meeting with Sonny Cross tomorrow afternoon?"

"Sure, anytime after two would be fine with me. I've been having some throat problems, so I'm trying to get more rest."

Stan went to the phone, contacted Sonny, and set up a meeting for the following afternoon at 3 o'clock. After informing Jerry, he said, "When I talked with Sonny two days ago, he sounded chesty. He must be upset over something. Before we get together with him, I'd like to know if you two have been having troubles."

"None that I know of," Jerry replied. "I ignore him most of the time, and he manages to stay out of my way."

"Jerry, this is important. If Sonny has some gripes, I'd like to know about them before our meeting."

"Why should he have any gripes with me? I fill his showroom and send satisfied customers into the casino twice a night. Don't worry about the meeting, Stan. I think we should just walk in and play it by ear."

"Okay, but I can't help feeling concerned."

"You worry too much," Jerry told him. "All Sonny wants to do is beat me down on price and fringes, but we won't let him. Is there anything else you'd like to discuss before I rest up for the second show?"

"I guess not, but I'd like to know the name of your lead trumpet man."

"That monster is Mike Moore," Jerry replied. "He plays like he's from another world, doesn't he? I've been using him in my nightclub band for a long time. Why do you ask?"

"We know Mike. The first time Doris and I were out together, Mike was with us. I haven't seen him since we left Chicago and moved West. Dear, do you remember Mike Moore?"

"Yes. He was a lush and a womanizer."

"He still is," Jerry Ross told her. "But it doesn't seem to affect his trumpet playing or anything else. A couple of years ago, he saved me from being worked over by two pros. We were on tour at the time, and I left my hotel suite around 3 AM to get some fresh air. I was walking around the parking lot when two guys stepped out of the shadows and pinned me against a car. They took my wallet, watch and rings before I hardly realize what was happening. Then they decided to punch me out. I covered my face with my arms as to blows started to come. They only hit me two or three times and then they stopped."

"Was Mike taking a walk in the lot also?" Doris asked.

"Hell no. Mike had been in the backseat of a car two rows behind us. He was in the process of seducing a local broad who attended our concert. I think she was a music teacher, but that's not important. I guess the activity outside distracted Mike and made him mad. Anyway, he was precise and fluid with the two hoods. I've never seen anything like it. In a matter of seconds, he broke their ribs and laid them out cold. They were hurt badly and had to be taken to the hospital. It must've scared the crap out of the girl, because she drove away without saying a word. When it was over, I remember telling Mike that I'd keep him on as a bodyguard if he ever lost his lip."

"He did the same sort of thing for Doris and Norma Anderson a number of years ago," Stan said. "I'd like to see him before we leave Vegas. And speaking of leaving, we better get out of here and let you rest."

As they walked to the door, Jerry said, "See you tomorrow afternoon, Stan. And don't worry about Sonny Cross. If he starts acting up, I'll straighten him out and give him something to think about."

Stan and Doris went to the musician's room, but Mike Moore wasn't there. One of the house band musicians was returning as they were leaving. Stan asked him, "Do you know where we could find Mike Moore?"

"He's probably down the street at the Aladdin Hotel. The latest love of his life is working in the lounge this week. She's a doll. Mike sure knows how to pick them. For an old cat, he's sure young at heart."

"When do you think he will return?" Stan asked.

"About five minutes before the second show. Since he isn't a member of the house band, he doesn't have to follow our rules and cuts it pretty fine. If you want to see him before he goes into seclusion for the night, I suggest you hurry down the street. It will be over an hour before Mike shows up here."

They took the advice of the musician and drove a few blocks south to the Aladdin Hotel. The open lounge was easy to find, and they saw Mike sitting at a corner table with his back to the casino. While they were approaching him, Stan asked, "Do you think he will remember us?"

"I doubt it. He hasn't seen us in over 30 years."

Stan leaned over the railing and said, "You still play a mean horn."

Mike turned his head and looked at them. Then he stood up, extended his hand and said, "Stan, you been putting on weight. You should start working out and taking better care of your body. I can't say the same for you, Doris. You look fine. Would you care to ditch this old fart and spend the rest of your life with me?"

Before she could replied, Mike put his hands on her waist and lifted her over the railing. He looked at Stan and told him, "You'll have to walk through the entrance. You're too heavy to lift."

When Stan joined them, Doris said, "That girl on the stage is Mike's friend. I think she's good."

Stan watched and listened to the girl perform in front of a three-piece combo. She sounded great, looked charming and made all the right moves. Her manner wasn't pretentious, and she acted like she was having the time of her life. The image projected itself to the audience, and they were enjoying her performance. As she concluded her final song and left the stage with a big smile on her face, Stan said, "I think you're wrong, Doris. She isn't good. She's outstanding."

Mike escorted them out of the lounge and introduced them to Connie Scott. While they were taking the elevator up to Connie's room, Doris asked, "Will you show me how you make some of those wild moves?" As the women move their bodies about, Stan asked Mike, "Where did you meet Connie?"

"The first time I worked with Jerry Ross, Connie was one of his backup singers. After Ross let the girls go, they returned to Los Angeles and worked in the Studios for a few years. When the other girls decided to get out of the business, Connie continued as a single. She doesn't have steady backup musicians, because she can't find enough work to hold on to them. When a job like this one pops up, I usually find a group for her. It gives me an excuse to stay in touch with some of the guys I admire, so it isn't a problem or chore."

They reached the room, and Mike made drinks for everyone. Everyone except Connie, explaining, "She won't drink a drop until her last performance of the evening is out of the way."

"I think that's commendable," Doris said between sips. "Stan, this girl doesn't have an agent, and I think you should take her on as a client. Connie has been trying to deal direct with entertainment buyers, and that must be a terrible experience. I still remember what it was like to peddle myself, and it wasn't much fun. In this business, a girl should have someone running interference for her."

"But Doris, I'm not taking on any new clients."

"Won't you make just one exception for me?"

"Since you put it that way, I'll keep one ear to the ground. Who knows, I might hear something rumbling around that would be of interest to Connie. If you had a choice, what kind of work would you like to do?"

"I'd like to be an opening act for a superstar," Connie told him.

"That's interesting," Stan replied. "Can you sing country music?"

"Sure. I can sing that shit. I can sing anything."

Stan thought about her statement for a moment and asked, "When you go back on stage, would you include a couple of country songs in your next set?"

"You bet I will," she replied. "Which ones you want to hear?"

"Anything that you're comfortable with would be fine."

Mike departed to play his second show, and a few minutes later, Connie decided to leave early and talk over the country songs with her musicians. While they were waiting for Connie's next performance, Stan and Doris went to the casino and lost a few dollars. When Connie started singing, they returned to the lounge. After Doris heard the second country song, she asked, "What do you think?"

"She seems to be able to adapt herself to any style of music," Stan replied. "She has a great ear, and everything she sings sounds good. I think Connie is capable of performing in any music idiom. According to Mike, she's been doing TV and radio commercials since she was sixteen years old. That's probably where she developed her versatility."

"Connie looks like she's young enough to be Mike's daughter. Stan, don't you agree?"

"I think Connie is almost young enough to be his granddaughter. Mike keeps getting older, but his girlfriends stay about the same age. Why not? Mike's just trying to live up to his image."

Doris glared at him as he continued to watch Connie's performance. When the fifty minute performance concluded, the three of them return to Connie's room.

Stan asked, " Do you have any demo tapes?"

"I've got all sorts of them," she replied. "How many do you want?"

"Three or four copies of a typical cross-section of what you do should be adequate. I'd like some photographs as well. The one that's posted outside the lounge is a real winner. If you have extra copies with you, I'd like to take them with me."

"I've got them," Connie said as she started going through one of her cases.

"How about a listing of your credits, the places you've worked?"

"It's in here someplace. I'll find it."

"Could I have a copy of your itinerary, so I'll know when you'll be available for work?"

"That I don't have, but it isn't necessary. After this engagement, I have three weeks in Reno and then I'm free as a bird."

"I don't think anything will happen that fast," Stan said, "but who knows."

As Connie handed him the items he requested, Mike let himself into the room. He looked at the tapes, photos, credits and said, "Stan, it looks like you're serious about trying to help Connie. Do you have anything specific in mind?"

"I'm thinking about a few things, but I don't want to get Connie's hopes up and then disappoint her. I'd prefer not to discuss them until I get back to my office and make a few calls."

Connie told him, "I've been disappointed before, so it's not a new thing that cuts me up anymore. If you have something in mind, I'd like to hear about it."

"Okay, client, here's the picture. I know a guy who books talent into class motels throughout the Midwest. I'm sure he could give you plenty of work, but you won't get rich or establish any sort of a name. For seconds, a friend of mine in Dallas has just opened a club, and he's looking for new talent. The pay isn't bad, but the work would be spasmodic. It would come and go along with the large conventions and special events."

"Spasmodic work is better than no work," Connie told him. "I think the Dallas thing sounds pretty good."

"It's something to consider, but what I'm really thinking about is Carl Kay's next tour. It starts in two months, and he needs an opening act for some of his engagements. You would probably make about twenty-five hundred a week working for Carl, but before we can pull it off, we must overcome two possible problems: First he will have to meet you, hear you perform and like you. I'm sure you can cut that part of it, but the other part may be more difficult."

"What's the second part?" Connie asked.

"Arrangements," Stan told her. "Carl will be using a fourteen piece orchestra, and he will expect you to use the same instrumentation. Do you have country song arrangements that would be suitable for fourteen musicians?"

"No. I don't have a thing," she replied. "How much do you think they would cost?"

"Carl would expect you to do about twenty minutes, so the music costs would probably total out at about four thousand dollars. Maybe a little less."

"I don't have that kind of money to spend on music," Connie told him.

Mike interrupted the conversation by saying, "I do. If Stan can get a firm commitment from Carl Kay, I'll buy your music."

Connie threw her arms around Mike. As he patted her behind, he told her, "It's just money, so don't get carried away and screw up your makeup. If we don't move our tails downstairs pretty soon, you'll be late for your last performance of the evening."

During the walk to the lounge, Stan said to Mike, "Jerry Ross mentioned that you saved him from being punched out a few years ago."

"Yeah, that turned out to be a rather interesting evening. Prior to that night, Jerry used to fire me about every other month! I believe he gets his jollies from firing people and seeing if they'll beg to get their job back. I've been fired before, so it never bothered me. Anyway, after Jerry's brief encounter with a possible facial disfigurement, he stopped firing me. Come to think of it, he even raised my pay."

They seated themselves in the lounge and ordered another round of drinks. By this time, Doris was very high. During Connie's performance, Stan told Mike, "I like your friend and I think she's an unusual talent, but you certainly surprised me with your generous offer to help."

"I like her too," Mike replied, "and the money isn't a big deal. I've got more money than I need. I'm sure she'll pay me back, but if she doesn't, it won't bother me. Hell, I've probably taken that much out in trade with Connie. I owe her."

Doris looked at Stan and told him, "Honey, I think I've had too much to drink. Let's get out of here before I pass out and you have to carry me home."

They helped her to the front entrance. When their car arrived from the valet parking lot, Stan said, "Thanks, Mike. I can manage her now."

"Are you sure you don't want me to ride along and help you get Doris into her room?"

"No, that shouldn't be necessary. We are on the ground floor, and we can drive right up to our door."

Doris mumbled, "Stan, please stop talking and get in the car. I'm freezing to death."

When they reached the room, Doris went straight to the bathroom, kneeled and put her face over the stool bowl. She moaned, "I think I'm going to be sick. How much did I drink tonight?"

"Well dear, let's count. You had two drinks at Jerry's show. When we arrived at the lounge, you had a drink with Mike. Then you had two more at Connie's room. When we went back to the lounge, you had two more. Then we went back up to Connie's room and you had another one. The last drink in the lounge doesn't count, because you didn't finish it, so that makes eight plus."

"Why did you let me drink so much?" She bellowed.

"Doris, I'm going to get us something to eat."

"Don't get anything for me. I can't keep down what I ate at the dinner show."

By the time he got her undressed and into bed, it was 4 AM and she was saying, "I think I'm going to throw up again."

Stan handed her the ice cube bucket and got ready for bed. When he woke up at noon, Doris was still clutching the bucket. He felt a little hung over as he showered, shaved, dressed and ordered breakfast. When room service arrived, Doris woke up and disappeared into the bathroom. He had just about finished his breakfast when she returned and said, "Take me home. I just want to die in my own bed."

"Now dear, I'm afraid we can't leave just yet. I have a meeting at 3 o'clock."

"Can we leave after your meeting?"

"I don't know if that will be possible. It depends on how the meeting goes."

"Stan, you've got to get me out of this city. I always drink too much when we're here, but this time was the absolute worst. I want to go home."

Doris drank her juice, and nibbled at some of her food and went back to bed. When Stan left the room, she was sound asleep.

Within thirty minutes, Stan was looking across the desk at Sonny Cross. Moments later, Jerry Ross arrived and sat down beside Stan. Sonny started the conversation by saying, "We all know why we're here, so I'll get right to the point." As Sonny handed each of them a sheet of paper, he said, "I can give you any or all of these open dates if you'll meet my terms."

Stan looked at the paper and said, "This is a significant amount of work, Sonny. What are your terms?"

"Ross has to take a twenty percent cut from his usual salary, and he has to be more cooperative. The hotel has special guests who want to have their pictures taken with him, I expect him to comply. And we're not going to tolerate unlimited complimentary admissions, meals and drinks for his business associates and friends. This nonsense of having thirty members of a Jerry Ross Fan Club admitted with only an hour's notice has got to go. We turned away paying customers for that show, and the maître d' was furious. So was I. In the future, we'll only give a maximum of ten comps per show, and we insist on a reasonable notice. If Ross wants to show a lot of his friends a good time in my show room, whenever the count goes over ten, he picks up the bill for the extras. We'll throw in the free suite when he's appearing, but we're setting a limit on the catered food and liquor at $200 a day. The hotel won't furnish a free automobile anymore, and we're not going to pick up the cost for additional musicians. Our basic house band is 15 men. If Ross wants to continue using 24, he has to pay the cost for the additional musicians. And one more thing, we're not paying for your long distance calls. They will be billed back to you."

"Sonny, those conditions are absurd," Jerry Ross told him as he got up from his chair. "If you think I'd even consider this proposal, you're not only full of shit, you're a dullard." Jerry walked out of the office and slammed the door so hard it shook the entire room.

Sonny Cross jumped up from behind his desk and roared, "You'll never work here again, Ross. You're through at this hotel." As Sonny straightened the pictures on the wall, Stan started to circle dates on the sheet of paper. When Sonny returned to his desk, he said, "I think your client is an egotistical asshole!"

"Maybe so. Maybe so," was Stan's replied, "but he fills up the showroom. Sonny, I think you made many good points with Jerry. I hope you'll overlook his outburst, he hasn't been feeling well."

"He's sick in the head," Sonny yelled. "That's what he is, sick, sick, sick!"

"I don't know about that, but he has been having a lot of trouble with his throat."

"You don't think he'll cancel out early on this engagement, do you? That would be awful. We're booked wall-to-wall during the next three days."

"I don't think that will happen," Stan replied. "Jerry has been trying to sleep in and get extra rest. He won't take calls before 2 o'clock, because he is trying to save his voice. That's probably why he didn't have much to say during our meeting."

"He said more than enough. God how I hate that guy."

"I know he can be difficult at times, but I think you asked him to give up too much. I agree with you on the comps, catering and long-distance calls, but a 20% cut in pay is pretty extreme. Won't you reconsider that item?"

"Stan, we're trying to cut costs at the hotel, and I had to ask for it. With the current business climate, I don't think it's out of line."

"Perhaps you're right, but Jerry simply won't accept it. I've circled some dates on the sheet of paper that we would be interested in, but if you insist on a twenty percent cut in pay, we can forget about the whole thing."

Sonny looked at the paper and said, "Do you think Ross would work these dates if I compromise and asked him to take a ten percent cut in salary?"

"I could ask. It's a lot of work, and I think Jerry might consider it appropriate if you will continue to let him have 24 musicians."

"Stan, nobody needs 24 musicians to back them up."

"But Jerry likes to hear them, you know how he is about things like that."

"No. I won't do it. I'll give him twenty, but that's all."

"I think that might be acceptable. Now, about the automobile. Are you going to withhold it from just Jerry, or is this an across-the-board thing with all of your headliners?"

"Let's just forget what I said about the car. I didn't intend to bring that subject up during our meeting, but somehow it slipped out. Talking up to Ross felt so good, I got carried away."

"Yes. Yes. Sometimes our emotions act faster than our heads."

"If he wants it, Ross can continue using the car," Sonny told him.

"Good. I know he'll appreciate your thoughtfulness. I'll contact Jerry and see how he feels about this tentative agreement. Sonny, it's a pleasure doing business with you, and I'll be back in touch this evening or tomorrow."

After Stan left the office, he went to a house phone and asked for Jerry's room. The operator informed him that Mr. Ross wasn't accepting any calls until 5 o'clock. Stan returned to his room, but Doris wasn't in it. He found her sitting beside the pool. As he sat down beside her, she asked, "How did it go? Can we go home?"

"I'm afraid not, dear. The meeting wasn't a roaring success. Jerry lost his temper and walked out on us. Sonny was very upset, but I stayed with him and discussed a tentative agreement. I'll present it to Jerry in a few minutes, but I'm not looking forward to his reaction."

"If Jerry doesn't like what you have to say, I wish you'd tell him to shove it."

"Perhaps I will, Doris. Perhaps I will. It has been a difficult day, and I'm more than a little tired of being pushed back and forth by strong-willed people. Stay here and rest while I make the call and get it out of the way."

Thirty minutes later, Stan returned with a big smile on his face and said, "Jerry bought the entire package as is. He even told me I did an outstanding job of getting him a good deal. Sometimes, I simply don't understand Ross. His mind works in devious ways. I think walking out of the meeting was a preconceived plan so he wouldn't have to sit around and haggle over terms. Anyway, I just told Sonny the good news and everyone is happy, including me."

"I'm glad, and I'd like to suggest something that might make your day a complete success."

"What is it?" he asked.

"I think we should get out of fairyland before something else comes up."

"But it's almost 6 o'clock."

"Stan, forget about the time. Let's hit the road."

As Doris packed, Stan called Connie Scott to let her know that she would be hearing from him in a week or two. Then he called Mike Moore to say goodbye. When he asked him to stay in touch, Mike gave his usual response, "I don't write many letters, but the next time I'm down your way, I'll drop in on you. Perhaps the three of us can get together for a drink."

"What did he say?" Doris asked.

"He said he'd look us up the next time he's down our way and perhaps we can get together for a drink."

"Don't mention that word," she replied. "Go pay the bill, and I'll get our things into the car."

Stan did as he was told. When he returned, Doris was sitting in the front seat all set to go. They drove to I-15 and headed south. Before they reached the state line, the sun had set. As they zipped down the highway, the darkness made the barren mountains look more impressive. After three hours of driving, the motion of the car started to upset Doris, so Stan decided it was time to take a breather. He turned off the highway at Barstow and stopped at a restaurant. As they walked around the parking lot, he asked, "Shall we find a motel and stay overnight?"

"No. I'm feeling better now, so let's have a light meal and keep moving."

After their meal, they walked around the parking lot for a while before continuing their drive. About one hour later, Doris said, "Stop the car. I think I'm going to throw up."

When she returned to the car, Stan told her, "You're too sick to travel anymore tonight. We're stopping at the next decent motel I see."

He left the highway at Victorville and registered at a motel. After he helped her to their room and brought in their luggage, he went to the all-night restaurant and picked up two large cups of coffee and a custard pie. When he returned to their room, Doris was in bed and sound asleep. Stan was wide awake, so he turned on the TV set and watched it until the late movie ended. When he joined Doris in bed, it was close to 2 AM and sleep came in a rush.

In what seemed only a few moments, Doris shook them out of his sleep and said, "I'm hungry."

"There's coffee and pie on the table. Help yourself."

Doris turned on the light and got up. A moment later she was back in bed shaking him again. "Stan, wake up. There isn't anything on the table except two empty cups and a pie tin. Did you eat an entire pie by yourself?"

"If there isn't any left, I must have. Now shut up and come back to bed. I'm sleepy."

"What kind of pie was it?" Doris asked.

"I think it was custard, what difference does it make? If it's gone, it's gone."

"Stan, how can you eat an entire pie and not leave a piece for me? Custard is my favorite pie. "

"I know. That's why I bought it."

"Will you buy another one?"

"Someday I might, but right now, I plan on getting a couple hours sleep."

"You've done that already. It's almost 5, and I think you should get up and feed me."

"My billfold is on the nightstand," he told her. "Go feed yourself."

"Is that any way to treat a sick person?" she shouted.

As Stan got out of bed he said, "Shit." Thirty minutes later, they were having breakfast. Doris finished hers by having a piece of custard pie. After paying the check, they went outside and noticed two men carrying golf clubs. Stan asked if there was a golf course close by, and they told him the clubhouse was just across the street. It was daylight as they returned to their room, and they could see some of the fairways. The course look like it was in good shape, so Stan asked, "Would you care to play a round of golf?"

"That sounds like a good idea," she replied. "It will settle our breakfast and give me a chance to see if I'm ready to get back in the car."

The golf course turned out to be interesting. For the most part, the fairways ran between houses. About every other hole, they had to drive their cart across the city street to reach the next fairway. As they putted out each hole, their balls left a trail on the greens from the morning dew. They pretty well had the course to themselves and were not pushed by other golfers. Doris felt good, and Stan didn't feel too bad until they played the second par three hole. His drive went into a sand trap, and it took two more strokes before he was on the green. He three putted the hole and was in a foul mood as he walked from the green. Doris picked up the flag and told him, "Don't forget your sand wedge."

Stan walked back and picked up his club. Then he lost his temper and threw his putter toward their cart. It didn't make it. Midway in flight, it struck the pin and fell to the ground. When he picked it up, the shaft was bent at an almost perfect 90° angle.

Doris didn't say a word as she watched him put the shaft across his knee and bend it back. Stan held the shaft straight out at eye level, made a minor correction with his hands, and dropped three balls on the green. After putting numerous times, he returned to the court and said, "I believe that slight modification is going to improve my putting. I should have bent that club years ago."

The rest of the game went by as smooth as silk. Since it was still a few hours before checkout time, they return to their room and showered, changed clothes and decided to chow-down one more time. Doris topped off her meal with another piece of custard pie, but Stan declined, saying, "I had my fill last night."

It was a short drive to Los Angeles, and their evening was spent leisurely reading over old newspapers and mail. They retired early and slept late. Doris enjoyed sleeping in her own bed, and Stan enjoyed getting an uninterrupted night's sleep.

When they finished breakfast, she told him, "I'm going to call Allyn and tell her all about our trip."

"Will that include the night you got drunk?" He asked.

"No. Besides, I didn't get drunk. I got sick."

"Whatever you say, dear. Say hello for me in between your blow-by-blow account of our excursion. I'm going outside and putter around in the yard."

After a few hours of mowing grass and trimming shrubs, Stan became restless and decided to look in on his office. He changed clothes and drove to Wilshire Boulevard. As he walked into his office, Helen Hall said, "You're back early."

"Yes. We got tired of traveling."

"What's all that stuff you're carrying?" Helen asked.

"Demo tapes, photographs and credits," he replied. "While we were in Las Vegas, I heard a marvelous new talent. Her name is Connie Scott and she's something else. Such a dynamite personality, and she's a friend of a friend. I want you to set up a file for her."

Helen took the bundle from him and said, "I thought you weren't going to take on any new clients."

"I'm not," he replied, "but Doris asked me to do this as a personal favor. You know how forceful she can be when she wants something, so what choice did I have? Before you file these things, I'd like to have you rough out a letter to Carl Kay. I want to tell him about Connie and forward one copy of everything she gave me. In a nice way, suggest he consider Connie for his opening act during his next tour. Use the usual superlatives about her voice, dancing and personality. You know what I want, so I'll leave it up to you. I'm going to take a look at my mail while you're getting the letter ready."

Thirty minutes later, Helen walked to his desk, handed him the letter, and said, "The file for Connie Scott has been set up."

"Good. Good." He made a few minor revisions and handed the rough draft letter back to her. Then he asked, "Did anything interesting happen during the past few days?"

"I don't know how interesting it is, but I finally talked the authorized agent for this slum into extending your lease for six more months. They were holding out for at least a year, but yesterday they weakened and gave in to my request."

"Is that so? Helen, I don't want you to think I don't appreciate your efforts, but while we were on the trip, I had a change of heart about my business. I believe I'll stick it out for another year and then reevaluate my feelings. Will you take care of that item tomorrow?"

"They're going to think we don't have our act together, but they probably felt that way for a long time. Sure, I'll take care of it."

She went back and retyped the letter. Stan continued to examine his mail and found a letter from Norma Anderson. She had enclosed a check for $5,000.00. Her note thanked him for the loan, but she said she wouldn't need the money. Her house was sold, so she was in good financial shape.

When Helen returned with the retyped letter, he signed it and suggested they call it a day. During the elevator ride, he asked her to remind him to call Carl Kay, saying, "I want to discuss Connie Scott with him before our parcel arrives." His final words to her were, "Since I'm still supposedly on vacation, I'll probably be a little late getting to the office tomorrow."

The return drive on the freeway didn't seem all that bad, because it was good to be home. Apparently, Doris felt the same way. She had spent the remainder of the afternoon preparing a marvelous dinner. Afterwards, they spent the evening discussing their trip, old friends, and how good showbiz had treated them over the years.

When Stan walked into his office the following day, he greeted Helen with, "So what's new this morning?"

"You received a rather interesting phone call a few minutes ago, and the details are in a note on your desk... on top of the morning mail."

Stan went to his office and found the note. It stated: Mr. Sonny Cross-telecom-10:00 AM. "Tell Stan to call me back as soon as he gets in. He can reach me at (702)555-8555. That so-called artist he booked into my room has gone too far this time. I've had it with his crap."

After reading the note, he walked back to where Helen was sitting. Stan handed her the note and asked, "Isn't this the same message we received a few weeks ago?"

"It certainly looks like it, doesn't it?" She replied. "But it's a brand-new one that says the same old thing."

As Stan walked back into his office and picked up his phone he was thinking, staying in the business six more months may be more than enough!

Chapter 8

Cleo F Ansteth

Biography

Cleo Ansteth was born in Hartford, Michigan to Frank and Mildred Ansteth. His brother, Gene, was the victim of an accident in 1946. After this tragedy, Cleo joined the House of David Band. He was a graduate of Midwestern Conservatory and awarded the degree B.Mus. Trumpet Major. The famous Chick Bell gave him trumpet lessons. It was said that Chick made Cleo hang his trumpet from the ceiling on a cord... then, not using his hands but only the pressure of his lips, learn to blow and form the notes. The idea was to teach him not to put pressure against his lips; because as musicians get older, their lips give out due to years of continued pressure.

Cleo performed with several traveling bands, including Clyde McCoy, and later Hank Winder out of Omaha. "One-nighters" were the standard fare in those days, and along with the trumpet, Cleo also played the piano.

Cleo took a correspondence course in Engineering and moved to St. Joseph. He played with the Harry Diffenderfer Orchestra and also did arrangements for his own orchestra.

Cleo did play trumpet for a while but found his true calling in becoming an arranger and successful music copyist. After years on the road, Cleo married Alice. They settled in Las Vegas, Nevada and Cleo decided to 'try his hand' in the music business there.

Over the years, he arranged and orchestrated music for many Headliners: Including Paul Anka, Natalie Cole, Frank Sinatra, Neil Sedaka, Tony Bennett, Vic Damone, Wayne Newton, Debbie Reynolds,

The McGuie Sisters, Engelbert Humperdinck, and Segfreid & Roy. Other Headliners to whom he provided music services were: Diahann Carroll, Red Skelton, Diana Ross, Tony Orlando, Shecky Greene, Regis Philbin, Tonie Tenille, Mary Wilson and the Supremes, Louis Mandrel, and Larry Gatlin and the Gatlin Brothers.

Cleo's career in Las Vegas included arranging and orchestrating music for: Sophisticated Ladies (Duke Ellington's Music) at the Desert Inn Hotel; Splash at the Riviera Hotel; Fire & Ice at the Hacienda Hotel; Solid Gold at the Riviera Hotel; Starlight Express and Music of the Night (Sir Andrew Lloyd Weber's music) at the Hilton Hotel; Beach blanket Babylon at the Sands Hotel; and One Of A Kind at the Desert Inn Hotel. He also penned arrangements for opening acts, variety acts, network, cable, PBS, high schools, colleges, symphonies, and other venues. (Many of his scores have been donated to CCSD by his wife, Alice.)

When Cleo and Alice reached their 50th year of marriage, they planned a 6,000-mile trip around the United States, ending up in Sedona, Arizona where they enjoyed their final evening meal watching the sunset with a candlelight dinner.

"Cleo's golden trumpet is stilled now but he left his mark on the musical world. Even now, when we listen to some of the great ones, they are singing and playing arrangements put together by a Hartford kid who has woven some great music into the tapestry of our lives along the Paw Paw River" (stated by Roy M Davis.)

Cleo Ansteth

NOTES

Made in the USA
Lexington, KY
01 November 2013